My sister in Christ
Karen El.
Find encouragement knowing
that you are valuable to
God and His Kingdom
Be blessed by this reading

RELATIONAL BUMPS
CONNECTED TO GOD

Love ya much

Maureen . S. Eckert

Author
Maureen Susan Eckert

Edited by Melanie Grayned

ISBN: 978-0-6151-7507-2

Printed in the United States of America

Lulu Publishing

This book is dedicated to the memory of my mother, my grandmother (whom I never knew), and my great grandmother (Ouma) who were responsible for my spiritual formation. I am surrounded by a great cloud of witnesses daily.

I thank God for selecting me to endure the process beginning with my Dad whom I love very much. Through Dad I came to realize that God's Hand has been upon me before the foundation of the world.

Acknowledgements

It is with thanksgiving from the heart, such as the tongue can never express, and with deep humility that I wish to thank the following people.

For your constant encouragement, prayers and support
Brenda, Portia, Rhoda, Deborah, Iris, Sudonna, Harvey, Karen, Charlie, Lillian and Edwina.

For motivating me through the process
Rev. Fran
For being my God given prayer partner and counselor
Rev. Carolyn
For walking, laughing and believing with me through the book
Theresa keep on believing
For your selflessness and encouragement
Phyllis
For helping me become computer literate again
Beverly
For not meeting a stranger and embracing me
Frankie
For being my bank, my gas tank, my pantry, and most of all
my sister
Vallorie
For spiritually embracing me, in spite of what it looked like
and being in tune with my every spiritual need

Rev. C

For enduring and loving me
My God Given Children: Imani and Chinelo

I cannot thank God enough for every fond and valuable memory that He has granted my children and me, to have with grandma. I am still blessed to have and enjoy her in my life to this day. She was sent by God and kept for me.
I love you grandma. Thank you for consistently loving the kids and me.

Imogene Elizabeth Cary Cooper
1903 -

I Praise God for my siblings who prayed me through and consistently reminded me that I am loved.
Janet Eckert Adams, Marjorie Eckert, Robert Eckert, Lynette Eckert and Cecelia Eckert

Loving thoughts and thanks to my God Given big sister and husband who knew me before I knew myself
Catherine Walker (Cissy) and Edward Walker

Melanie Grayned, you are the best. Thank you for your sacrifice of unselfish love and kindness that you extended to me. Continue to hold to the law of love and giving. Thank you for being a doer of the Word.
Love you much

Foreword

All peoples of the world are experiencing their journeys. But not all peoples are sharing their personal experiences with others. Maureen gives us a vivid, crisp retelling of her life's events, holding into focus those events that required constant prayer if victory is to be had and celebrated. Because there's always a marketplace for evil in every situation we find ourselves, we must be willing to be persistent in prayer. It is Jesus who teaches people to pray and never give up. This is important because in family, friendships and even in faith, we can become discouraged and cynical with no hint that things are going to get any better. Jesus gives this encouragement: persist in prayer; do not loose heart. In Luke 18, it is the widow who seeks justice for her cause and pesters the judge who finally settles the case in her favor. In this writing, it is Maureen who through many trials and tribulations, has prayed, stood her ground, passed the test and is now sharing with us her testimony. I hope this reading will bless you as it has blessed me.

Rev. Dr. F. James Clark
Pastor and Founder
Shalom Church (City of Peace)
St. Louis, Missouri

Foreword

Born in South Africa, Relational Bumps Connected To God, chronicles aspects of the author's life experience virtually, from birth, through adolescence, and into adulthood. As the title suggest, the reader incorporates an understanding of certain spiritual principles, often positioning faith as a means whereby a person might overcome even the most daunting of perceived obstacles. Along the way the author explores the relative complexities of human nature, highlighting qualities relating to identity, loyalty and love in various forms.

This book will appeal to a large base of the population who has lived long enough to find out that life does not always go as one expects. The author finds herself deeply relational with so-called men and women of God. However, what she thought she saw in their lives brought her to the realization that it was just a mirage, and that they were great pretenders.

Despite the "relational bumps" she experienced, God intervened and created an opportunity for genuine growth. The author experiences a sacred call to self-discovery. She is drawn to serve God in a true relationship of love, joy, peace and sincerity. She comes to realize Who really is the most important person in her life, and to trust Him that her times are in His hands. Maureen's transparency allows you to see the hand of God working in her behalf throughout her entire life. This book will provoke thought for the reader, who presently is in a similar path. I pray that it will inspire you to strive and grow in your relationship with God.

Lois Patterson
Christian Family Therapist/Social Worker
St. Louis, Missouri

Chapter 1   Living Sane in an Insane Home

Chapter 2   Dating

Chapter 3   God's Covering

Chapter 4   The Wedding

Chapter 5   The Maintenance of Marriage

Chapter 6   My Perception of Ministry

Chapter 7   Leaning on Jesus

Chapter 8   Itinerant Surprises

Chapter 9   Evaluating My Life

Chapter 10   Fasting

Chapter 11   Stand

Chapter 12   Draw Close to God

Chapter 13   He's Jehovah Shamaa

Chapter 14   God Sits High and Sees Low

Chapter 15   No More Pretense

Chapter 16   Connecting

Chapter 1

"You fell in love because your old brain
had your partner confused with your parents.
Your old brain finally found the ideal candidate
to make up for the psychological and emotional
damage you experienced in childhood."
GETTING THE LOVE YOU WANT

HARVILLE HENDRIX, Ph.D

"When I was a child, I spake as a child,
I understood as a child
but
when I became a man,
I put away childish things."
I Corinthians 13: 11 KJV

Living Sane In an Insane Home

My dad was a weekend alcoholic. During the week he was the best dad to be found, but come Friday, watch out! Silence was my mother's attitude. I did not realize until much later in life that mom was not saying anything because she was constantly praying. We would ask mom a question but there would be no response at all. Sometimes I would observe her lips just moving, but hear no sound coming forth. You talk about Hannah described by Eli? Well, I know what Hannah looked like.

We never ate dinner without the presence of my dad, except on weekends. Mom would have us set the table earlier than usual on the weekends, and we would have dinner without my dad. My dad would come home late on Friday nights, and the only way we would see him was if mom needed us to help her pull this drunken body into the house. My dad would leave again early Saturday morning, and we would not see him again until five o'clock Sunday evening.

I was five years old when I noticed this pattern in our weekend lives. Dad would be drunk Friday nights and leave early Saturday morning. Between one and two o'clock on Saturday afternoon, our neighbors, Mr. & Mrs. Davis whom we affectionately called Uncle Arthur and Aunty Jane, would come and take us to the store where we bought candy, soda and chips. We could not play outside. Uncle Arthur and Aunty Jane would keep us in their home occupied until after 2:00 p.m. When we returned home, my mother would look like a different woman and sometimes had to be taken to the hospital. I could not understand what brought this horrible physical change to my mother but I was going to find out.

It was a beautiful Saturday afternoon, and Uncle Arthur and Aunty Jane had come to the house to get us. I had hid under the bed and after calling me for a while, they left assuming that I had left with my friend Linda who came by earlier that afternoon. I laid quietly under the bed, waiting. About twenty minutes later (which seemed like forever) there was a loud noise. My father entered the house cursing and swearing at my mother. My mother was sitting in the bedroom and when he saw her, he pulled her by the hair and started hitting and kicking her like a rag-doll. My mother did not say a word. She just allowed this man to hit her as if she was his punching bag. She was physically able to defend herself but just allowed this man to hit her again and again. I laid there scared to death. I thought, "What would happen if he killed my mom?"

My mind started working and I decided to help my mom get out of this evil dilemma. When I saw my dad pulling back his fist to hit my mom again, I stuck my foot out and tripped my dad. Dad fell and hit his head against the corner of the dresser and he was bleeding. I felt a hand pulling me out from under the bed. It was my mother and in her other hand she had a four-inch wide belt. Did I get a whipping from her that day? I remember screaming at the top of my lungs, "Why are you hitting me? I was helping you. You should be hitting him!" I was so hurt that day not because of the spanking, but because I was trying to help mom, and this was the thanks I got.

There was a loud knock on the door. There were two white police officers who came to take my dad to jail for the rest of the weekend. Before this experience, whenever mom was asked where dad was, her response would be that he had to go to work out-of-town for the weekend and that he would be back home Sunday evening. Well, I now knew what the truth was. I was mad. I had to spend the rest of the day in the backyard all by myself. That was the day that I decided that I would never marry a man like my dad, and no man would ever lay a finger on me.

That Sunday night when dad was released from jail, he could hardly look me in the eyes and I stared at him with so much hatred in my heart. This was the weekend pattern. Friday night dad went straight from work to his drinking place wherever that was. Saturday morning he would leave to go and get drunk again. He would come home about 2:00 p.m. on Saturday, physically abuse my mother, and then he would be arrested and kept in jail until Sunday evening. Sunday evening he would come home, take a bath and go to bed. But that was not all. This is the best yet. Monday morning at 5:00 a.m. my dad would go through the house like a roaring lion. "Get up, get up, it's time for prayer." Crazy or crazeee! I hated my dad.

During prayer time I stood in the prayer circle meanly staring at him and in my mind I screamed, "HYPOCRITE! HYPROCRITE!" My mother pinched me and motioned for me to close my eyes. I closed them just until I knew her eyes were closed again. I was so confused. I had witnessed all this mess this weekend, and now I stood in a prayer circle, listening to this drunkard calling on the name of Jesus. "How could he open his mouth and call on the name of the Lord?"

That weekend for the first time in my life, I witnessed a look in my mother's eyes that I would never forget. It was a look that I would recognize two more times in her life. She was sad because she knew that we knew what was happening on weekends. But God always provides a way of escape and my mother accepted it.

All of our grandparents died before we were born. (We never knew our grandparents on either side of the family.) I always envied my friends who enjoyed the tender, loving care of grandparents. However, they were always kind enough to share them with us. My mother had a grandmother (Ouma) who was still living. She had outlived most of her children. Ouma had a farm in Elsies River, about an hour drive, outside of Cape Town.

We got out of school one Friday afternoon and all we knew was that we were going somewhere. Mom had our bags packed and we were on our way. We had to travel on two busses and this was a luxury for us, because we normally went everywhere by foot. We were delightfully surprised when we arrived at our Ouma's farm. I

4

loved being at Ouma's home. We had so many uncles, aunts and cousins galore. We were happy at Ouma's.

Ouma was very strict. We knew that we had to be on our best behavior around her. Ouma was in her ninety's but she was strong and had the best ears. You never whispered around Ouma. She could hear things that we never thought she would pay attention to, like the sound of a snake. I remember all of us playing hide 'n seek in the grass. Sometimes the grass was six-feet tall and we knew when we heard the sound of a whistle, we had to get to the porch (stoep) immediately. Ouma would take off into the grass like a mighty wind with her six-foot stick and a brown sack in her hand. My aunt would be screaming across the yard for my Uncle George to come and help Ouma. When Ouma came back she had killed a cobra snake. It would range from 3 to 8 feet in length. How she did it I don't know, but she did. We were safe around Ouma.

Ouma would sit on the stoop with us and show us the snake that she had killed. Whenever we misbehaved she would "torture" or punish us by putting us in the bag with the dead snake and we could not come out until she said so. It only took one snake-bag experience for me. Talk about mental abuse. It taught us though to be obedient, and so we were.

Ouma baked the best monkey bread. At dinner time there would be so many family members. Even though all the children were seated on the floor, I had to sit next to Ouma. The reason I had to sit next to Ouma was because I was always telling our family business and when Ouma said for me to be quiet, I was quiet. I believe I was Ouma's favorite. I was the apple of her eye. She really loved all of us, but I was the one who could always get away with certain things that the others could not get away with.

After dinner, everyone would sit around and talk. There was so much laughter and noise that you sometimes had to wonder how we could possibly hear each other. Then we would sing. My mother would go to the piano and give every section their key. The family would start singing and oh the beautiful sound that was rendered. You never wanted it to end. Ouma would be watching the clock though, because nine o'clock was her bedtime. My Uncle would give us a Word from the Bible and Ouma would tell us some family story. Those were the best times of my life. Everyone, from the youngest to the oldest had to pray one sentence prayers and then it was off to bed. We would awaken to the smell of fresh air and breakfast and enjoy another day with Ouma.

When Ouma was ninety-six years old she fell and broke her hip. She died soon after that. That was the demise of our big happy family. Aunts and uncles fought over Ouma's property and belongings. The only time we would see the family after Ouma's death was at weddings and funerals. It was not the same.

Ouma was the best gift God gave me in my childhood. We spent many weekends with her. I will never forget her. She was bold, strong, courageous and a praying great-grandmother. I thank God upon every remembrance of her. She was the best Ouma we ever could have had and she had a great impact on my life. I am sure that she was aware of what was happening in our home. Every Sunday afternoon before we left, Ouma would lay hands on each of us individually, speak blessings over our lives, kiss us and stand with us at the bus stop until the bus came. We would run to the back of the bus and wave at Ouma until we could see her no more. Our way of escape had ended. At least so I thought. We had to go back and face my dad, the weekend alcoholic.

I carried the negativity of this experience with me for a long time. I never remembered or celebrated the good things my dad did for us when he was sober. Later when I became married I found myself looking to my husband, to do the things for our children that my dad did for us as children.

So I made the decision at five years old that I would not marry a man like my daddy. My daddy accepted the Lord Jesus Christ as his Personal Savior. My dad struggled tremendously with his new found life in Christ Jesus. My mother patiently and lovingly encouraged him. Sometimes it seemed that he was not going to make it, but he did. My parents enjoyed and celebrated over forty-nine years of marriage. Mom died six months before their fiftieth anniversary.

Chapter 2

True love is a process of growth and development
like the ripening of fruit. An individual can actually
love being loved, or love the feeling of being loved,
or even love the feeling of loving and yet not be in love.
Love at first sight may be merely a compulsive need finding
expression in a romantic attachment.

ANONYMOUS

"Doth not behave itself unseemly,
seeketh not her own,
is not easily provoked,
thinketh no evil."
I CORINTHIANS 13:5 KJV

Dating

Dating is handled so differently in the United States. In my opinion, there are so many expressions in terms of romance and other freedoms, than in South Africa. People are not ashamed to hold hands publicly, or kiss each other openly. In South Africa you are so conscious of people and your surroundings, that you waited till everyone was gone (which rarely happened), or you went for a ride to a secluded place to romantically express yourself.

In my time of dating in South Africa, parental approval was very critical. The entire family was a part of the relationship. I started dating at the age of fourteen. I was mostly infatuated. It was never the start of real love and was short lived. I lived out my own desires. My mother knew that I was interested in boys. Mom never worried, because she knew she had scared me to death as far as sex was concerned. No boy in South Africa knew the hem of the dress that I was wearing because sex was not going to be a part of our relationship.

My mother once told me if you had sex outside of marriage the man's penis would fill up your body and come out of your throat. It stuck with me. Another story she told me was that this young girl had sex before marriage and the man's penis got stuck inside her and the doctors had to cut out their private parts.

Today I laugh about it, but it was not funny back then. My mother had the most creative imagination. Years later, after I had been married for a while, I asked my mother why she told me all those lies. She just laughed and I could not do anything else but laugh with her.

She had a story about a refrigerator and pubic hair. I won't even go into that one but that was the only way my mother knew to prevent me from having sex before marriage. My younger sister, however, did not listen to my mother. I do not know if my mother ever told her the same stories she told me, but my younger sister came home with a baby outside of wedlock.

Most of the guys I dated between the ages of fourteen and seventeen were for very short periods of time. As soon as they tried to have sex with me they had to go. It was not until I was eighteen years old that I had my first lengthy courtship. I never was friends with the girl next door, but she decided one day to introduce me to her boyfriend Michael, just showing off. He was always with a bunch of guys. Every time he saw me he would wave and I would wave back.

It was Christmas of 1975. In South Africa back then, we would greet each other on Christmas with a kiss on the lips, whether we were family or not. Michael wished me Happy Christmas that day and while kissing me on the lips he thrust his tongue in my mouth very briefly. I was shocked and asked, "What is the meaning of this?" He laughed, got in the car and drove off.

In January 1976, I was coming home from school and had a ten-minute walk home. Michael waited for me one day after school and walked me home. Soon thereafter we started dating. I felt bad, but not too sad for my neighbor.

My parents did not like Michael at all. My mother told me one day (in Afrikaans), "If you do not stop seeing that guy I will pray him into his grave." Though it sounds harsh it still sounds more beautifully expressed in the English language than it did in Afrikaans.

We dated anyway. I would meet Michael in places that my parents never knew about. Michael could dance, and I loved to dance. Wednesday, Friday and Saturday nights, we would meet each other at the Civic Center. I was allowed to dance with everybody and anybody. When it came to slow dancing, Michael was very possessive. It was flesh of my flesh and bone of my bone.

Michael smoked cigarettes and weed and he drank alcohol. These were some of the same habits my father had. I hated them in my father but endured them with Michael.

I was the youth president at church. On Monday nights the youth club would be packed because I brought Michael and all his male friends to youth club. Our youth club was more than one hundred strong. Pastor would always come by to check on the youth when he saw all those "afroes" present. Many of the young women attending youth club started dating Michael's friends. I always had to meet Michael in the street. My parents did not like him at all and would not allow him in the house.

In August of 1976, Michael came to our home boldly one Sunday night, and asked my parents if he could take me to meet his mother who lived in Ocean View, about an hour drive from where we lived. My dad slammed the door in his face. I was so embarrassed and mad at my parents for their rude behavior. Michael sat and honked in front of the house and upset the rest of the neighborhood. This prompted the neighborhood-watch to come out and put him out of the neighborhood. He left and I waved goodbye, standing in the window.

I did not see Michael again until a month later at a soccer game. Michael held me in his arms and it felt as if it would be the last time. When I left he said to me, "Kaffir, always remember I love you forever." It felt so sad and final, that I turned back and hugged him so hard. I did not want him to let go. I asked him if he was going somewhere. He never answered, he just laughed.

A few days later on September 9, 1976, Michael was shot in the head by the riot police. I met his mother for the first time the day of his funeral on September 16, 1976. So mom prayed him into his grave. After he was shot, I heard my mother telling someone that he was a good guy.

Years later, mom and I sat and talked about the experiences of life with Michael. We laughed about our behavior and experiences.

Mom told me that she always wanted the best for me and did not always know how to express it. She laughingly asked me not to treat my children the way she treated me. I did not have lengthy courtships after Michael's passing.

The twenty-first birthday is a very important celebration in South Africa. It is a coming of age celebration, and is normally very big. People rent auditoriums. There is a formal elaborate dance which forms the number twenty-one, and then the guest of honor is presented with a key representing independence. People party until the wee hours of the morning. My dad told me that he was not going to feed other people for my twenty first birthday, but that he would rather spend the money on a trip for me to the United States by way of London and France. I enjoyed the United States the best. It was the best birthday gift ever.

My dad scheduled the trip to the United States in May of 1980. My brother who had lived in the United States for four years was getting married, and my dad and I were coming to attend the wedding. I loved life in the USA. I was blessed with a full-time scholarship. My dad was going to leave me behind and I was going to be on my own.

Well, it was not God's time yet for me to stay. Word came that my mother had taken seriously ill and I could not stand the thought of mom being sick or dying and me being in a far country. I went back to South Africa and the day we deplaned, mom welcomed us back home at the airport. She had a virus that was over-exaggerated. However, it was all part of God's plan for my life.

I started dating a young man a few days after my twenty-first birthday. He impressed my dad, but my mother did not like him at all. Whenever he came to take me somewhere, my mother would always find something for me to do just as we were walking out the door. His parents loved me and treated me royally. Every time his mother shopped for his two sisters, I was included in that shopping spree.

We had many challenges. He had an eye for other women. He was a deejay. He did not like going to church. He was very jealous. If I spoke to any other male friend, he would go into a rage. He smoked cigarettes and weed and drank alcohol on weekends. He would stalk me at work and accuse me of having affairs with white men. He always walked into my place of employment when I was in a meeting with my white manager. Every Saturday he would pick me up after work and all the way home, we would fuss about who I worked with that day and how I was handling my customers. When I told him that my dad was taking me to the USA, he consistently tried to get me to have sex with him by saying, "If you love me you will prove it by doing it with me." Lie born in hell. If you love me you will wait.

He was very happy when I returned home. My courtship continued for two-and-a-half more years. Our relationship lasted for three years. I was helping his mother with laundry one day, and she asked me to bring his laundry from his bedroom. I did. When I sorted the clothes I saw that his underwear was bloody. I was shocked. His younger brother had been telling me that he was having an affair with another young lady who worked with him. I did not want to believe his brother. When I confronted him about the bloody underwear, he confessed that he had been sleeping with this girl because I did not want to have sex with him. I cried bitterly that day but decided that enough was enough. When I finally came to my senses and ended the relationship, my mother's words were, "Praise the Lord." I worked for two-and-a-half more years, saving and planning my way back to the USA.

On February 5, 1985, I returned to the USA. This time I would stay no matter what happened back home. I lived in Battle Creek, Michigan for six months. In August, I moved to Austell, Georgia to attend college.

I first met Rezin on the college campus in Austell, Georgia. It was in August, 1985. Janice and I had just met on campus and we were waiting on the church bus to come and transport us to church. It was not long after that that Rezin came and stood with us, also waiting on the church bus. He and Janice were talking about roaches and rats. I thought, how gross. "Could you please change the subject and talk about something more pleasant?" At 10:40 that Sunday morning, the bus had not yet come. Rezin went into the building and asked his friend to take us to church. I ended up sitting next to him in the car. We got to church and it was beautiful. I joined church that Sunday. I also learned that Rezin was an associate minister at this church. I had no interest in him at all because at that time I was dating a six-foot-three inches tall, dark and handsome guy named Leo.

I had met Leo while visiting Austell, Georgia in March of 1985. He showed me around the city. One thing led to another, and soon he asked me to consider becoming more than a friend to him. I had spent about three weeks in Austell, and Leo showed me a wonderful time. I liked him but tried to keep my emotional distance. Have you ever been with someone that you felt just was not with you? Well, after my time was spent in Austell, I returned to Battle Creek, Michigan, and we spoke to each other once a week, usually on a Saturday morning.

When I returned to Austell for the fall semester, Leo picked me up from the airport and stood in line with me all weekend trying to get me registered and moved in on campus. I told him that on Sunday I would be going to church and he did not seem interested but told me he would pick me up for dinner that evening.

Leo was a very handsome guy, well established, two years older than me and he was an engineer. He was not the spiritual person that I was looking for and sometimes came across as very materialistic.

Well, our courtship moved to another level and the lessons that mom taught me and the scary stories that she had told me were now forgotten. I tried to resist the temptation to sin but was not victorious. Temptation happens to all of us. It does not take into account how spiritual you are. James 1:14-16 says, "But every man is tempted when he is drawn away of his own lust, and enticed. Then when lust hath not conceived it bringeth forth sin, when it is finished, it bringeth forth death. Do not err (be deceived) my beloved brethren." I prayed daily "and lead us not into temptation but deliver us from evil." I was not that strong in mind and spirit anymore so that I could resist the temptation. Needless to say, I lost my virginity at age 27 while dating Leo. Mom would never find out though.

I introduced my mother to Leo by phone. He would take me once a week to his mother's house so that I could speak to my family in South Africa.

After several sexual encounters, I decided that I did not want to see him as much. We decided that we would see each other on weekends only. I knew better but it still happened. I was confused and could not remain objective about him anymore. I soon found out that we were intimate with each other, but we were not necessarily committed to each other. I started mistaking the physical relationship for love. I learned that love is great, but an important part of love is the willingness to love the other for life. That is why sex within the context of marriage is so important. God intended it to be with the same person in marriage forever. It is one of commitment, trust and intimacy. Sex as God ordained it to be, is not just a physical act but an experience which involves the body, soul and mind. It distracted me from the willingness to obey God. I would repent and confess my sins unto the Lord but the next time he called, it happened. I was being convicted by the Holy Spirit and for a while, I did not answer Leo's phone calls.

Leo showed up on campus one Saturday morning and took me to breakfast. At breakfast, I expressed to him that I was not willing to have sex with him anymore and that if he still wanted to be with me, it would have to be a sex-free relationship from thereon in. He respected my wishes and agreed, but it still happened.

I remember shortly after having the first sexual encounter with Leo, I was so downhearted and felt so disgusted that everyone I came in contact with would ask me why I was looking so sad. It was my conscience and I was now in a defective dating relationship. I rushed God's timing and spoiled the beauty of His plan for my life. I was away from home and lonely and found comfort and pleasure in having sex with Leo. I chose what was good for me instead of what was pleasing to God.

In the meantime, I would see Rezin on a daily basis. Whenever he saw me crossing campus or on my way to a class, he would always impress me by telling me that he had already prayed for me that day and that every obstacle that I was facing God had already taken care of it. He always said it to me just as I was experiencing some trial.

Rezin's timing was always perfect. He started watching my class schedule and would meet me in the cafeteria and enjoy a meal with me. I knew he was flirting. I was six years older than him. I was not interested in anyone younger than me. I remember him flirting with me in the Library one evening and I pulled out my passport and showed him my date of birth. His response was, "What does age have to do with anything?" I also told him that I was seeing a guy named Leo. He ignored me completely and kept on pursuing me. Everyone kept encouraging me to go with Rezin but I just did not feel it. I just knew that when I told him that I was not a virgin anymore that he would stop pursuing me. He did not.

We were at church one Sunday and they were serving dinner after service. I was seated at one table, and the head table was set-up for clergy and their spouses or significant others. I heard him tell one of the ushers, "Please bring my girlfriend to this table" and then he pointed to me. I was shocked. The usher told me that Rev. Rezin wanted me to sit with him at the head table. I complied not wanting him to be caught in a lie; after all he was a minister. I did not have much to say to him because I wanted to know what he meant by saying I was his girlfriend. I waited until we were back on our way to campus. His reply was that whether or not I believed it, I was going to be his wife one day.

It was Christmas break and everyone was going home for the holidays. Rezin asked my girlfriend Tiny (who was from South Africa) and me what we were doing for the Christmas season. We both replied that we did not know. His response was that we were more than welcome to spend the Christmas holidays with his family and that his mother was a very gracious hostess. Ooh, he got me! That was so nice of him to think of us foreigners. I thanked him for the kind invitation and told him that I was going to Michigan for Christmas. He gave me his phone number and asked me to call him from wherever I was on Christmas.

I allowed Rezin to give me my first kiss in the window of his dorm room before we left for the airport. I thought to myself, "Oh my goodness, he had soft lips! I'll have to get used to this. Uggh!" We left for the airport and were on our way to enjoy Christmas wherever we were going to find ourselves. I called him over the Christmas season. He had his calls monitored by his sister. After clearing the caller with him, he finally answered. He sounded very excited. I spoke to him for a minute and gave him a number where I could be reached and hung up. We spoke a few more times and then it was back to college.

I was still dating Leo. Leo met me at the airport. He took me to the gymnasium where registration was taking place. We entered the gym and from a distance I saw Rezin. I always was a quick thinker. I told Leo that he could go and that if he wanted to hook up for dinner that evening to pick me up at about 6:00 p.m. He said that he had something to take care of and he left. Thank you Jesus!

I was standing in line pretending that I had not seen Rezin. He was wobbling his way over to me and when he came to me I acted surprised. "Hi!" I exclaimed. "When did you get here?" Well, we spent hours in line that afternoon and had to come back the next day. That evening I told him that I had an appointment. He never questioned me about anything and just believed whatever I told him.

My relationship with Rezin started blooming. We started seeing more of each other and soon I was being spoiled with flowers, cards, surprise weeks, candlelight dinners, gifts, and just everything sweet. We made it to Spring Break and he said that he needed to get away. He left for Alabama, and I spent the spring break with Leo.

The dorm director was aware of my relationship with Rezin. That week she was on duty and every time Leo would pick me up, she would give me the strangest look like "What is going on here?" I just ignored her and kept moving.

That Sunday when Rezin returned, she told him that I had another visitor all week while he was gone. He asked me who it was. I asked him who told you all this. Someone walked up to him and they started talking about their week and we never got back to the issue at hand.

Summer came and Rezin and I traveled to Miami Florida, where I would meet his parents for the first time. His mother was a very big woman and his dad was an average-build man with a strong face. I immediately knew that I was going to love his dad but had some reservations about his mom.

We made the introductions and were standing in line waiting for a hotel room. Rezin and I were sharing a room with his parents as we could not afford our own rooms. This however was a good way of making the initial introduction.

Rezin's dad was wonderful, straight and to-the-point. He was very interested in life in South Africa. His mother would go around in circles asking me questions. For example, she knew that I was older than her son. Now let me set the record straight, I did not look a day older than Rezin. To say the least, I looked younger than him. She asked me, "How many siblings do you have and where do you fit in?" She asked me how old was the youngest, and that was followed by how old was the sibling who was older than me. Dad interrupted her and said, "Just cut through the chase wife and ask her how old she is instead of asking her all of these unnecessary questions." I laughed and said, "that's my man." I loved his honesty and openness. Rezin scored a point with me because I fell in love with his dad that day. I was still trying to make up my mind about his mother.

Plans were made for me to spend August with his family to celebrate his mom's fiftieth birthday. I met the rest of Rezin's family without him being present. He had four brothers, three sister-in-laws, one sister and seven nephews and nieces. I fell in love with Rezin's family long before I fell in love with him. His family was very close-knit. Every major holiday they would all get together and celebrate. Dad would always call for prayer time before everyone left and would bless us in his own peculiar way. I loved the environment of harmony, unity and community within the entire family. There would be good food, great fellowship, games, laugher, and a house full of grandchildren. His mother was a preacher too, so the church would be packed to capacity on that Sunday when the whole family went to church.

One day, Rezin's mother took me aside and told me that she did not know how I was raised, but she just wanted me to know that their family did not believe in pre-marital sex. My response to her was that my mother raised me well. My flesh was screaming at this point but I kept my cool. "Guilty!" Rezin and I had had a few times when we were caught up in the moment.

I visited with Rezin's family quite a few times before he would ask for my hand in marriage. I said "yes," and we decided and pledged before God that we would wait until marriage before we had intercourse again.

There were lots of warning signs that I ignored during the dating tenure. Rezin was a very selfish person except when it came to his mother. So I took that as the saying goes: a man who treats his mother well will treat his wife well. That is the biggest lie ever told. It might be true for some men, but not for all.

He was nasty. His room would always look and smell like a trash can and I was Mrs. Clean. The guy he rented from called me one day and said, "I'm calling for a Jesus meeting tonight with these boys because this house looks like a garbage dump. Come over and help me out."

When I got there I would feel so sorry for Rezin and help him clean up and tell him very nicely to try and keep his room clean because a dirty room says a lot about you. He was a preacher, and I believed that cleanliness is next to godliness. Or so I thought. Is it or is it not? I hate a dirty house. I believe unclean spirits dwell and fester in dirty places. I grew up in a very small house, but it was always clean. I was and still am surprised whenever I visit a preacher's house and it is dirty.

Rezin spoke very unkindly and sometimes very disrespectfully to me, and I accepted it believing that it would get better after awhile. If only I knew back then what I know now. His mother heard him one day and said, "He is a son that only a mother can love." She said that several times to me. If only I knew what that meant to her. That's another chapter. In my mind, I heard the words: "Run, Mary run!" But I was stupid and naïve and so I ignored it.

Rezin was not very affectionate. He was also very forgetful and always losing money or his keys. He always had to have the last word. He was very controlling. However, with all of these warning signs, I said "yes" to him when he asked for my hand in marriage in May 1987.

I was still dating Leo and decided to end our relationship in March 1988, a few days before his birthday and three months before my wedding date. I knew our relationship was not going anywhere and would never become a permanent commitment according to the Word of God.

The wedding date was set for July 2, 1988. Then, Rezin's father had a serious bout with cancer. In April 1988 he called the entire family home and we took pictures for the last time with dad. I really loved and admired this man.

That Sunday afternoon, everyone was gathered in the living room and dad spoke his last words to us as a family. I will never forget the words he said to me. "Mary, if I die on July 1st don't postpone the wedding, but celebrate it as if I am with you. Always remember that our family does not believe in divorce, so divorce is not an option for you." He spoke to me and not to his son.

Dad died on May15, 1988, six days after my birthday and six weeks before the wedding. The home going celebration was scheduled for that Friday. Rezin was graduating from College that Sunday. The itinerary called for us to be in California that week until that Friday, for dad's homegoing celebration. We had to fly back to Austell that Saturday and attend graduation that Sunday. We would leave for Tuscaloosa, Alabama that Monday morning where Rezin's dad would be laid to rest that Tuesday. Rezin was so grief-stricken when he received the news. He was the only one who could not be at his father's transition in California. Grandma (whom you'll learn more about in the next chapter) allowed him to spend the night with us in her home. We traveled to California where Rezin preached his dad's home-going celebration. Dad asked us not to cry and I did not. I left the celebration with a headache so big, because I had held back the tears. The entire family traveled back with us to Austell where Rezin graduated that Sunday. We left early Monday morning for Tuscaloosa, Alabama.

Dad's death initiated the demise of the family that I fell in love with. Dad was a strong, sincere, ethical, moral and deeply spiritual man who loved his family and was the glue that held them together. I had lots of laughter and wonderful conversations with him. I was sad that my children would be denied the opportunity of meeting such a fine grandpa who loved his grandchildren very much.

Chapter 3

"I passed by you again
and looked on you;
you were at the age for love.
I spread the edge of my cloak over you
and covered your nakedness.
I pledged myself to you and entered
into a covenant with you,
says the Lord God, and you became mine."
EZEKIEL 16:8 NRSV

CHRIST MY COVERING THROUGH
ELIZABETH CARY
1903 - present

God's Covering

Seeking to be under the covering of a man rather than that of Jesus is a dangerous form of idolatry. God uses His covering to express authority and also depicts His full measure of His protection and provision. He also assures us of His Shekinah presence.

Rezin and I became engaged the first Saturday in May 1987. Our pastor called for me to stand during worship the Sunday after our engagement. He congratulated Rezin and me on the celebration of our engagement. After worship several people came to express their joy and blessings to us on this marvelous occasion. My heart traveled back to South Africa and envisioned how different the scene would have been.

In South Africa, my pastor would have called us to the altar and made the announcement from the altar. He would have directed us to kneel and would have prayed for us and for the steadfastness of the commitment that we had made with each other. However, I was not in South Africa, and after all, I was engaged to a preacher.

After worship a lady came to me and said that there was a certain Mrs. Cary who just had to meet me. She was blind and so I found my way over to her. I hugged her. She was beautifully dressed and was wearing eye-glasses. I fell in love with her the very minute I laid eyes on her. I squeezed myself next to her on the end of the pew and she held my hand. Her first words to me were, "I feel like I have known you forever." I froze. She measured my wrist and said that Rezin had gotten himself a good thing. She could not see. She was blind. I marveled at how well her makeup, especially her lipstick, was applied. We sat there for another fifteen minutes talking, her holding my hand all the while. Rezin finally joined us, and she extended to us an invitation to dinner that following Sunday at her home. She said she would cook it herself. We accepted. This was the start of an unexplainable yet explainable glorious journey. I call her my covering, Christ Himself in the flesh. The Bible says in the beginning was the Word and the Word became flesh and dwelt among us. God is still doing it today.

My experience with Mrs Cary reminded me of a lady in South Africa from my childhood. Let's travel back to South Africa and my childhood for a moment. Five doors from our house lived an elderly lady whom we fondly called, Ma Lackay. Her family lived all around her but did not take care of her. My mom would take care of her during the week and Aunty Jane our neighbor would take care of her on weekends. Whenever I was punished by mom, I would be held responsible for a whole week or sometimes a month to take care of Ma Lackay. I had to empty her pee-pot on a daily basis. I had to sweep her room and make sure that all the old food was taken out of her room and disposed of. I had to take her breakfast and dinner. I was glad when weekends came, because it was Aunty Jane's turn to take care of Ma Lackay.

Ma Lackay would, in turn, look out for us especially when mom had to go somewhere and had no one to baby-sit. Ma Lackay would tell us stories and we would hang on to every word she said. She disciplined us as if we were her own. Most of Ma Lackay's grandchildren were gangsters. Our family was safe because they knew and appreciated the fact that we were taking care of their grandmother.

Ma Lackay became ill one day. She was very feeble after recovering from that illness. We had to go and help mom wash her and dress her, and every time we entered we would be met by a foul smell that would make me vomit. I was not only punished for vomiting but I also had to clean up my vomit and find everything that contributed to the foul odor. My mother, however, would sit us down and explain that Ma Lackay was God's representative. She explained that however we treated Ma Lackay we were treating God. I took that very seriously.

Ma Lackay died at eighty-eight, and we missed her very much after that. She was a part of our family. Mom trained me early for what was about to happen in my current life. I was prepared, and Mrs. Cary would soon become the beneficiary of the exchange and experience that I had as a child with Ma Lackay and Ouma. Or is it the other way around? I would soon become the beneficiary of God's covering for my life.

We went to Mrs. Cary's home that Sunday afternoon after service. When we got there, her home was decent. I smelled the food she had prepared and was going to receive it with all the love that it was prepared for us. She had set the table in fine linen and cutlery. Everything was beautiful. I am not going to lie and say that the food was good, because burned food is not tasty, but I appreciated it and ate it because in my custom, it is disrespectful to refuse that which had been prepared for you at someone else's expense.

After dinner that afternoon I took over, cleaned up the kitchen and put up the leftovers in the refrigerator. Mrs. Cary scared me that afternoon with something she said to me. She said that the Lord told her that I should have been living with her a long time ago. Remember, I froze in church last Sunday. Well, let me explain.

I came to Austell in August of 1985. My very first Sunday in church I drew Mrs. Cary's name from the Missionary prayer basket. Now it was not mandatory to take a name but if you did, the request was that you would contact the person by phone or send a "thinking of you" or "get well" card to that person. I never did any of the above.

In September, I drew her name again. I still did not do what I was supposed to do. In October 1985, I drew Mrs. Cary's name again. I tried to call her but her phone was busy and I did not try again.

For the next few months, I got different names. In April 1986, I drew Mrs. Cary's name again. That also happened in May and June. Three months in a row again and I never called. I stopped taking names from the basket because I realized I was doing this for show.

I believe this was God's way of trying to set me up with Mrs. Cary. God had given me several opportunities to meet her, but I did not accept them. Rezin once had the opportunity to serve her holy communion at her home. He came back after that experience and expressed to me that he had served this blind lady communion and that he thought it would be nice for us to go and clean her home. I agreed but it never happened.

God gave me seven opportunities to meet Mrs. Cary and this was the beginning of the next go-round. She asked me where I was staying. I told her that I was in the process of looking for a new place as I was not getting along with my roommates. She asked me that Sunday if I would consider coming to stay with her as she needed a younger person in the house. She said I would not have to pay anything as long as I would keep the house clean and cook sometimes. I knew this was a blessing. I could save for the wedding.

I did not have to think about it and responded "yes." I had two more weeks in the apartment, and slowly started moving my things out.

The bedroom that she gave me was full of junk. Mrs. Cary's deceased husband was a barber. She had taken every mirror and every chandelier out of his shop and stored it in this unoccupied room. I told Mrs. Cary that I had to sleep in her room for a few weeks until I could get rid of some of the stuff she had in this room. She was a packrat. Oh my gosh!

When I started cleaning, I had the hardest time with her. She did not want to let go. Not only was her husband's stuff in there, she had her deceased sister and brother's belongings as well. This room was precious in the sight of Mrs. Cary.

I asked her one day whether she knew what she had stored in that room. She named the mirrors (she had six of them which were 6' x 6' wall mirrors), the trunks (she had two of those big trunks), a roll of carpet and men's clothes galore. I made up my mind that day, because of Mrs. Cary's eyesight, that I was going to do what I had to do in order to get the room clean. So I started bagging all the men's clothes. The useable items I gave to the Salvation Army and the rest I threw away. Everything that she did not make mention of that was in the room I threw away. The rest of the things I put up in the attic. That is how I treated her whole house. The house was clean everyday as long as I lived with her.

I hate clutter. I'm amazed at people who have so much junk in their garages like they're afraid to give it away or just trash it. The garage is made for parking cars, not for storing junk. Packrats! Get rid of it. I cannot stand junk and clutter. I feel that I am suffocating. It depresses me. Unclean spirits dwell and fester in dirty places. "Jehovah M'Kaddesh please sanctify this place!"

The house was clean, and Mrs. Cary always smiled when her friends or family came over and complimented her on her clean house.

I finally got settled and God blessed my stay with Mrs. Cary indeed. It was during the summer months that I met her. I was working part-time as a telemarketer for a telecommunications company. My hours were from 5p.m. until 10p.m. That summer my hours increased and I was able to make some extra money to pay for my tuition and for the upcoming wedding.

I told you that I came to Austell in 1985. That first semester of college was a financial burden because everyone who had committed to paying the tuition did not come through. But God was watching over me. I was able to re-enroll the next semester but had another financial hangover.

The following happened a year before I met Mrs. Cary. The summer of 1986 I started looking for a job by faith. There was an elderly brother in our church who offered me a place of residence at a minimal fee. My girlfriend from the Bahamas and I shared a room at his place. He was gone for most of the summer.

I worked the graveyard shift at a major food company. Now I had a social security card but not a valid green card. I worked all that summer and the hand of God kept me. I worked a lot of overtime that summer and I came out ahead. I paid my tuition and still had some money to move into an apartment. However, I moved into a home with one of the church mothers and paid her rent. I soon had to look for another place. This lady was treating me as if I was her personal maid. I could not commit my time to studying and doing for her the way she wanted me to. I moved again.

I moved into an apartment and shared it with two fellow students, a girl and her brother. I was going to school from 8 a.m. to 3:00 p.m. and then to work from 5 p.m. to 10:00 p.m. I was hardly ever home. My roommates were not very clean. Whenever I came home, the house was nasty and the kitchen was always stacked with dirty dishes. I came home from work one night and went into the kitchen to make myself a cup of tea. I was so sick when I saw roaches going up and down the wall from the kitchen.

I had interviewed and started working at a telecommunications company. I was hired as a telemarketer and God gave me favor in so many ways. I had been working there for six weeks. My supervisor came to me one evening and told me that he was going to give me my first evaluation. The report was excellent. However, the next thing he asked me to do blew my mind but God covered me with the spirit of peace. My supervisor said that because I was doing such a wonderful job, he wanted to have me help him get some clerical work done. He told me that I needed to ask everyone in our group for their social security cards. He wanted me to make sure the cards were valid for employment and to make a copy of them and take them up to Human Resources.

My heart sank, but I was at peace. My social security card said "not valid for employment" and I was working illegally. What was

I going to do? I remember asking the Lord, "Why me?" and he answered, "Why not you?" Well, I took up everyone's social security cards and followed the instructions that were given me. I did not include my social security card. A few nights later my supervisor came and asked me whether I got the social security cards to Human Resources. I did not look up and just answered "yes."

Two years later I was still working for this company. In 1988, I got married and was able to have my social security status changed immediately. I started working as a telemarketer then I was promoted to telemarketing trainer. From there I worked in the computer room loading programs and then on to management. I traveled across America to attend programs, workshops and conferences for this company. I thank God for my supervisor entrusting me with that duty. It was all God. God covered me.

Some think this was deceptive. The Bible is full of stories of how God used his hand in certain circumstances to protect his children. I worked for this company until 1991. I thank God for His grace and mercy.

I was now living with Mrs. Cary whom I fondly refer to as grandma. God had given me another chance and I was not going to let it slip through my hands again.

Chapter 4

The Family begins in
a commitment of
Love
ANONYMOUS

"For this reason a man shall leave his father
and mother and shall be joined to his wife,
and the two shall become
one flesh."
EPHESIANS 5:31 NRSV

The Wedding

Presumably, weddings take place between two people, a woman and a man that are madly in love and intend to spend the rest of their lives together. Our wedding preparation took close to fourteen months. Our marriage preparation was six weeks. Wow! I now wish it was the other way around.

We were students living and making it on part-time jobs. This wedding needed money. I was blessed with free accommodation and was able to save for the wedding. I asked two ladies who were very kind to me when I first came to the United States to serve as our wedding directors. I did not want a single woman to be my wedding director because I was not going to allow her to let my wedding planning become her fantasy wedding.

I do not believe that a wedding director or coordinator should be a single person whom has never been married. I am not saying she does not know what she is doing; after all anyone can pick up a book and read about how to plan a wedding. However, I believe experience is far better than just having read some book. It's like giving an alcoholic advice on how to become sober and yet you have never taken a drink in your life. I chose two ladies from Battle Creek, Michigan to serve as the wedding directors.

My bridesmaids were from all over the world. I had five bridesmaids and two junior bridesmaids. The bridesmaids were from Cape Town, South Africa, Battle Creek, Michigan, Los Angeles, California, Kingston, Jamaica, and the Bahamas. The junior bridesmaids were from Apple City, California and Bermuda. The groomsmen were his four brothers and a friend from Maine. The person who would steal the show that day was the flower girl who was the groom's niece. She was not even two years old and she was so adorable.

The officiates were my pastors from South Africa. I purposely chose the second of July as our wedding day, as I knew that most of my people from South Africa would be coming to attend an International church conference in the United States which started after the Independence Day celebration. I chose my Pastors Rev. Jantjies and Rev. Messias. Rev. Jantjies was to perform the wedding vows. Rev. Messias was to bring the wedding sermon.

The invitations were mailed. It was going to be a spiritual event and I wanted God to be in attendance. **"Unless the Lord builds the house, they labor in vain that build it."** (Psalm 127:1) We applied for the license. The planning process was challenging, and I cannot say that God was always present in the planning and details of the wedding. The colors were peach and cream. The bride and groom were wearing white. I found my dress at a boutique in the Galleria Mall in Georgia, that I was going to wear that day down the "runway." The men's tuxedoes were reserved.

The make-up artist I met working in Perimeter Mall in Georgia. She made the commitment to come do the make-up for the wedding party. She and her fiancé were going to be attendance. The photographer was in place. The florist was recommended by my soon to be mother-in-law. I expected the flowers to be exceptional because she came highly recommended and was very pricey. The limousines were reserved. Rezin's family was paying for the reception. We would tie the knot at the church where Rezin grew up in Los Angeles.

We reserved about twenty rooms at a motel for the out-of town guests. The airline tickets were bought and we were ready. It was one thing to make all the preparation for a wedding and include God in the plans, but I have learned that God expects an invitation too. He will not be present if He is not invited. No matter how much you include Him in the planning activities, He does not like being taken for granted. He wants to be invited too. I remember including Him in the plans.

At marriage counseling I paid very close attention to our counselor's prayer, and he was the one who for the first time prayed that God would be present and to take the Headship at the wedding ceremony and marriage. Alan invited God to the wedding on our behalf. I do not remember much about the marriage counseling, except that I was always nervous thinking that this was going to be the day when I say something that will make Alan say to me that we were not marriage material. I remember him asking me the question, "Why do you love him?" I was quiet for several minutes trying to think of reasons to give him. I wanted to give him an impressive answer, but all I could come up with that day was, "I don't know." He said that it was the best answer. Alan blessed us and asked God to show favor upon this union. Alan was the Christian intervarsity coordinator. Thank God for Alan who has now gone to be with the Lord. The fourteen months of planning went so quickly, and then we were in the month of June, 1988.

My father came three weeks before the wedding was to take place. He stayed with Mrs. Cary and me. He loved Rezin and said that God had blessed me good. My "Aunt" and friend came at the same time. My aunt and friend stayed at the apartment that would become our place of residence after the wedding. They had us over for dinner everyday. They were doing all that good South African cooking and just spoiling me. They really were jealous because they tried to put some weight on me so that I could not fit my wedding gown. Just kidding!

We were ready for this event to take place. I went for the last fitting and my aunt, friend and dad went along with me. The front of my dress had a sheer "V" from the neck to my navel. It was about two inches wide just enough to show some cleavage and a little skin, at least so I thought. My dad immediately said that they had to put some material in that area of the dress. I said, "No, this is my wedding dress and I am going to wear it the way I want to. It is sexy." My dad said, "then you can walk yourself down the isle, but I am not walking you half-naked down the isle." Oh, I was mad but my seamstress who had sown the bridesmaid dresses said she could fill that space with some beautiful lace and so she did.

We left Georgia on the twenty-eighth day of June and did we have an entourage and luggage. I carried my wedding dress and three of the bridesmaid's dresses. When we boarded the airplane we were welcomed and congratulated by the head stewardess. Later in the flight we were gifted with a bottle of champagne. We had a wonderful and safe flight and arrived in California where the crowd was awaiting us.

We stayed in Apple City for two days and then left for Los Angeles. We checked into the motel where we were happily greeted by our guest from Cape Town, Battle Creek, and Austell. We were we all at the motel. I spent a lot of time visiting with my folks from South Africa and catching up on news. We all had dinner together that night and afterwards the men took Rezin out for his bachelor's party.

I was making sure that everything was in order because one of the wedding coordinators had an unexpected illness in her family and could not make it. We finally went to bed, and that night when I undressed, I had hives all over my body. They said it was wedding jitters. I thought that I was cool and calm. My girlfriend asked me if I realized that in a few hours time I would not be single anymore. I said "Oh well," and that was it. Someone was sent to the pharmacy to find something for the hives.

The next morning I awakened as usual. I was expecting to be excited, anxious, and ready for this day to take place, but I was of the attitude that it was just another day. My soon to be mother-in-law called me and said to me these words: "Mary, I cannot figure you out, but today you're going to become my son's wife and my daughter-in-law. I want to welcome you to our family and let you know that we do not believe in in-laws but we are all family. I hope that you and Rezin will have a happy life together just as dad and I had." I thanked her and hung up.

The words "I cannot figure you out" stuck with me. Why did she have to say that to me? Why couldn't she just wish me well? Why did she have to let me know that she was still unsure of me? Well, my roommate who was my friend from Jamaica and my girlfriend from the Bahamas were in the room when I got the call. They told me, "Forget her. You are not marrying her, you are marrying her son."

Doubt immediately set in. I was not sure whether I was making the right decision or not. My mind immediately went to Leo. "Maybe Leo is the one I should be marrying." My Jamaican girlfriend who knew most of my secrets told me to go call him. She had no good sense. I was on my way to the phone when I saw Rezin. I asked myself, "What you are doing?" I turned around and went back to the room.

When I got back to the room my Jamaican girlfriend asked me whether I had made the call. I said no, I saw Rezin and came back to the room. She said, "Oh Mary that is not good. You saw him before the wedding takes place." I laughed and said, "Girl stop being so crazy. You are so superstitious." We both laughed and left that alone.

It was time to get dressed. My girlfriend from South Africa told me to cry as much as I could before I got dressed because she was not going to allow me to mess up the wedding gown as it had to be passed on to her. We all laughed. At the wedding rehearsal that previous night, Rev. Jantjies told me that he would bring me a sheet to wipe my tears the next day because he knew that I cried easily and this was going to be the day in my life where I would make a life-long commitment.

I cry whenever anything beautiful or sad happens. They all knew it and everyone was giving me advice on how to contain my tears. The only thing they did not know was that deep inside of me I wanted to run as far away as I possibly could, but how could I express that to anyone who had spent so much money to come and share this happy day with me?

My aunt helped me get dressed. Everyone was oohing and aahing. When I walked down the stairs to the limousine there were people everywhere applauding. We were on our way to the church. When we got to the church, the bouquets were given to us. My handle on my bouquet was put on incorrectly, so I had to carry my bouquet upside down.

My South African friend kept on checking with me to find out why I was not crying yet. I was quiet. Rezin had to borrow a clergy robe from the host pastor for one of the wedding officiates. The host pastor gave him a hard time because he believed that Africans did not wash under their arms, and he said that he did not want the robe to be given back to him stinking like an African.

The processional had started, and it was time for me to enter when I asked the question whether grandma had been escorted to her seat. She was sitting in a room somewhere and they had to get two persons to escort her down the isle.

After she was seated, the flower girl entered and I heard the applause and peeped in through the window. Instead of looking at the flower girl, I looked for the beauty of the sanctuary and there was none. There was supposed to have been flowers and candles everywhere and there were none. I was so upset. I had paid this woman all this money for the flowers and decorations and it looked like she did nothing. I was concentrating on everything except the presence of God. Oh, if I only knew then that which I know now.

It was my time to shine. My dad did not want to unbutton his tuxedo coat, so we started walking down the isle. I smiled and greeted everyone as I passed them. When I got to the eighth pew from the front of the church I saw all these South Africans. I asked myself happily, "Where did they come from?" Well, my girlfriend who knew that I was getting married and who also knew how concerned I was that my side of the church would be empty had taken it upon herself to invite some of the South Africans who were living in Los Angeles to come and be with me at the wedding. So I had a full side too. I thanked them for coming and told them to be sure to stay for a South African picture after the wedding.

When I passed Mrs. Messias, my pastor's wife, she said to me in Afrikaans, "Ek kan nie glo dat jy nie huil nie." She was saying that she could not believe that I was not crying. I laughed, and the next thing I knew, my father was placing my hand in Rezin's hand. The wedding service had begun.

We opened with the singing of that great hymn "Great is Thy Faithfulness." We were led in prayer. The scripture was read. My pastor's sermon topic was "The five C's of life." We recited our vows. The pronouncement was made that we were now husband and wife. My husband gave me a peck on the lips and we were on our way to the wedding reception.

I can still hear his mother saying the following words, "Cling no longer to your mother's skirt." She must have said it about ten times that afternoon.

On my wedding day I was menstruating. It did not really matter on the wedding night except that my menstrual cramps were so intense that night after the love making and the next day that I decided we would not make love till I was through menstruating. We left the next morning for San Diego.

We were broke. We hardly had any money left after all the unaccounted expenses were paid for. We found the most economical place to stay. We had early dinner that evening at a Mexican restaurant and I hardly ate because my stomach was so upset. We spent two days in San Diego mostly relaxing and enjoying each other's company lying on the beach rolled up in blankets.

We left the morning of the third day driving back to Apple City. I spent most of the day packing our wedding gifts in boxes and washing and packing clothes for the next stop we were about to make.

The next day we left for the International church conference held in Detroit, Michigan. We stayed at the Hyatt Regency Hotel in a honeymoon suite. The room was beautiful. They had a newlywed congratulatory package waiting for us. This was my first time attending this kind of international church meeting.

This was mostly a business meeting. Worship services were held once a day. I was not too impressed with the meeting and spent most of my time socializing with my friends and family from South Africa. Rezin and I would meet for dinner or otherwise I would be awakened by him trying to make love to me. He was very into the meeting. The highlight of this meeting was normally the election of leadership. I had decided that I was not going to miss this event. To my dismay I went. I left so disgusted because of the things that I saw and heard and went home and cried myself to sleep. This was not God. It was so political, that if God had tried to enter the politicians were going to kill Him. I asked God that night never to let me attend a meeting like that again. Be careful what you ask God for and always remember what you ask of Him.

Chapter 5

A marriage may be made in heaven
but the maintenance
must be done on earth.
GOD'S DEVOTIONAL LITTLE BOOK FOR COUPLES

"All that you have learnt and received and heard and saw in me put
into practise continually and the God of peace (of untroubled,
undisturbed well-being)
will be with you."
PHILIPPIANS 4:9 TCNT

The Maintenance of Marriage

We arrived in Austell, and my husband carried me over the threshold and put me down. No kiss no nothing. I was hoping it would be more romantic like in the movies. But that was it. We both were tired but come on, this was the beginning of our new life together.

For us to have been newly weds, lovemaking was very sporadic. Sometimes it was twice a week, sometimes more, and some weeks there was no lovemaking whatsoever. It was not a spontaneous explosion but very sporadic and always had to be initiated by him. Whenever I tried to initiate lovemaking, he would hold my wrists so tight in both his hands and not let go. I started feeling that he wanted to be the one in charge, so I allowed him to be. It still did not happen as I thought it should.

I was looking forward to a glorious life of intimacy with my husband. There were very few times in my marriage that I felt sexual intimacy took place. I grew up in a very dysfunctional family. I had no role model who could demonstrate to me the caring, warm, tender ways to share thoughts and the innermost desires to one's mate. My parents did not have the verbal skills and language to share their deepest feelings and emotions. Rezin would say mean things to me. The approach that I took to avoid a confrontation with him was to allow things to go unsaid and sometimes remain unsaid forever.

When I was growing up, I had to sleep in the same bed with my mother. My dad's alcoholism caused me sleep walk. Our neighbor who worked till 2 a.m. found me walking in the neighborhood twice at night, and it was recommended that I sleep with an adult. I often wondered when my parents would make love, because that was what marriage was for. My mother told me that she and dad made love on a consistent basis until after my youngest sibling was born. After the birth of my youngest sister, nothing happened anymore.

She also told me that her mother did not have a very active sex life. She said that my grandmother was married to my grandfather. My grandfather was an Indian. My mother's father was born in Calcutta, India and at a very early age in his life moved to Bombay, India. His parents moved to Cape Town, South Africa when he was nineteen years old. There he met my grandmother and they were married. From this union seven children were born. Mom said she always wondered how the children came about because her father was never home. Every time he came home, her mother would be pregnant after he left. My mother said that Ouma (my great-grandmother) had the same experience. I saw it as a generational curse in my family.

I never had the knowledge of what intimacy was really about, yet I was craving it. The closest mom and dad came to it was when they kissed each other goodbye. When dad came home from work, he would greet mom with a kiss again. She and dad never truly expressed intimacy.

Intimacy requires making a serious commitment to the relationship that each person will experience a sense of dependency on each other. It is sometimes very difficult. Men are taught to strive for independence and are labeled as weak when they show their dependency because it has been feminized over the years. It was very hard for Rezin and me to establish an intimate marriage relationship. Whenever we got as close as we both could tolerate, we would have an argument and pull back to a safe distance. We would decide not to talk to each other or have fun together, go to bed at different times, rarely make love and live like roommates instead of a married couple.

God intended from the beginning that we develop intimacy with each other to the point that the two will become one. One in flesh -

sexual intimacy, one in Him – spiritual intimacy, and one in heart – emotioanl intimacy. I found solace in our prayer time together.

I grew up in an insane home. The one thing that kept our family together was prayer. The family that prays together stays together. Our family praying together is what kept us together. It was the number one priority. My mother focused intently on teaching my brother and me how to pray. I always wondered why she did not involve my two sisters in her times of spiritual teachings.

My dad was a weekend alcoholic but every morning at five he would call the family to pray. Mom would close out the day with us in prayer. Despite everything else that was happening around us, prayer was a vital part of our family.

Rezin impressed me with prayer. When I crossed campus and ran into him, he would always assure me that he had already prayed for me. He said that everything I was going through was going to work out because he believed God answered prayer. Sunday mornings at church when Rezin was asked to pray people who were late would get upset for not being able to enter the sanctuary while Rezin was praying. "He prayed God into the house."

We were married for three months and every night Rezin and I would kneel down and pray. It did not matter what happened between Rezin and me during the day; at night I would find comfort, strength, peace, love and forgiveness in our times of praying together. We had just gotten up from our knees when he turned to me and said, "I know you do not like praying with me so we do not have to pray together anymore." I was baffled and exclaimed, "What do you mean? I love praying with you. We are doing what the Word of God calls for us to do as a family. A family who prays together stays together."

Oh I was livid. How can you know what I feel and not be able to explain why I feel like it? He did not want to pray with me anymore. From that night on we did not pray together anymore. Our prayer altar had been demolished. I hated going to bed at night because the man of God did not want to pray with his wife anymore. I would sit up and study until late at night, and when I got to bed he was sound asleep. In my prayer time I would implore God to bring us back to the altar of prayer.

Life was not the same anymore. I was angry with him about us not praying together but never could communicate it to him. He had and still has such a command of the English language. He would use words that would penetrate my spirit and hurt me so deeply, and I was going to avoid that. I withheld myself and did not open up myself to him. Life continued. I started questioning the apartment we were living in and convinced myself that there must be an evil spirit in the place. Very soon I was looking for a new place.

We spent our first Christmas together in the mountains of Colorado. That was the first gathering of Rezin's family after his dad's death. The whole family had rented a large bungalow. Every married couple was responsible for a meal. It was a beautiful cold sunny day and most of the family had gone out to enjoy the snow. The married couple who was responsible for the lunch meal decided to serve while most of us were out. There were about six persons left in the bungalow. They were the persons whom were blessed with a meal that afternoon.

When we came back from the outside, cold and hungry they informed us that they had already served and whoever had missed lunch had to wait for dinner. There was not enough food for everyone. I laughed so hard and said that they were so cheap. How could you bring enough food just for yourselves? Rezin's twin brother's ex-girlfriend and I started walking down the hill to go and buy our nieces and nephews something to eat. We laughed and teased the couple about their cheap selves.

Rezin was always very affectionate when we were around people. He was always rubbing on my behind or hitting it lovingly. The cheap brother and sister-in-law shared a bedroom with us. Our bedroom was attached to his mother's bedroom. My husband decided to make love to me one morning after his brother and wife had left the room. His mother accidentally walked in on us. I was so embarrassed but not embarrassed enough to stop what we were doing. These were rare and precious moments. Instead of her just closing the door she stood and looked. I lifted myself to look at her and she closed the door. I am sure it made her proud to see her son making love to me. We had a wonderful vacation that Christmas. That was the last time the family got together collectively on an annual basis.

Rezin had a preaching engagement that Sunday. While we were in the mountains, my mother-in-law revealed to me that she had forgotten to buy me a gift but that she had something stored in her closet for me. We were ready for worship that Sunday morning and my mother-in-law gave me my first Christmas gifts. They were two old, old-lady-looking hats. I received them graciously and was told to wear one to church. I was wearing a gray pin stripe suit to church. That morning I reluctantly put the gray hat on my head.

I hate wearing hats. My mother forced me to wear hats all my life. My salvation was dependent on wearing a hat. I got so many beatings when my mom learned that I did not have a hat on in church. When I came to the USA, I was on my own and did not have to wear hats anymore. My mother-in-law told me that day, "Now you look like a preacher's wife. That hat suits you perfectly." In my mind I was saying, "yeah, right."

We left for church that morning. Rezin delivered a powerful message that day. I was seated next to the first lady and she really encouraged me in the Lord. Her husband gave Rezin a check so big that day that he was able to pay his entire tuition for the next semester at seminary. We returned to our apartment in Austell and everything was back to normal. We had decided that we were going to look for a new place to stay. I had in mind for us to purchase a home and make an investment for our future. Rezin said that we were not going to be in Austell that long and that we should look for another apartment.

Looking for a home reminded me of the home I grew up in. The home that I grew up in, in Cape Town, South Africa was spacious and had an enclosed backyard. In 1971 under the apartheid system the group area act was introduced by the government. People of color living in Cape Town were forced to leave and move to municipal areas (projects) about fifteen minutes outside Cape Town. The government built these small houses hardly seven hundred square feet big. The surrounding grounds and play grounds were very dirty. They really looked like dumping grounds. We qualified for a three bedroom home, but my dad somehow settled for a two bedroom home.

We were moved from beautiful, clean Cape Town to unattractive, dirty Hanover Park. The house had two bedrooms, a bathroom, kitchen and what we called a front room. Our home in Cape Town was twice the size, and so you can imagine how cluttered the house was when we moved every piece of furniture into that small house. I always told my mother that I could not wait to get out of that small house. The municipal areas were very dangerous. Gangs would travel from other areas and have the fiercest fights in Hanover Park. I thank God for His Hand of protection over us. We were settling in that small house. It was cluttered but always clean. My mother believed that cleanliness was next to godliness.

My father's brother used to pick us up on Sundays and take us for drives through the most beautiful neighborhoods in Cape Town. We would go visit Constantia, Rondebosch and Newlands where white people lived. I always looked forward to it. When we got there, my uncle whom we called Boeta would tell us to pick our homes. That was the best home window shopping that we did and we enjoyed it.

One Sunday afternoon my uncle stopped in a white neighborhood. He asked a white man if he would allow us to see his home. The man said yes, and I noticed a smirk on his face. The man went inside the house and as soon as we set our feet on his property he set his two bulldogs loose on us. We ran as fast as our legs could carry us. We made it. The man and his two sons were laughing and my uncle said, "Let's laugh with them." We did, but I did not see the humor in it. My uncle instilled in us to look for something better than where we were or what we had.

The one bedroom apartment Rezin and I lived in was comfortable but not sociable. I could not entertain. Rezin and I were about to find something better. We started looking for a new place. We were driving in Lithonia, when we came upon a new apartment building. We stopped and it was beautiful inside. It was new apartments. I would be the first to take a shower or a bath in the shower or tub. My bottom would be the first to greet the toilet. I would be the first one to introduce myself to the stove and refrigerator. A dishwasher! I did not have to do dishes anymore. Thank You God! It was new, clean and spacious. We had to move there. It had a retreat like atmosphere. Lots of trees and a walking path. We signed the lease and moved in happily.

We had a two bedroom apartment, two and a half bathrooms, kitchen, living room and dining room. The "Mary Hotel" was open. Whenever South Africans came through Austell they would stay with us for extended lengths of time.

We moved into our new apartment and had our first social event which was the house blessing. The house was full. The fellowship was great and the food I must say was very delicious. I prepared it. Everybody was having a good time, and at 11:00p.m. I started reminding everyone that we had church the next day. I would not allow them to blame my house blessing for them not being able to attend worship the next morning. The last guest left at 12:40 a.m. My girlfriend and her husband stayed behind to help me clean up. Rezin went to bed and by the time I got to bed, he was in his fourth dream. The house was clean and I could sleep peacefully. The next morning we were awakened by grandma (Mrs. Cary) who reminded us to pick her up for worship.

I noticed some strange things happening in my new home. It was only Rezin and me living in the apartment. Every time he would take a bath or a shower he would lock the door behind him. I asked him why he was doing that. His response was that he needed his privacy. I asked him not to do that anymore. Sometimes he would be resting in the guest bedroom and the door would be locked. He would not move to open it for me. I could not understand.

One evening I tip-toed into the bathroom while Rezin was taking a shower. The door was unlocked and I decided to surprise him, and join him in the shower. When I pulled back the curtain I saw him masturbating. I was devastated. I thought he loved himself more than he loved making love to me. I walked back into the bedroom and went and showered in the guest bathroom. I cried so hard while I was showering. That night Rezin made love to me three times as if he was apologizing. I laid like a robot, numb and not responding, just allowing him to do whatever he wanted. "Who are you?" I thought.

In Cape Town, the alleys were a place where men always openly masturbated. We as children knew and were forewarned to stay away from the alleys. We also knew where these men lived in the neighborhood. A girlfriend of mine was raped by one of these masturbating freaks. As children we would always gather cans, rocks, and pieces of glass. Whenever we saw men masturbating we would stone them. We hated these men. We did not want them in the neighborhood. Someone would always run and call a parent who would instruct us to go inside. Sometimes the police would be called, but after a short time these men would be back on the street again. I was stunned.

I did not want my husband to touch me anymore after seeing him masturbate. Why could you not make love to me to keep your body from exploding? God allowed us to get married to have sex with one another and not ourselves. According to scripture illicit sexual fantasies are forbidden. The bible says, "If your right eye causes you to sin, gouge it out and throw it away. It is better to lose one part of your body than for your whole body to be thrown in jail." (Matthew 5:28) Masturbation to me was shocking, shameful and unmentionable. I wanted nothing to do with this man. Who was he? Where did he come from? This was not the man I married. "Oh God where are you and how am I going to get out of this?" He had fallen in love with himself. I do not believe God designed sex to be a solitary experience. It is supposed to be shared with another. "The man should give his wife all that is her right as a married woman and the wife should do the same for her husband: For a girl who marries no longer has full right to her own body, for her husband then has it rights to it too, and the same way the husband no longer has full rights to his own body for it belongs also to his wife. So do not refuse these rights to each other. The only exception to this rule would be the agreement of both husband and wife to refrain from the rights of marriage for a limited time...." (I Corinthians 7: 3-5).

I called my old friend Leo. We decided to meet and talk. Rezin and I had been married for close to a year. Here I was seeking counsel with my ex-boyfriend.

At work I seemed so far removed from everything and everyone. My co-workers asked me several times what was wrong. My shift was from 3 to11. Leo picked me up from work one night and we went for a drive. I cried all the way. He stopped and held me and gave me his advice. One thing led to another and soon we were kissing. I felt so confused. We did not make love but I knew that if I saw him again, sooner or later it would happen. He would come to my place of employment and spend his lunch breaks with me. He would always over emphasize to me that I did not know who I had married, and that I should be very careful.

My marriage seemed to be based on duty and responsibility. We were living together in a relationship that was less than God intended it to be. Romance and intimacy is needed in every marriage. Was I that blind to the person's weaknesses and faults? I did not know about his perversion. It would have made a difference to me. I was married to a man who was not willing to sacrifice his personal desires and needs in order to please and satisfy me. Love was not controlling this man's sexual desires.

I could not allow myself to communicate my love for him.

Chapter 6

The Ministry Journey

"Therefore, since we are receiving a kingdom
that cannot be shaken, let us be thankful
and so worship God acceptably with reverence and awe."

My Perception of Ministry

The persons who were my pastors until the age of twenty-six were excellent testimonies of holiness and righteousness. I never observed my pastors being rude or disrespectful to their wives. They lived lives that reflected that their word was their honor. Simply stated, they practiced what they preached.

The two pastors that had the most significant impact on my life were Rev. Jantjies and Rev. Messias. Rev. Jantjies challenged me to live a righteous life. He taught me about the spiritual things of God. Love your neighbor as yourself. Do not look down on other people. Share whenever you can. Forgive. Don't let the sun go down on your anger. He was also very humorous. I was a very mischievous person. If anything went hilariously wrong, the first person they would look for was Mary.

Rev. Jantjies had two daughters named Connie and Bonnie. I had a girlfriend named Lorna. We favored each other and whenever we were out in public, we would introduce ourselves as sisters. Lorna and I were working at the headquarters of this company in Koeberg, a suburb outside of Cape Town. During our lunch break, Lorna and I would go to the café a half mile from work.

We met a very attractive guy in the café. Both Lorna and I liked what we saw. He started the conversation and asked us if we would like to go and see a movie with him and his friend. We asked him where he lived. He told us that he lived in Hazendal. He sounded very well-rounded, but both Lorna and I could not go out with him. I asked him his name. He replied "Clive." He asked us what our names were. This was the moment I was waiting for. I answered that my name was Bonnie and she was my sister Connie.

Bonnie and Connie were both fair-skinned. Lorna and I were dark-skinned. Connie wore thick eyeglasses. Bonnie had thick long hair. Lorna and I had good eyesight and our hair was shoulder length. Lorna looked at me and she could hardly contain her laughter. Clive asked us if we would consider going out with him and his friend to the movies that evening.

We both wanted to go out with him but not his friend. He asked us if we thought our parents would give him a hard time. I replied that my dad was a very nice person and he would like him. I jotted down the address to the parsonage and he was going to pick "us" up that Wednesday evening at seven. The reason I remember that it was a Wednesday was because we had choir rehearsal on Thursday evenings. We left. Lorna and I were laughing like two crazy persons who could not stop.

The next day we saw Clive from a distance and we just laughed some more and decided to give him some time and space to cool off before we spoke to him again. Cedric, Connie and Bonnie's brother told us later what happened that Wednesday night at their home. He said that Clive came to the door and was greeted by Mrs. Jantjies.

Clive greeted and introduced himself and told Mrs. Jantjies that he was there to take Bonnie and Connie to the movies. Mrs. Jantjies called up the stairs and went into the kitchen, leaving Clive sitting by himself in the living room. Connie came downstairs and walked passed Clive and went into the kitchen. She in turn called Bonnie who came downstairs, walked past Clive and went into the kitchen. All of this time Rev. Jantjies was sitting in his study waiting for the opportunity for Connie and Bonnie to ask him for his permission to go to the movies.

Apparently, Bonnie and Connie both went back upstairs and Clive was left sitting there for about twenty minutes when he got up and asked Mrs. Jantjies if Bonnie and Connie were home or not. Mrs. Jantjies told him that Bonnie and Connie were just down there. She called them again-this time waiting for them to come down and when they did, she introduced them to him.

By this time Rev. Jantjies had come into the room. Clive said that he was sorry but he did not know them and then he explained what had happened. I believe that he left very disappointed.

The following night I went to choir rehearsal. I had completely forgotten about the prank that we had played on Clive. When I walked into rehearsal, Rev. Jantjies was sitting on the front pew and I greeted him merrily. The response was kind of odd but I did not pay it any attention.

It was not until Lorna came in and motioned me with her eyes, "What is he doing here?" that I remembered. Rev. Jantjies was sitting and staring me dead in the face. I could not sing anymore and he knew I was about to laugh aloud when he asked for "Bonnie and Connie" to see him in his office immediately.

Lorna and I pretended that we did not know what he was talking about so we just sat. The next time he raised his voice somewhat and said, "Mary and Lorna get to my office." Lorna and I both fell out laughing and those who did not know what was going on accused us of disrupting the choir rehearsal that night.

Rev. Jantjies ended up laughing with us but warned us to be careful, because Clive was a nice guy but someone else might hurt us for treating them like that.

When we got back to choir rehearsal we could not continue rehearsing anymore because we continued to laugh. Everyone wanted to know why we were laughing. Cedric stopped choir rehearsal and told them what happened. We went home early that night.

One thing I will never forget is how Rev. Jantjies fought on my sister Magdalena's and my behalf to get the leading roles in a play called "Man Born to be King." The director knew that we were the best persons suited for the leading roles-Mary mother of Jesus and Mary Magdalene. According to the director, we were too dark and had coarse hair. He wanted fair-skinned girls with long silky hair.

Rev. Jantjies put his foot down that night and my sister and I had the leading roles.

The newspaper write-up about the performance was pasted on every church door and window. My sister and I were interviewed and our pictures, along with the guy who played Jesus, were in the newspaper.

Nobody knew why I cried so bitterly that night during the play. In the last scene when they had taken Jesus from the cross, my lines were "Give me my Son into my arms..." I had forgotten that "Jesus" was wearing a crown of thorns. As I pressed him to my bosom one of the thorns pressed into my breast and it really hurt. That was the scene that gave us all of those beautiful accolades written-up in the Argus and Cape Times the next day.

Rev. Messias taught me how to implement the practical spiritually. I served as Youth President for more than eight years. Under my leadership we had more than one hundred young people in the youth department.

For every outing that the youth had, I had to get permission and confirmation from Rev. Messias. Rev. Messias taught me how to work with business people. He over-emphasized that my "yes" should mean "yes" and my "no" should mean "no." He taught me timeliness. I hated (and still do) being late for anything. If the invitation or event calls for 7:00 p.m. then I am there.

I recently went to a revival. The service was supposed to start at 7:00 p.m. Normally the preacher would get up at 8:00 p.m. The host pastor and the preacher did not get there until 8:30 p.m. They were celebrating the host pastor's birthday. They had the audacity to tell the people. I started calculating how much time this man had wasted. There were about 4,500 people in the auditorium - multiply that by 90 minutes and divide that by 60 which is 6,750 hours divided by 24 which is 281.25 days. Wow! Lord, have mercy. Imagine what we could have done with all that time. That was the church. What about these African-American banquets? I love timeliness and hate wasted time.

Rev. Messias allowed us to have fun in church. He taught me to believe in myself. He was a very serious person, but courteous, respectful, loving, kind and generous. He would always give financially to the causes that the young people undertook. We were allowed to have youth dances and parties and mystery drives under his administration. He would check-in on the youth ever so often but gave us our freedom of space, believing we would do right.

Whenever I went somewhere, Rev. Messias would always remind me to be the best reference found for God. Thank you Pastor! Whenever I did something incorrectly, he would correct me right there and then, no matter how many people were present. On the job training! Well, he and his wife gave me a lot of good pointers to go by when I became a preacher's wife.

Mrs. Jantjies recited a poem once, which I learned while she was reciting it. I'll say more about the poem later. Mrs. Messias was our youth mother and advisor in many ways. She used to sway in church from side-to-side. I did not understand then and used to mimic her. She was moved by the Holy Spirit.

The pictures that I stored in my memory bank about my pastors were that of excellence. The picture I stored in my memory bank about my dad was that of a drunk. So when I met this man who would later become my husband wearing a black suit and a collar turned backwards, he appealed to my senses.

I was one of those persons who placed preachers on pedestals. I thought that preachers did not sin. Preachers were examples of holiness and righteousness. Preachers had the mind of Christ. Preachers enjoyed the presence of the Lord. Preachers loved to pray. Preachers did not give in to temptation. They acted Godlike and were not disobedient to what God called and commanded them to do. Preachers did not get caught up in the disguise of sin and become comfortable in it.

Preachers went where God sent them. Preachers worked for saving of souls and for substance, not for numbers. Preachers were called by God and not by the echo of their ego. Preachers had a place of ministry and did not seek fame and fortune. Their ministry was to glorify God and ecclesiastical theology. Preachers developed the congregants to love God with all their hearts, and all their souls and all their minds and all their strength.

Preachers loved their wives as Christ loved the church. Preachers taught people to lean to the spirit and not the flesh. Preachers did not neglect their families. Preachers did not allow their successes to lull them to sleep so that an inferior force, and inferior weapon or inferior cause that had already been defeated got ahead of them in the struggle.

Preachers were not duty-bound to take whatever negativity came from the congregants. Preachers did not smoke or use drugs. Preachers did not consume alcohol. Preachers exemplified God to the utmost. Preachers were not bigger than life. Preachers did not live wasteful lives. To be wasteful with anything much less with life is to be very irresponsible. Preachers had lots of benefits.

Preachers did not become satisfied with their gifts; they developed and deployed them. Preachers did not want to be rewarded for their successes. Preachers did not ask God questions and guidance and then debate Him over His responses. Preachers were humorous.

Preachers obeyed God. Preachers were not satisfied with an occasional moving of the Spirit. Preachers knew that the Holy Spirit required a denying of self. Preachers relied on the power of God and not on their own resources. Preachers were loving, considerate, hospitable, forgiving, faithful, patient, sharing, and beared one another's burdens.

Preachers relied on the Holy Spirit who had both the answer and authority of the Father. Preachers mended folk and they equipped them. Preachers used God's truth to bring wholeness and healing to the hurting.

You made a good choice Mary. This is what you wanted. This was an accurate picture of reality for me. This was the desired future I was looking for. My life would now begin as a preacher's wife.

Chapter 7

I can receive nothing that has not been
granted to me from heaven.
Ultimately there is no other source of supply.
It is God Who has made me what I am.
Every good gift that I have comes
from my heavenly father.
JAMES RIDDLE

"John answered and said,
A man can get only what Heaven
has given him."
JOHN 3:27 Beck

Leaning on Jesus

It was getting close to our third anniversary. I had a sneaky suspicion that something was wrong with me because I was not yet pregnant. Although lovemaking took place very seldom, I never used any contraceptives.

In June 1991, I saw a gynecologist who decided to give me an ultrasound. The ultrasound showed that I had severe endometriosis and that I would not be able to conceive. The doctor recommended that I should have a hysterectomy. I was completely dumb struck and numb. I sat and listened, but my mind was everywhere else. I felt so weak and sad, as I always wanted to have children. In my spirit I was asking God, "Why me? why do I have to go through all this? Is life really supposed to be like this?" I wanted to cry and scream but did not. I was thinking about Rezin and how he must be feeling learning that I, the woman he married, would not be able to have children. I kept my cool.

The doctor scheduled surgery for that Saturday morning. I was supposed to meet him at the hospital at 6:00 a.m. that Saturday. We left the doctors office and hardly spoke a word to each other in the car.

We went straight to grandma's house. When we got there Rezin went and sat in the backroom and I shared with grandma what the doctor had just told us. Grandma said that this could not be happening. She said, "I did not have any children and I regret not having children." She did not help the situation, and I burst out in tears. Grandma responded, "All we can do is pray and believe." We sat there for the rest of the afternoon very quietly. Grandma got up to play the piano and I asked her not to because I did not want to cry anymore.

We left to go home. When we got home, I went directly to the guest bedroom. I turned on the television which was on TBN. Benny Hinn was on, and as the television came on the words that were spoken by him were no coincidence. He said, "Woman the doctor says you cannot have children but God says that you will have as many children as your heart desires. Believe God for your miracle." I started screaming and praising the Lord like a mad woman. Rezin came in and asked me what was going on and I told him. He said, "God is able." I received that prophecy by faith. I did not call the doctor until that Saturday morning to inform him that I would not be coming in for the surgery. He asked me if I knew what I was doing. I told him about the Benny Hinn experience. He told me not to be crazy and play with my health. I responded that I was going to be crazy for Jesus this time and was willing to take that risk. He was very angry and hung up on me very abruptly.

I never believed in healing services. I know of many healing crusades that had taken place over the years in South Africa. I had a few cousins who were paid to come down the isle in wheelchairs and at the touch of the Evangelist they would jump up and scream that they were healed. I did not really believe in healing ministry. I always thought that it was fake. Here I was in a desperate situation and God spoke to me through a man named Benny Hinn and I believed. I did not or could not regard it as a coincidence. I was coming from the doctor who said that I would not have children and then the man of God on television spoke life to my womb just hours later. I believed God. It did not matter anymore what had happened at those healing crusades in South Africa. This was and felt so real.

In May of 1991, Rezin had completed his work at the seminary and was looking forward to moving back to Los Angeles. While he was in seminary he was pastoring his first church in the heart of the projects in Austell, Georgia. The projects were so big but the beauty of the church was that the building was centrally located on top of a hill in the heart of the projects. The church had seven adult members and twelve children.

Every Sunday morning, Rezin and I would go through the projects and pick up children to come to church. Soon the church was growing at a fast pace and more adults were coming to worship. Parents followed their children to church. Rezin pastored that church for ten months. He made seventy-five dollars a week and of that he gave back to the Lord fifty dollars in offerings. In less than ten months the church membership increased from nineteen to more than one hundred and thirty members with eighty of them being adults. He refurbished the church and it looked beautiful when it was completed. Rezin was committed to ministry and showed a love for people who were hurting and seeking God.

He developed programs that were best suited for the believers so they could grow and get nourishment in the Word. He would come home on Sunday and start preparing his sermon for next Sunday. I had to hear it three to four times a week, and by Sunday I was able to preach the sermon with him. He was excited about ministry. He treated his commitment to God as a commission. They were a loving church.

We had our friends to help in the music ministry and also the children's ministry. I took some of the children home with me on weekends so they could experience life beyond the projects.

Before we left, the congregation blessed us with a thousand dollar gift. The church had sold barbeque dinners on the first Saturday of each month to raise that gift to give to us without our knowledge. We cried as the people so lovingly expressed their love for us. The people were so humble and sincere in their actions. They were truly hungering and thirsting after the Word of God.

Some of the children were given unusual so-called African names. They said it was African but it was really made up. One lady tried to name her daughter Neferititi. She ended up naming her Nafeteria and the kids teased her by calling her Cafeteria. We were blessed in our ministry in the projects. Whenever I was at a church meeting with other clergy families present, I would introduce myself as the wife of the pastor of the major metropolitan church in the city. I was honored and blessed to serve God's people in the heart of the projects.

The month of July came with all kinds of challenges. Rezin did not know what the church had to offer him on the west coast. We had to plan by faith and believe God that He would have everything worked out for us when we got to wherever He was sending us. We sing the song so regularly "I'll go where you want me to go dear Lord," and yet we never think about the words. I knew that when I married this man that he was called to the itinerant ministry and that it would be required of him to pack up and go whenever he was called to do so.

We had an apartment full of furniture and did not know whether to keep it or sell it. Well, we just assumed that the appointment would come with a parsonage. Rezin and I were arguing about selling the furniture, and I just wanted to give it away. My Jamaican girlfriend asked me if she could buy the furniture from me. I wanted to give it to her, but Rezin would not allow me to do that. I never had a problem with giving things away and not expecting anything in return, but I was married to Rezin.

I finally gave in to him and sold the furniture for a hundred dollars to my friend. Rezin was furious. He left it up to me to decide the price and I did. My girlfriend came and got the furniture when she was certain that Rezin was not around because she knew that he was furious about the hundred dollar sale.

It was finally time for us to move but there was one problem. Our friends who were having a home built asked us if they could move in with us for a few weeks. This couple helped Rezin cheerfully and generously with the ministry in the projects. We allowed them to stay with us. They moved in at the end of May 1991. The builder had given them three weeks to their move-in date. Three weeks came and went and by the end of July, they were still waiting on their home to be finished. I convinced Rezin that we should ask for another months lease and have them to close out the lease. We did. Our friends stayed for another month and we were on our way to California.

We arranged to stay with my mother-in-law while we were waiting on his pastoral appointment. My mother-in-law met us at the airport. She nonchalantly informed me that she had made arrangements for me to baby-sit her two grandchildren. They were waiting for me at her home. The youngest was three months old and the other child was three years old. Being the person that I am, I accepted the assignment although I was very tired.

Rezin and I had to use the office space as our bedroom. It had a pull out couch in it. It was terrible sleeping on it because the mattress was very thin, so we ended up sleeping on the floor most nights. I was awakened two to three times a night to see about the baby. I will never forget whenever we were surrounded by people, Rezin would always display his romantic side. I enjoyed those moments. I remember the room we were occupying had no lock on it. I was very conscious of someone walking in on us when we were making love, however it did not happen.

We were there for a few weeks and money was running low. I noticed that everyday we were running to the grocery store and buying groceries. Rezin's family in Los Angeles never invited us for dinner, but they always came for dinner on us. We were both unemployed and living off the little money we had saved until Rezin could get his appointment. This became a little too much for me. I decided to call my dad in South Africa and ask him to send me some money so that I could go back to Austell and wait for Rezin until he got an appointment. My dad sent me the money - not that he could afford to but he did and I was on my way back to Austell to grandma's home.

Grandma was so glad to have me back in the house. I stayed in Austell from August to October speaking to Rezin on a daily basis. I noticed that my menstrual cycle was timely but very abnormal. I did not pay it any attention. It was wonderful to be at peace and to enjoy grandma and be spoiled by her.

It was the last week in September that Rezin called me and told me that he was assured of getting an appointment at the closing of the conference. He told me to make arrangements to be present for the closing of the conference. I bought my ticket to Lenexa, Missouri and left the first Friday in October, 1990. Rezin received his first appointment in the First Episcopal District.

His friends were disappointed in the appointment but Rezin accepted it with so much excitement and honor, and he was ready to start the next round of ministry. Rezin and I were blessed by a pastor and his wife to stay with them until we got settled. The first Sunday in October, 1990, Rezin was assigned to a three-year-old congregation that had about thirty members. He called for the necessary church meetings to make the new adjustments for us. The church had no parsonage. In the meantime, we were still living with the Marlin Family.

The Monday after the assignment, I accompanied Mrs. Marlin to the Hypermart. When we entered the store she decided to take a shortcut through the liquor department to get where she needed to be. While walking through the liquor department, I started vomiting all over the liquor. She asked me if I could be pregnant. My reply was "no." We kept going and I could not stop vomiting. I was kind of happy to be vomiting in the liquor department. No one was going to buy liquor that day. She convinced me to buy me a Clear Blue Easy Pregnancy Test. When we got home, I immediately took the test. It was suppose to give me the results in three minutes. Everyone was anxiously awaiting the results so it seemed like it took forever. Three minutes later the test showed that it was not in the blue. I was not pregnant. We had no health insurance and we were not financially ready to have a baby yet. At least so we thought.

That night while sleeping, the Lord awakened me at four in the morning. I was directed to go back to the trash can and retrieve the test. It was in the blue. I awakened Rezin and the rest of the house and screamed "I'm pregnant!" Everyone was up and then I started vomiting again. We prayed and thanked the Lord for being true to His Word and blessing my womb. Rezin was thinking about finances, but I was just gloating in the goodness of God.

The next day I made an appointment to see a gynecologist. I could not see her for another ten days. Rezin and I had to go back to Austell to get our car and the things that we had left with grandma.

We left traveling Greyhound for twenty four hours to Austell. I was physically exhausted when we got there. I shared the news with grandma that Clear Blue Easy had diagnosed me pregnant and she was overwhelmed with joy as she was going to have her first grandbaby. Grandma called her friends immediately. I laughed when she called people who did not really care about the good news that was happening in our lives.

We loaded the car on the Friday and everything that we could not get in the car was sent by UPS. We left Austell and we were driving back to Lenexa. It was supposed to be a twelve hour drive. I had Rezin to stop so many times to vomit and relieve myself. I hate using public toilets, but I was forced to use them and sometimes the public facilities made me more sick than anything else.

I remember being so cranky that Rezin turned up the radio as loud as he possibly could to drown me out. We finally made it to Lenexa, still married.

Our first Sunday at the new church was a beautiful experience. The people welcomed and received us sincerely and promised to make our stay a comfortable one. There was no parsonage and the church was looking for a place to rent for us. They looked without my input but I did not know any better. They found us a home in the city about twenty minutes away from the church. They had taken out a three month lease. When we entered the house, I could feel spirits all over that place. I was a new preacher's wife and did not know what to do or how to be treated, so we humbly accepted this dwelling place as our new abode. I was not happy but did not complain. The church purchased a new bedroom suite for the house and that would be the only new furniture we had in the house. The living room set was purchased from somebody's home and it was stained and stinking. I would not have bought it for my enemy.

I noticed that whenever I was away from the house I did not vomit as much, but as soon as I returned to the house I would vomit profusely. I finally had my appointment with the doctor. She took several tests and called me back the next day to inform me that the most definitive test, the blood work, came back negative and that I was not pregnant. Something within me would not take that response seriously. I was supposed to see her again the next day so that she could determine what was wrong with me and why I was vomiting so much.

I saw her the next day and she put me on the pill. That night when I tried to take the pill the pill fell out of my mouth. The spirit within me warned me not to attempt to take it again. I obeyed. I saw the doctor everyday that week and our bill was more than two thousand dollars by that Thursday. That Friday as I walked into her office I was led by the Spirit to make this negotiation with her. I asked her to give me an ultrasound and if there was no baby, then I would have to pay the medical expenses. I also said that if there is a baby she would have to refund me for all the unnecessary services she gave me that week. She tried to persuade me that she knew her job very well and that an ultrasound would cost me an enormous amount of money. I said that I was willing to pay. Rezin tried to assist her in her explanation, but I did not want to hear any of it except for what God had told me to do. She and I had an agreement.

She finally did the ultrasound and when I saw a little black dot swimming around. I cried like a baby. She never told me that I was pregnant. She asked me if I wanted to have it aborted. She did not understand my tears. I jumped off the bed and got dressed and did not respond to her statement. I knew she was not the doctor for me. She kept her part of the deal and refunded the money we had spent that week. I never saw her again.

I visited the beauty shop that Saturday morning and shared my experience with the beautician. The beautician asked me if I would allow her to introduce me to the best gynecologist in the world. She also informed me that the gynecologist was a Christian. She walked to the other side of the shop and was told that the doctor had just left. The doctor's four year old daughter whose hair was still being done gave me the phone number to her mother's practice.

I called Dr. Rose that weekend and left a message on her answering machine. She returned my call that Monday morning and asked for both my husband and me to be present at the first appointment.

When we entered her office complex, I felt the spirit of peace welcoming me. We were genuinely greeted by the office staff and sat waiting on our turn to see Dr. Rose. She took us into her office. She asked us some questions and then gave me the best news. She said the reason she asked both of us to come was for us to understand that she did not have a medical practice, but that this was her ministry. I screamed, "Thank you Jesus!" It was determined that day that I was twelve weeks pregnant. I conceived a month after Benny Hinn spoke that prophesy in my life.

My thoughts were, "God I bless you and thank you for this miracle called life within me. Thank you for Benny Hinn who has made me a believer."

The church we were assigned to had rented a parsonage in the city. The house reminded me of a ginger bread home. We were living in the parsonage for six weeks. I had all-day sickness. I vomited and thought at one time that all of my insides were going to come out. Rezin had decided to go ahead and start working on his doctoral studies. I was left by myself at least five to fifteen days a month when he was away at school and whenever he went out of town to preach. I did not like staying by myself and living in a neighborhood that I was not familiar with. I could not sleep at night when he was away.

I would lay awake and listen to the house talking to me. We were blessed to have a ministerial couple to live close by. They lived in a beautiful clean parsonage. I never liked our parsonage because it was very dark on the inside. Whenever I visited them I did not want to go home. God so ordained it that every time my husband was out of town, her husband would be away preaching. She would invite me to come and stay at their home and enjoy the peace of God. The beauty of all this was that she gave up their master bedroom for me to sleep in and I would sleep like a baby. My body got the necessary rest it needed and my mind and spirit rested too.

When Rezin returned from his first class, I insisted that we should start looking for a home. I was not going to have my baby live in that house. There were too many spirits in it and it was not the Holy Spirit. His income was two hundred dollars a week and he did not know how we were going to be able to buy a home. I insisted that we believe God.

It was snowing one day, and we were on our way to service. I went outside to get in the car when I slipped on the ice. I was six months pregnant. I slid downhill and went underneath the car. My stomach prevented me from going all the way under the car. I believe that I hurt my baby that day. I started bleeding and was put on bed rest for three days. I was denied three days of looking for a home.

We found a home about two hundred feet away from the church. Grandma helped us with the down payment and we were blessed to be homeowners for the first time in our lives. It was a ranch style home which was about eighteen hundred square feet. It had three big panoramic windows in the living and dining rooms. The bedroom windows were so high up I could not see out of them. It had four bedrooms, two and a half bathrooms, a nice size kitchen and dining room and living room area. The basement was the size of the upper house and we remodeled it later. I felt good. The house did not talk to me at night. God is so good. The Lord provided for us to get new furniture for the home. It was beautiful. We moved in when I was eight months pregnant. The church people were so kind in helping us get settled. Rezin did not assist in anything as far as the moving into our new home was concerned. He was busy with church work. It was still hard for me to sleep in the house by myself, but I survived. When I did not have a good nights rest, I would make up for it during the day.

The church was growing. God truly was giving the increase. Rezin was happy being the pastor of this church. I did not like church meetings because those were the times when folk would not act saintly. Sometimes I felt that Rezin had many opportunities to teach, but decided to appease the people of God rather than instruct them in the ways of the Lord.

My baby was due May 21st. I was hoping that the birth would take place on my birthday, May 9th. The baby had a mind of her own. I did not know the sex of the baby and was not interested in it either. I was just happy to be pregnant. Every time we visited the doctor, I always came back with a good report. My husband was praying for a boy and in my heart I would be praying "Lord please let it be a girl." For the entire pregnancy I had gained twenty pounds but I was as big as a house. I was bent backward.

The church gave me a baby shower. It was a beautiful and generous event. God provided through the church the furnishings of the baby room. The baby had everything. This was the first baby born to the church and they were just as excited. I did not have to buy anything. Grandma and I were talking daily on the phone and she always concluded her conversation, "Let me know if there is anything my grandbaby needs." She was excited. She was my family.

May 21st came and went and so did May 30th. My doctor scheduled to induce labor on June 4, 1992. I was supposed to be at the hospital at nine that morning but I decided (not knowing anything that giving birth entails) to go to the beauty shop. The hospital called several times and when I arrived it was after three that afternoon. My doctor exclaimed, "Where have you been?" and I answered that I had gone to the beauty shop. She replied that you do not go to the beauty shop when you have to deliver a baby. She placed a magazine in my hand and asked me how I was doing. I replied that I could not wait to have this process over with. I looked at the magazine and it said "be anxious for nothing....." I said I repent and refute what I had just said. I breathed in Jesus and breathed out impatience and anxiety.

Time went very slowly from there on in. Seventeen hours later I had only dilated two inches. My doctor explained that she was going to have to perform a cesarean. There was a lot of chaos and confusion between the anesthesiologist and my husband. The anesthesiologist felt that Rezin would be too weak to stand the birthing process, and he was not going to put up with him. I do not know why. They went back and forth and Rezin finally gave in and stood outside the room looking through a window. We prayed before he left.

They applied the anesthesia and I was out. When the baby was born Dr. Rose said that it was a girl. She was born June 5, 1992 in

Lenexa, Missouri. I was still very groggy and was beginning to cry. My doctor asked me not to cry. So I stopped and went back to sleep. I had given birth to a beautiful girl, six pounds and seven ounces, twenty inches long and she came out cooing. She had ten fingers and ten toes and everything needed to be called a perfectly healthy little girl. At least so I thought. There was something that I had not yet been told, and I had not yet had the opportunity to see my baby.

I was sitting half naked, spread eagle on the toilet. The nurse was spraying my vagina with water so that I could urinate. This male doctor walked right into the bathroom. I was so disgusted and embarrassed because I thought he should have waited or had himself announced. He said that we have an emergency. "The left leg of your baby is deformed and in order for us to correct it we must act immediately." He gave me two options. My heart started racing and I asked God to help me to focus and not to allow me to have a pity party or a panic attack. I asked the doctor to do what he thought was best. He left.

I started praying out loud while the nurse was still attending to me. I called to remembrance the prayer that Bishop Philo had prayed for us just a few weeks ago.

We were attending a revival service in Lenexa, Kansas. The last night of the revival the host had invited all visiting clergy and their spouses to come and have fellowship at his home after the worship service. They served real food that late at night. I did not eat because I knew what the consequences would be for me later that night. Rezin ate and as we were getting ready to leave, I asked Bishop Philo to pray for us as a couple and the baby that we were about to bring into this world. You know how we ask people to pray for you and then they say they will but never do. Bishop Philo placed his arms around both of us and prayed a sincere prayer for us and the baby right there. I still remember him asking God for a healthy baby.

I was a desperate African woman seeking God for a miracle. Not saying that I would love my baby any less if she was to remain deformed for the rest of her life. I do believe that it is the desire of every mother to give birth to a healthy baby. I implored God to hear my prayer and if my prayer was not heard to remember the prayer his son Bishop Philo prayed on the baby's behalf.

I saw my baby for the first time two hours later. She was beautiful and her left leg was now in a white cast. The cast was supposed to stay on her leg for eight weeks. I named her according to my experience, Imaan which means Faith. **"Now faith is the substance of things hoped for the evidence of things not seen."** (Hebrews 11:1) I kept on walking by faith because I heard the Word of God.

I had called grandma in Austell and told her that she was the new grandmother of a beautiful baby girl. She was so excited and thanked the Lord and thanked the Lord. She would call me every twenty minutes daily. At night time we spoke for hours while I was still in the hospital. She had called someone to go to the store and shop for her new grand baby.

I had spent three days in the hospital and it was finally time to go home. It was a beautiful hot summer's day. We placed Imaan in the car seat which seemed so big for her and drove home. I was not feeling good mentally but just kept it to myself. I felt like I wanted to cry but did not know why. I got home and would sit in the bathroom and just cry. Whenever Rezin was around I would pretend that everything was okay. It was three weeks later and I was still crying. I went down stairs to the basement and just let it out. I was crying uncontrollably until Rezin came down and asked me what was wrong. Rezin held me in his arms for a long time and then we called my doctor. The diagnosis was postpartum depression. I do not wish it on my worst enemy. My doctor prescribed some medication but I refused to take it as I was nursing Imaan. I was determined and intentional not to let the depression get a hold of me. I was on my way to recovery and soon I was back to my normal self.

The church people supplied us with a meal daily. Imaan's wardrobe was bigger than mine. She had so many clothes that I could change her two or three times a day into something new. I never had the opportunity to buy her any clothing for the first sixteen months of her life. My mother-in-law asked me one day why Imaan was always so dressed up. I said she was blessed by God to be dressed up. Between Grandma in Austell and the church she was set for clothes. She was the church's baby and I never acted selfishly with her. I shared her with everyone and she did not pick up any diseases.

It was the fourth week of Imaan's life on earth when we had to go and see the orthopedic surgeon. They removed Imaan's cast and did not have to replace it. Her leg was completely healed. Thank you God! I just stood there in the doctors office, crying tears of thankfulness. The doctor said that he could not believe it and did not understand how it happened so quickly. I said that God did it. He shook his head and said, "I suppose so." She still had to go back on a monthly basis at first and then every three months and then once a year. Thanks be to God for His healing power.

We received a seventeen-thousand-dollar hospital bill. I did not know how we were going to pay, it but I believed God. Rezin was pouting about the bill, but I had surrendered it to the Lord so there was no place for discussion. Grandma was aware of the situation and took it upon herself to call the hospital and work out a payment plan with them. Her blindness restricted her from doing what she wanted to do the way she wanted to do it. She did not want everyone in her business, so she called Rezin to come and to pick up a check to pay off the bill at the hospital. Jehovah Jireh my Provider. He is more than enough for me.

Imaan was two weeks old when she had her first flight. At two months old she was on her way to Austell and had her second flight. For the first time she was about to meet Grandma Elizabeth. Grandma held Imaan every time she was awake and Imaan would coo and make all kinds of guttural noises and enjoy grandma. Grandma loved Imaan. Grandma would sing to Imaan and teach her to count and call the name Jesus. She would call her friends and hold the phone to Imaan's ear and tell them to say hello to Imaan.

Before we left for church that Sunday she called her friends to make sure that they would come see her and her grandbaby after worship. I was instructed to make sure that I sat in the place that I normally sat and that she would hold the baby during service. Grandma's in-laws did not like the fuss that she was making about Imaan but she did not care; this was her f
irst grand baby. I complied to grandma's every wish. She was very sad when I had to return to Lenexa, but vowed that she would be with us for Christmas.

In October of 1992 we were to celebrate Imaan's baptism. Family and friends came from far and near. My "aunt" who was with me from South Africa from the day Imaan was born was visiting in Miami, and flew back to Lenexa, to celebrate Imaan's baptism. A lady who was a bridal dress seamstress in our church, made Imaan's Baptismal outfit. We took pictures that Saturday night and presented Imaan for baptism that Sunday morning. She was beautiful. One of the Bishops of the church came to preach that Sunday and baptized Imaan. Imaan's grandmother, (Rezin's mother) met her for the first time in her life that weekend.

After the baptism, I could not understand what happened but instead of my child being given to me, the Bishop gave the baby to my mother-in-law. When a child is baptized in South Africa the child is presented to the preacher by the godparents and the preacher intentionally gives the baby back to the mother with words of wisdom and instruction. "Your responsibility in raising this child is unto the Lord. So train this child in the way she should go that when she is old she will not depart from it." There my mind flew off into a different direction again and I was fighting in the spirit trying to maintain the flesh. I cannot even remember the baby being placed in my arms that morning. I controlled myself and kept going.

I was the only foreigner in their family. They were supposed to be my family. Publicly they always said that we do not believe in in-laws, we are family, but privately it was another matter. Whenever someone in the family had a baby, or was celebrating a birthday or an anniversary, my mother-in-law would call us and remind us to call them and wish them according to the occasion. My problem was whenever something great happened in my life they would never call. Not for my birthday or our babies birth, and I was the only one who had one blood relative in the United States. Well I am still living.

After the baptism and dinner, our guest had to be transported to the airport which was about forty minutes away. The rest of that day was spent going back and forth to the airport. Two of our guest remained till Monday morning and I happily but sadly took them to the airport. We enjoyed a good weekend, and it was just nice to have friends and family visiting with us. I celebrated the beauty of the earth as I traveled to and from the airport.

Rezin was a proud daddy. He would lay and just look at Imaan as if to say, "I cannot believe you came from us." Imaan was a very pleasant baby. She hardly cried and I had to check on her in the crib to see if she was still sleeping. She would sleep for long periods of time. When she awakened she would quietly enjoy the bright colors of her room. I read to Imaan a lot. Whatever her eyes followed I would tell her the name of what she was looking at. At four months old Imaan was saying her first words, "Daddy," "light," "fan" and "give." She did not say "mommy" till she was eleven months old, and here I was, the one spending twenty four seven with her.

Rezin was still working on his doctoral studies. On a monthly basis he would be gone. He would have preaching engagements and was not home very much. The baby and I would be home all by ourselves. He never called me immediately when he got to his destination to say that he had arrived safely. I would have to wait sometimes until the next day before I heard from him. This would really upset me. He interpreted my concern as tracking him down. I started pouring all my energies into my daughter.

In February 1993, he pledged to become his mother's campaign manager without discussing it with me. His mother desired to be elevated in the church and to be the first woman elected to the office of bishop. When Rezin graduated from undergraduate school, he promised me that he would allow me to finish my degree that year and then he would start seminary. He started seminary the same year that I was completing my baccalaureate work. When he finished seminary he told me that he would give me the opportunity to go and work on my Master's Degree, and when I finished he would start his doctoral studies. I never got to the Masters Degree, and here he had started on his doctoral work and also now committed himself to be his mother's campaign manger. My concerns and opinions did not matter.

As the "to do" list increased, it sabotaged our closeness and partnership even more. I felt like a single parent and his roommate in our marriage relationship. He had less time for me or was it just another way of dealing with the scariest aspect of the relationship; intimacy.

I was harboring so much frustration within me that I should have expressed. I felt unappreciated, I felt like his maid and most of the time taken for granted. I had absolutely no help from him in the house and hardly any help with Imaan. I was feeling so bad one day and Imaan wanted to be held. I asked Rezin to hold her and he abruptly and disrespectfully said, "no." I became so enraged that I pressed Imaan in his arms and just started pummeling him like a punching bag. I was livid, and it seemed like I could not stop. Imaan started screaming and I ran downstairs and just cried. He did not once lift his hand to hit me back. I was so ashamed. That came about because of pent-up feelings. I was not freed of old emotions.

Whenever Rezin and I had an argument I would always allow him to have the last word. I would walk away from it unfulfilled and feeling like there was no closure. I never had the opportunity to release the unexpressed emotions. I reacted with disproportionate anger and frustrations to this event. It reminded me of all the other times that we did not communicate through and had no closure.

God blessed me with an intense inner strength. The best way for me to release the emotions was to cry, pray and believe that God had heard and seen everything, and that He would have the last word. I had mixed emotions. I had to deal with the consequences of my repressed emotions. I ignored my feelings by overeating, always keeping busy and spending an excessive amount of time watching television. My behavior that day was a reaction to past events as well as the present. I encourage you the reader to deal with your emotions no matter how difficult or painful it is when they occur. It takes a lot of work to keep them stuffed down.

We had no sexual relations from the day Imaan was conceived until August 1994. I was in the window looking and admiring the beauty of fall. I was thinking to myself about Benny Hinn and the prophecy he spoke into my life. I looked up to heaven and said prayerfully "I would love to have another baby. You did say as many children as my heart desires." My desire was to have two children and for the next one to be a boy. Two days later our friends Nona and Lonnie made their announcement that they were expecting. That night Rezin made love to me for the first time since Imaan's conception. Two weeks later I was diagnosed by clear blue easy that I was pregnant, and it was confirmed by my gynecologist a week later.

During the pregnancy Rezin did not touch me again. The pregnancy was much more pleasant than the first one. I gained more weight with the second pregnancy but enjoyed it. I was blessed by God. It was a beautiful day. The snow laid like a thick white carpet spread across the fields. It was so beautiful. I saw the colors purple and gold in the form of a star in the snow. I said to Imaan, "look at the Star of David." In my spirit I heard God whispering, "It is a boy."

Again I was not interested in the sex of the child because my womb was blessed by God. All through my pregnancy I confidently referred to this baby as a boy. When people asked me how I knew, I would excitingly reply that God told me.

In November of 1994, I had the house repainted. When we got through with the painting I told Rezin not to hang the pictures because the Lord had told me we were going to move. I had this dream one night and Rezin was in a different pulpit. I was sitting in the congregation and praising the Lord. I remember when we left church we went to a different home. I interpreted that dream as confirmation to this "gut feeling" that we were going to be moved.

In January the call came, and Rezin was informed that he was being moved to California. All of his family lived in California except for his oldest brother and his family. I was excited because we were going to be close to family. So I thought.

I was eight months pregnant and was very sad that I was going to have to leave this wonderful Godly gynaecologist who had spiritually and physically prepared me through this phase of life. She gave me the okay to travel. I had to pack up the house. I was blessed with church members who were kind and loving enough to extend themselves to come and help me pack our belongings. Rezin had no part in it whatsoever. The house was clean and we left some money with our friends to have merry maids to clean the house.

During the week that we were scheduled to leave, the lady who made Imaan's beautiful baptismal gown died. Her funeral was that Saturday morning, and that Saturday afternoon we said our final good byes to our congregation. We were sad and they were sad to see us go, but we had to go. We made the commitment, "I'll go where you want me to go dear Lord." We arrived safely in Los Angeles and traveled down the road to the Marriott Hotel where we would stay the next few days.

Rezin's commitment to ministry seemed so real. Everything that he did for God was always his best. I could not understand how he could be so good at what he was doing for God and neglect his family. The church was a challenge, but he stuck with it no matter the cost. Sometimes money was needed to pay certain bills at church and he did not think twice to sacrifice our finances and make our bills run late to accommodate the church. He saw things through to completion no matter what the cost.

We attracted people to the church because we were a living example publicly. People were hungering to see a true commitment, and he gave them an opportunity to see a living example and not just a word definition from a dictionary. He would go when the sick called him in the late or early hours of the night or day. He would help those who could not pay for the entire grocery bill in the store. I'll never forget us standing in line and an older couple was trying to find the last bit of change to pay for everything they needed. They came up short and Rezin paid the rest. He gave them a business card, and the next Sunday this couple and twenty eight of their family members came and joined church. The man expressed that he could not believe that there were still kind people living.

When storms came to the church, he had the enduring ability to make people believe in miracles. He had a spirit of compassion and kindness for others that he could not express to his wife. Whenever the church was doing well we were doing good. When the church went through difficult times I had to suffer privately. I still had to smile, to sing, to encourage, to endure, to lead, to give and still love the church and God. He was an excellent preacher and could teach bible study that you did not want to miss it. He renovated the church and left it with more than two hundred members. His public relationship with God grew the people into an expectant people.

Chapter 8

May the Master take you by the hand

and lead you along the path

of God's love and Christ's endurance."

2 THESSALONIANS 3:5 MESSAGE

The Lord continually directs my heart into the Father's love, showing me how to trust and walk in it, and into the steadfast patience of Christ, which is a sure confidence in my inevitable victory.

JAMES RIDDLE

Itinerant Surprises

The denomination that I am a part of makes use of the itinerant ministry. Pastors are assigned to a particular church for a limited period of time. It takes a lot of adjustment spiritually, physically, economically and mentally. It is hard on young families and those who have established themselves through employment in the community.

For me it was always an exciting adventure. I was being given an opportunity to enlarge my territory and to meet new people, live in a new culture, experience a different life style, enjoy the beauty of the earth as it is presented differently everywhere, and spread the love of Jesus somewhere else.

In Lenexa there were no mountains, just flat lands. The first thing I noticed in California was the beauty of the mountains, and it seemed as if it surrounded us everywhere we went. Psalms 125:2 says, **"As the mountains surround Jerusalem so God surrounds His people (children) both now and forever."** That scripture became my favorite while living in California. Just to know that the presence of the Lord was surrounding me was comforting.

Our home in Cape Town South Africa faced Table Mountain. I was blessed as a youth to be able to climb Table Mountain. So I loved the mountains and was somewhat reminded of being back home.

I was also welcomed by the beauty of the oceans. I loved the beaches of California. Back home Cape Town is surrounded by oceans. At Cape Point, the Indian Ocean meets with the Atlantic Ocean. The water calms my spirit and I normally do my best meditations at the water. We left cold Lenexa and here I was in sunny California. The water and mountains were just a beautiful sight to behold.

I do not know of anybody who would refuse going to California. It is the most beautiful country in all of the United States. California also came with family. All of Rezin's family was living in Southern California. So I was at home eight months pregnant, with the mountains, the oceans and family. I thought I had it all.

We were driving for a while down I-405 to Orange County. My body was tired and I wanted to get to a restroom. Rezin had been driving for more than an hour when I realized that he was lost. I asked him if he knew where he was. He told me to enjoy the ride. I replied that I had been riding all day. I was tired and wanted to get to bed. He just ignored me. I kept on nagging him until he stopped and asked someone to give him better directions. What is it about men and driving in circles and not wanting to stop and ask for directions?

Rezin had already met with the church and had attended two services before we made it there together as a family. We finally got to the hotel, and I showered and went straight to bed.

We were awakened the next morning by one of the church officers who brought us a delicious homemade breakfast. During breakfast Imaan was enjoying the limited hotel space and I was looking in the newspaper for a temporary apartment to stay in because we only had a few more weeks to go before the baby was due.

We were blessed to be welcomed joyfully by the church. We had good worship that Sunday morning. The officers had a light repast on our behalf after worship so that we could meet the members. The church was full and an elderly lady presented me with a beautiful necklace that morning. A couple who were both engineers took us to dinner. This was a step up for Rezin. Every round goes higher and higher. I realized at dinner that afternoon that the "to do list" just got much longer.

I was happy and in the right place. The church had a parsonage, but the officers felt that the community was not a safe place to raise a young family.

Monday came and my top priorities were to find a place to stay and a gynecologist. The first apartment complex we stopped at was in Yorba Linda. I was pleased but wanted to see something a little closer to the church. We stopped in Costa Mesa and found a nice Town home. Our furniture and cars were still traveling. We were happily informed that we would be able to move in that Thursday, the same day the moving truck would arrive in California. God was doing it.

I made an appointment with a gynecologist in Newport Beach for that Friday.

The church members again came to my aide by helping me unpack and helping me make the transition as comfortably as possible. We had a six-month lease. The apartment complex was beautiful. The only thing I did not like about it was that the door opened right in the street. I had to put a bell on the inside of the door to warn me when Imaan was trying to get out. Our neighbors had a daughter the same age as Imaan. They always came to my rescue when I was in need of a nap. Imaan did not meet a stranger, and people loved her for being so sociable. The neighbor's daughter had the most beautiful curly blond locks.

I met my gynecologist for the first time that Friday. I left her office pleased but missing the godly woman who had assisted me and encouraged me in my faith back in Missouri. I saw my new doctor twice a week and we bonded gradually. She was pregnant too. Every time she would have a negative comment about her body, I would remind her of how blessed she was.

The church had six hundred members and it kept Rezin busy. He was gone most of the time. Imaan and I explored our way around Orange County. Everyone was very kind and helpful.

Before we left Lenexa, a pastor's wife who encouraged me through difficult times of ministry gave me a name of a sister whom she knew in the new church. She felt I would be able to speak or confide in her if necessary. Service was over and I saw this lady approaching me. I said to her, "You must be Sister Pearl," and she replied "How did you know?" I fell in love with her immediately and our spirits connected. She became my God-given mother for my stay in California.

I was sitting in church that first Sunday in April 2005, feeling a lot of discomfort and increased pressure in the lower abdomen. I did not say anything. After service I went home and rested most of the afternoon. I went downstairs that evening and felt a little trickle down my legs but did not pay it any attention.

We went to bed, and the next morning at five I was awakened lying in a pool of water. The rupture of the membranes had taken place. I excitedly awakened Rezin and said that we needed to get to the hospital. We called my doctor and she said for me to go to the hospital immediately. I was praying for a normal delivery this time. We could not take Imaan with us and a sister-friend volunteered to hold Imaan for the day.

I got to the hospital at six. They were hooking me up to tubes and poking me, getting me ready for this delivery. I was calm. My room was facing the ocean. The hospital was on top of a hill overlooking the beauty of the sea. I was happy because the water calms my spirit. The monitor gave us the necessary indications. The contractions were progressively long and close. Although the machine indicated when there was going to be a very strong contraction, I was only moderately aware of the contractions. My doctor was in the room when the nurse told me that a big one was coming. I just laid there as if she was talking to the walls. My doctor said that it was a little too early in the morning for her to deal with my so-called optimistic spirit. She asked me to let her know when I wanted the anesthesiologist to give me an epidermal. She left and I did not see her until an hour later. She asked my husband if I was always this calm. He laughed and said that she is no matter how bad you treat her.

The day continued slowly and at four that afternoon, those who were around me had worn me out mentally and I was ready for the epidermal. The anesthesiologist was so kind and gentle unlike the anesthesiologist I had for my first born. I really saw Jesus in him. I continued being prepped and tested for a few more hours when one of the brothers came by the hospital and took my husband to dinner at a very exclusive Japanese restaurant in Huntington Beach.

I had some quiet time and enjoyed God, imploring him to move the process along as quickly as possible. I had been there for fourteen hours already and was getting just a little anxious. I had only dilated four centimeters.

When Rezin and the brother returned they brought all that good smelling left over food into the room. It just made me aware of the fact that I had not eaten all day long. I was hungry and could not eat. They laughed and took the food away quickly.

My doctor came at nine-thirty that evening and asked me to give up the thought of having a normal birth, as I was not dilating anymore. She gave me another hour and then she was taking me into surgery to perform a cesarean. Earlier that day I asked her if I could have my tubes tied if she had to do a cesarean. My doctor was not very happy about my desire. She asked me if I had given thought to the idea that anything could happen to my children or that I would want to have another child. My response to her was that my children are covered by the blood of the Lamb. Her response surprised me when she blurted out that she was sick and tired of me always talking about God and acting as if I was not living in the real world where real things happen to real people. I started praying in the spirit, for this was the gynecologist who was going to deliver my baby in a few moments. I remained calm. I told her that God created this world and He controls everything that happens to me in this world. I was very aware that I was living in this world but not of this world.

My doctor was pregnant and tired. She was kind and had graciously committed to delivering my baby. She could have given it to some other doctor to do, but she stayed the course to deliver my baby herself. She looked at me and shook her head. She stuffed the papers into my hand and said, "Sign on the dotted line. I can see I am not going to get through to you." I said, "No, God has given me the desire of my heart a girl and a boy." I was thirty seven and considered old by the present population but blessed to be able to give birth to my son. She did not understand the things of God yet as well as I did, but I sensed that she was seeking.

My son was born at 10:31pm. This time I was able to see him immediately. He was a fine, handsome-looking healthy baby. Everything was in tact. No surprises. He looked so clean. No wrinkles or frown, just a happy little curve around his mouth that said he was so glad to be here. I again named him according to my experience. Niamke which means "thought of God" or "God remembers." We thanked God for this miracle called life and asked him to bless and protect this new bundle of joy. I was moved to another room and had the privilege of having the room all by myself. It felt very cold to me. I remember the nurse putting blankets on me, and at twelve she said you must be warm enough now. I laughed, thanked her and fell asleep.

They awoke me to nurse the baby three times that night. The next morning, Rezin showed up at the hospital with our daughter who was three years old and very excited to meet her new brother. She was so happy when she saw him and sat on the bed with me while I allowed her to hold him. She kept on kissing him. Rezin said that he had to leave, and he left Imaan with me in the hospital.

After a few hours, the nurses realized that I was babysitting Imaan. They put a phone call in to her dad to come and get her as she was not supposed to be there unsupervised with the patient.

When Rezin arrived, he and I got so involved with the baby that we forgot to keep an eye on Imaan. Imaan was doing everything that she was not supposed to do and unknowingly pushed the code blue button. Medical staff came running from all over the hospital and the nurse was followed by about twenty other medical workers into my room. I calmly asked what was going on and was informed that the code blue button had been pushed. The nurses had had enough. Rezin had to take Imaan somewhere where she could explore her territory without having any boundaries. My doctor was the last to arrive. She said she could not help but think about the conversation we had the previous day. I said that the Lord is to be praised, nothing happened. It was all an innocent mistake.

Rezin and Imaan left and I had time to walk around the hospital and start the healing process. They concluded my stay at the hospital with a candlelight dinner for Rezin and me in a beautiful setting, and we were able to watch the sunset together. The sun was so fiery bright that night that it mirrored the waters as if it was on fire.

I was in the hospital for three days. I had one phone call from Rezin's brother who lived in Marietta, Georgia to wish me well. I thought that we were family and that they would check up or stop by to see me in hospital, but they did not.

For my first few days at home, I was blessed to have Sister Pearl's daughter Ashley, to come and take care of me and the children. She made the best breakfast and taught me how to prepare breakfast potatoes the way they do it in the Wren household.

Rezin was traveling and attending to church business. Rezin's sister came the next week and stayed that entire week with me and the children. The following week Rezin's aunt spoiled me with good cooking, genuine cleaning and much love.

I thought that because we were living in California close to Rezin's family that everyone in the family would have made their rounds to come and welcome the new addition to the family, but not so.

Niamke met his grandmother, uncles, aunts and cousins for the first time at his grandmother's engagement. We had met at Rezin's twin brother's home for the engagement celebration. Everyone had an opportunity to say "hello" to Niamke for the first time.

Everyone tried to spoil Niamke by holding him, but I asked them to refrain from doing so because he still had to go home with me. I shared Niamke freely with everyone and he remained a very healthy baby. Niamke, like his sister, was a very content baby and had everyone fall in love with him. He was spoiled and whomever he did not want to have any business with, I respected his wishes. Babies detect unkind spirits.

It was time for my six-week check up. My doctor's office called me that morning and asked me to be on time for my appointment. I found that very strange, as she never did that before. When I got to the office, she seemed extremely pleased to see me. She gave me a good report and said that I did not have to see her again until my next pap smear.

She stood over me and very reluctantly said that she wanted to share something with me. She said that her faith is very different from my faith, but she liked what she saw me exhibiting during my pregnancy. She remained quiet for a few moments and then asked, "How do you do it?" I told her that I could not do anything without God. It is the spirit of God that leads me and guides me in all ways. She stood there and just played with her fingers. I got up and started getting dressed. I asked her to tell me what the real question was that she was afraid to ask. She just looked and smiled. When she opened her mouth a tear dropped from her eyes. I reached out and hugged her. She broke down and said my baby is in trouble and I don't know what to do. I said, "God is Able." I laid my hands on her stomach and prayed for her. I encouraged her to believe God that at the next doctor's appointment she would have good news. I told her to read Deuteronomy 28 verses 1 through14 to her baby for the next few days. She called me a week later and told me that whatever I did worked. I corrected her and told her that I did not do anything but that God did it and to always remember that. She said, "Goodbye I wish I could be surrounded by people like you daily." I replied that she should ask God to do it for her and that He would. I was happy that God had come through for her. I prayed that God would continue to draw her closer to Him.

Niamke was three months old and I noticed Niamke's skin just breaking out. I was so shocked and instead of going to the doctor, I jumped in my car drove to Sister Pearl's home. When I got to her house I just cried. Sister Pearl started praying out loud. She took some powder and started rubbing the baby's body down. Niamke looked like a white powdered baby but he was smiling and laughing and trying to have conversation with everyone. By the time we left, Niamke was healed in Jesus Name. Every time something happened I would call Sister Pearl. She would lovingly and helpfully comply.

One of the church members died. He was a very important individual in the community. I decided to attend his funeral that

Saturday morning. I was running late. You know how it is when you have to get two babies ready all by yourself. The family processional was about to begin, and they had just finished praying before marching into the church. It was a large family. I drove up on the church parking lot. My husband saw me and motioned to me that he would give me time to enter before he would start the processional.

I had released Imaan out of her car seat and she ran into the church. I walked around the car and the next thing that happened was so embarrassing that I wanted the earth to open and swallow me whole. I had just taken Niamke in his car seat out of the car when I saw the associate ministers running towards me. My skirt had fallen off and I could not reach down immediately to pull it up because my hands were full. The family tried to look the other way but I saw them. The associate ministers relieved me from Niamke, the diaper bag, the car seat and my handbag. I was able to reach down to my ankles and pull up my skirt. My husband came over and we laughed about the incident. I was glad that my mom had taught me at a very early age that my under garments were more important and should look better than the outer garments. I had on clean underwear, good looking legs, a little bit of a pouch and much embarrassment.

I walked by the family and greeted them as if nothing had happened. The wife of the deceased told me, "Sister Mary, I was going to cry today but you gave me something to laugh about." The family had their private show by the pastor's wife. I hugged her and we laughed.

We were nearing our sixth month in the leasing contract. I did not want to live in an apartment or town home anymore. I wanted a home with a backyard for the children to play in. My husband informed me that we could not afford to purchase a home at the time. I felt we could, but he was in charge of the budget so I believed him. I started looking for a home to rent or lease. I found a good agent, and she started showing me around. Everywhere we looked in Costa Mesa did not work out for us at all.

I went to a neighboring city called Irvine and found just what we needed. When we walked through the house the owners were entertaining guest. I had my mind made up that we were going to be denied again. The very next day the agent called and I could hardly believe my ears when she said it was ours. I thanked the Lord, for his mercy truly endures forever. We were set to renew the apartment lease for another six months the next day. God is an on time God. I started packing as fast as I could and we were ready to make the move again.

The neighborhood that we moved into was 99.99999 % white. There was one black family living in the neighborhood. They saw us coming down the street one day. The man jumped out of his car and did a dance in the street while chanting, "Black people in the neighborhood." I laughed and said, "Thank you" for the unusual welcome.

The house we occupied was located in a cul-de-sac. It had a very big tree in front of it, and the garden had a swing in it. I enjoyed watering the garden and washing off the driveway at night. My neighbors were very friendly. My immediate neighbors were raising their granddaughter who became best friends with Imaan very quickly. She and I would sit for endless hours in the evening and watch the children and just share with one another about the goodness of the Lord. She was helping her son raise his children and was available to him and his wife whenever it was needed. She gave so much to her grandchildren and made every opportunity she had with them a fond memory, and Imaan benefited too.

The church was growing. A young lady had attached herself to me. I noticed her the Sunday her husband came down the isle and recommitted himself to the Lord. The church was happy and people were shouting and crying about this event. The spirit nudged me to pay careful attention to this young couple. I became acquainted with the wife. She started opening up to me about things that she could not easily speak to anyone about. She informed me that he was a drug addict. I learned that the recommitment incident was a regular event. Every time her husband got out of trouble he would come back and recommit himself to the Lord. The church would shout and praise God for the occasion, but no one was willing to show him how to commit himself to a consistent life in God.

His wife shared with me about the many children he had outside of their marriage. She said she smiled every time he made his way to the altar but felt it was just a show, and she could not get excited about it anymore. He would be good for a day or two and then go back to his old ways again. There was no accountability required of him. As a married couple they had three daughters together. They were living with his mother who was an alcoholic. She and her children had to endure the verbal, physical and mental abuse. The children would come and spend weekends with me and they would share with me their pain and frustration. They were so young, and I wished in my heart that I could save them from this undeserving life experience they were living. The littlest one was the same age as Niamke. She would cry so sadly when she had to leave my home.

I started sharing the Word of God with his wife. Her attendance became more regular. She joined the choir. Her husband was physically abusing her, and she was looking for a way out. I told her that she needed to get into a place of her own. She said that he would kill her if she left him. I told her to trust the Lord. I never encouraged her to leave her husband by divorcing him but I encouraged her to look for a new place away from the alcoholic mother-in-law.

She was a beautician and could not afford renting space. We

started praying with each other, petitioning the Lord daily on her behalf. He had abused her again. I asked her if she envisioned her life to be like that forever. She replied "No" and that she wanted to do better for herself but most of all for the children's sake. I told her whenever she was ready to move let me know and that my car was available.

My son was five months old and a very good baby. I was changing his diaper one morning when the phone rang. It was Deborah asking me if I could come immediately and help her move out. I said I would be there in a few minutes. Everything I had planned for that day was put on hold, and I was on my way into Orange, to help Deborah move. I stopped by Sister Pearl's home and dropped Imaan and Niamke with her. My husband was unaware of the events taking place, but I was just happy to see a sister being set free.

We did not have time to pack anything neatly, so we dumped everything in trash bags and filled my car with it. I made six trips from Deborah's place of residence to her temporary home which was going to be with Sister Pearl. The seventh trip was interrupted by the sighting of her husband, and we both concluded that she had more than enough to sustain her. It was 7:30 that night when we got done.

Deborah and her children were happily settling in at the Wren's residence. Word got to her husband that I had helped to move her. His response was that I should be careful running into him. I was not scared at all. A few days after the move he was arrested for drug trafficking. While he was in jail he wrote his pastor Rezin the most beautiful letter. It brought tears to my eyes when I read it. He repented of his ways again and said that if the Lord would allow him to be free one more time, he would serve the Lord for the rest of his life and make up to his family for all the pain he had caused them.

He had twelve children outside of his marriage. God did grant him his request and again before the church he came sobbing and testifying of the goodness of The Lord. The spirit of God informed me that this again was but for the moment.

His wife told me after service that she did not know how long it was going to last, but she was staying where she was. Doors started opening for her. A lady who owned an apartment complex gave her an apartment to live in free of charge until she could get herself back on her feet. She moved from the Wren's residence and into her apartment. She was very happy and God continued to bless. One thing that I never encouraged her to do was to get a divorce, because I felt that God was still able to restore her marriage to what it was supposed to be.

Her husband was back on the street and doing everything and more than what he did before. She had been in her apartment for three weeks when there was a knock on the door one evening. She opened the door and there was her husband standing. He started an argument with her while holding his foot in the door so that she could not close it. She called out to one of her children to call me. She said as soon as she said my name he was gone.

He took ill shortly after that incident. I went courageously to the hospital to visit him. When I got there he had three male visitors with him. I walked in and greeted him politely. He did not respond to my greeting but told his friends that I was the one who broke up his family. I responded very kindly to him with a smile on my face that I did not break up his family that he did it all by himself. He thought that the brothers were going to jump on his band wagon but they started rebuking and admonishing him. I was in good company. I asked him what was wrong with him and he replied that he had a viral infection. I asked him when was he going to stop playing games with God. He said that he was trying to do better, but he just could not help himself anymore. I recommended that he should place himself in a rehabilitation centre and take the time to get well. Again he promised that if the Lord delivered him from this sick bed he would give God all his time and substance.

While he was saying that, a female walked into the room. She greeted him with a kiss on his mouth. I asked him whether he allowed any woman besides his wife to kiss him like that. The brothers who were present started laughing and said that I was a bold sister. The female told him that it was not necessary for him to answer me. I told him that he must let go of this adulterous behavior if he is truly seeking God's help and healing. He asked the female to leave and she did.

Every time he got out of his many troubles, he would come to church and go before the church and repent so sincerely, but the next few hours he would be found doing the same old things again.

His wife was blessed with a job managing and running the day-to-day affairs of a beauty salon. A gentleman from South America bought the place and told her that she could rent it out to whomever she wanted as long as the rent was covered. God was moving on her behalf. She was happy that she had made so much progress on her own for the short period that she had stepped out on faith. There were times when I had to remind her that it was all God, and she received it very graciously.

It was the Sunday of Memorial Day weekend in May 1996. Deborah had invited me and the children to come by her place after service. I told her that I had to take my husband to the airport. I asked her to come by my place instead so that the children could play in the backyard without us having to have them cooped up in the house. She agreed that she would meet me at my house within an hour. I allowed my kids to drive with her to my house while I took my husband to the airport. When I got home, there was no sign of Deborah or the children. I gave her another hour and then called her apartment. There was no answer. My spirit was alerting me that something was wrong. I could not do anything but pray. I called and called for several hours.

At eight that night I finally was able to locate her mother. She called someone else to find out about her and especially my children's whereabouts. Her mother called me back at nine-twenty and informed me that she was going to pick up my children and that I could come and get them from her home. She said she would give me more details when she saw me. I asked her to answer me one question before she hung up and that was to tell me if my children were okay. She said they were fine and to meet her at her home in thirty minutes. I got in my car and flew down the 5 Freeway to get my children. I was thanking God that they were okay.

When I got there my children were half asleep. I was told that Deborah was kicked in the head by her husband that afternoon and that she was in the hospital semi-conscious. She had a three-inch gash in her head. I drove back home and just concentrated on my children.

We got home and I bathed them and put them to bed. The next morning I asked my four-year-old daughter what had happened. She did not witness anything except for the hearing of Deborah screaming. I called Deborah to check on her, and all she could do was to apologize. I asked her if she had called the police and brought charges against him. She said yes and that he was in jail.

For the court case I would sit with Deborah every day. The district attorney asked me to encourage her to be as honest about the situation as possible. She was very hesitant in answering certain questions, and I would nod my head while she was watching me prompting her to tell the whole truth. We had spent four days in court. On the fifth day I was there with the district attorney waiting on Deborah. This was supposed to be the last day, and Deborah did not show.

The case was thrown out. I was furious but had to tell myself that I had not experienced what she experienced. Maybe she was scared that he would kill her or something. I left court that day deciding that my days with Deborah were over and that it was time for me to let go.

Her husband was on the streets again. Very shortly there after, he was hospitalized again. I went to the hospital and gave him a message from the Lord. I told him that God had told me that the next sickbed would be his last sickbed and that he would not have another opportunity to make things right with his family and God. He cried like a baby. I dreamed it and it was so real that I could not keep it to myself. After the release from hospital, he made his way back to the church again. He was good for a few minutes but then just went back to his old ways. He was enslaved.

Three weeks later he was back in the hospital again. I knew that the word was from the Lord. I told Deborah to allow the children to spend as much time with him as they could afford. Deborah went there daily no matter how embarrassing or humiliating it was to her. Women would show up at the hospital and disrespect her openly as the wife of this man. I asked him one day whether he was sure that he was going to heaven. We prayed the sinner's prayer together and sang his favorite hymn, "Why should I feel discouraged." I left that day and two days later he was no more. I thanked God that God had released him from this life of oppression and asked Him to have mercy on his soul.

The funeral was crazy. Deborah decided to show up an hour late with the family for the funeral. In the meantime at church all the mothers of his children had the kids say their final farewell to their dad. The girl that I encountered at the hospital was putting on a performance. I prayed mightily. When I saw her going out the door I seized the opportunity to follow her. Outside she was surrounded by two females and was just crying and screaming. I did not feel sorry for her at all and approached her very gently. I asked her to give Deborah the respect she deserves, especially today, and not to make a scene in the church. She screamed out loud, "He loved me and not her!" I asked her, "So why did he not want to marry you?" The ladies had to pull her back because she was about to swing at me.

The family cars were pulling up and she made her way back into the sanctuary. I sat myself directly behind her. After the wife and children had viewed the body, she tried to get up but I pressed her back down. She said, "Leave me alone. I have to say goodbye to him." I replied that it was too late and you have said your final goodbyes. She walked out of the church and never came back inside until the close. She thought that the casket was going to be opened again for her to give her final performance. We had had enough drama that day that would last us for eternity. I saw her a few days later in the grocery store checking out ahead of me with another guy. I said, "So much for Manny."

PAUSE

100

My mother-in-law called my husband on numerous occasions. When I answered the phone she would ask, "Where is the pastor, or where is my son?" She would never ask "how are you doing" or "how are the grandchildren doing? I remember asking my husband one day what he and his mother talked about so much. He responded that everything she says to him is confidential, and just because I was his wife did not mean that he needed to share everything with me. "My mother does not want you to know the things we talk about."

My mind immediately went back to an incident that took place in our lives caused by my mother-in-law that second year of marriage. After I got married, I still saw grandma four to five times a week. I would take her a meal and do some cleaning around the house so it would maintain the look it had when I was living with her. There was a closet in grandma's home that I never touched while I was living with her. It made me tired just looking at it. It had a cedar closet which contained a lot of clothes, papers and what I thought was a lot of junk.

We were married for about fourteen months. Grandma had gone into the closet one day and came out with her hand bleeding. She said that she had stuck her hand into some clothes and something cut her hand. I promised grandma that I would come and clean the closet for her only if she would allow me to throw away some of that junk.

I went to her home early one morning and started dumping things into the trash bags. I noticed that grandma had pulled up a chair right outside the closet door and every five minutes grandma would ask me what I was throwing away. I had dumped six bags already when I found this green paper bag and opened it. It had more than three thousand dollars in the bag. I said to grandma, "What are you doing with all this money in the closet?" She replied that her brother used to hide money in that closet. She told me to make sure that I did not throw any money away. I retraced my steps and went through the six bags again and found seven thousand dollars. I opened every piece of cloth, every piece of paper from there on in, and at the end of the day I had found more than sixteen thousand dollars. Grandma took the money.

When Rezin picked me up that evening, she handed the money to Rezin and me and told us to use it wisely. I remember Rezin and myself sitting in the guestroom closet behind closed doors and recounting the money. The next day we took it to the bank and the bank called us back a few days later to tell us that some of the money that we deposited was antique and that the deposit was greater than what we had made. I told Rezin that we should pay our tithes and offerings. His reply as the head of the house, was that people would know our business if we put in that amount as a tithe. I was shocked but allowed him to handle it the way he thought was best.

The bank statement came a month later and the amount was four thousand dollars less than what it was the previous month. When Rezin came home I asked him if he could explain to me what this meant. He dropped his head and said that his mother had asked him to give her four thousand dollars to help her in an emergency and not to tell me. I was shocked, furious, disgusted and mad. I said, "Why would you allow your mother to teach you to have secrets from me? Don't you know that I feel I cannot trust you any more? Do you feel that I would have said no to your mother's need, especially if your mother had an emergency?" He apologized and I received it. Here we could not tithe unto the Lord who gave it to us in the first place because the church folk would know our business, but he allowed his mother to run his business. He brought it back to my remembrance during our stay in California.

Rezin was working very hard on his mother's campaign. He was gone most of the time. I felt so sick one day and told him that I was going to lie down. I did and slept for five hours straight.

When I awoke the children were still up and I put them to bed. He was supposed to go out of town with his mother the next day. He called his mother and told her that he might not be able to go. She told him to go to the store and buy some medicine for me to take. He did. I took the medicine. The next morning I was still feeling pretty sick. I could not move.

He decided that I would be okay and that he had to go to support his mother. I laid there not even listening to what he was saying. All I remembered was hearing him say good-bye and telling my five year old daughter to take care of her mommy. I wanted to scream, "Why would you escape your responsibility and place it on my child? How could she take care of me? We are supposed to take care of them." I just laid there staring not saying a word.

Missy Imaan would make her way downstairs to go see who was at the door whenever the doorbell rang. After the first time, I told her not to answer the door at all. I felt so weak and my children were hungry. I told Imaan to get them snacks out of the pantry. I could not get myself out of the bed. The doorbell rang again and Imaan went to the window, knocked on it and told whoever was at the door that her mommy was sick and her daddy was gone.

I was fast asleep unaware of what Niamke or Imaan was doing when I felt Imaan pulling on me and trying to inform me that we knew the person who was at the door. I dragged myself to the staircase and had Imaan to open the door. It was a church member who was in the neighborhood. "Thank you Jesus." I asked her if she would be so kind to fix my children something to eat. She said that she would go to McDonald's and get them something. She took the kids with her and that was their first meal for the day at 2:20pm. She told me to sleep, and that she would watch the kids for a while. I slept well for four hours. It was after seven that evening when I awakened. She had fed the children again and bathed them and they were ready for bed. God always is faithful.

103

We all had a good night's rest and the next morning I awakened feeling much, much better. When Rezin returned the next day I ignored him as if he did not exist at all. I was so mad at this man for always putting me at the bottom of his priority list.

My mother-in-law had her wedding date set for June 1996. She was being interviewed by "The wedding story" aired on the Hall Of Fame channel. My house was being bombarded with telephone calls from early morning until late at night with concerns about her soon-to-be wedding. Some of them were anonymous calls and others were from folk who were bold enough to ask the questions they wanted answered. I was getting tired of these calls.

People were expressing their concerns about the man she was about to marry. They felt that her son who was a pastor should counsel and inform his mother about this man's whereabouts. I told them to call him and speak to him directly or to call his mother. It was becoming so bad that I called our leader's wife and asked her how to handle the situation. She told me to ignore the calls and just to pray about it. She prayed with me and asked me not to have the stress of these phone calls to be placed on my husband. After that I did not answer the phone anymore, especially if I did not recognize the caller.

The situation was taking a toll on Rezin. There were rumors and gossip all around us. He expressed himself openly one night to me of what he thought about it. I told him that that was his mother's life and that she knew what she was doing. I said to him that if he thought she did not, that he should speak to her. He could not stand his mother's fiancé and I would always say to him, "Just be nice."

I called the brothers and their spouses to arrange a family get together in honor of my mother-in-law celebrating her singleness for the last time. They all agreed. Those who were out-of-state came. We had reservations at a restaurant in the city. We were all excited and when we arrived at my mother-in-law's place, there was a surprise awaiting us. The Hall Of Fame channel was there interviewing her and her soon-to-be spouse. It took forever. Our dinner reservation time had come and gone. One brother-in law who traveled for more than two hours, had to excuse himself. He still had to drive back and his children had to go to school the next day.

At 9:30 that night we decided to go ahead to the restaurant. My mother-in-law came and joined us when she was through doing the interview. Before we left for the restaurant, her fiancé and I were sitting in the kitchen having a conversation. He told me that he had heard that I was the one putting this event together for his fiancé. He asked me why he was not invited. I said that this was a farewell celebration to her singleness and present name and that it was just her immediate family wanting to wish her well on this new journey. He said that that was very nice and that his family had done the same for him just a few days ago. The strangest thing happened next. Standing with his back to me while talking to his fiancé, I overheard him telling her that I had said that he was not welcome to come to this event because he was not a part of the family. I ignored the situation and walked out the door on my way to the restaurant. When we got to the restaurant I shared with everyone at the table what had just happened.

My mother-in-law walked in just as I finished telling about the incident. She came in with an attitude and said to me that I must remember the time when her family welcomed me into the family. She said that they did not have to, but they did. She asked me, "Where did you get the nerve from to make my fiancé feel unwelcomed in this family? After all he is not marrying you but he is marrying me." I just shook my head and for the first time in my married life, my husband would stand up to his mother on my behalf. He said to her, "Now wait a minute. Mary married your son and you must remember that you are her mother-in-law. You believed what that man told you just a minute ago and never questioned Mary to hear her side of her story. Mary just got through telling us about what happened at the house between her and your fiancé. Don't come and start some mess in here. We arranged this evening to be a wonderful celebration for you and here you are messing it up." I did not say a word. I was so surprised that my husband spoke up on my behalf that I was left speechless. My sister-in-law spoke up on my behalf and my mother in law unapologetically said, "Let's order so that we all can get home." The atmosphere was very tense and I just sat there shaking my head. My mother in law carried this attitude with her to the wedding.

The wedding day came and Imaan was designated to be a flower-girl. Imaan was very excited. It was my mother-in-law's second marriage but the first wedding with all the hoopla. The church which seated fifteen-hundred people was packed. There were more than forty people in the wedding party. She had reserved seats for everyone in the family except for my white sister-in-law and me. We thought that we could sit with our husbands after they had given her away. We were told by the wedding director that that was not the case.

My sister-in-law and I found our way to the bride who was very edgy. We asked her where she wanted us to be seated. She replied that we could sit anywhere. I looked at her amazed and left. My sister-in-law and I found ourselves two seats together three rows behind our husbands. The wedding got started.

Each of her five sons, from the youngest to the oldest took their mother down the aisle. As she was passed from one son to the other the audience would scream and applaud as if it were a show. The worship outline resembled mine tremendously. I felt complimented for her using the same outline as I had. Picture taking was very stressful. I was tired of the entire unnecessary attitude and just wanted to go home, but there were two receptions to go to.

I was sitting quietly in a pew when my mother-in-law asked from
the front of the church whether I was going to be in a picture with
her and her husband. My flesh was warring against the spirit but
my spirit prevailed. I got up, took the picture and sat down. We
went downstairs for the first reception which was cake, punch,
peanuts and mints. I had never seen such a big beautiful cake in
my life. It was huge and placed in the middle of the room.

We left the first reception and went on to the exclusive reception. I
was happy to meet family from their hometown and enjoyed them
very much. My brother-in-law took me aside and told me that his
mother was grown and that we should stay out of her life. I did not
know where that came from but decided to let it fall on deaf ears. I
started looking for my daughter. I found her enjoying this event
tremendously. She was having a very intense conversation with a
photographer of the hall of fame channel. I sat with them for a
while just listening to the kind of conversation this four year old
was having with this gentleman. Imaan was interviewing him. I
laughed, and he said that she was a very delightful old lady in a
child's body. I laughed and I took her with me.

She ran and started dancing with her family. I had no one to dance
with me so I went and took Imaan and had her to dance with me.
Her daddy was just sitting. He has two left feet and cannot dance,
and I love to dance. I enjoyed myself with my daughter while my
son was enjoying meeting all of his family. We left that night
tired, needing to get some rest for worship the next day. The
wedding was over and the marriage had started. I assumed now
that my mother-in-law had a husband again she would leave mine
alone.

The urgency of his mother's campaign was at hand again. They
needed a lot of resources for the campaign. The election was to
take place in July, 1996. A banquet was held as a campaign

fundraiser. The price was enormous for them to serve a chicken dinner that night. I would never have noticed the following incident if one of our church members had not observed it. She spoke to me about it. The head table was seated. Rezin was at the head table with his mother and I was in the audience. Every person who was part of the program was seated with their spouse except Rezin. His mother had him at the head table by himself.

A lady came and asked me that evening what kind of a relationship my mother-in-law and I had. I looked at her confused. She said to me it was amazing that my mother-in-law would have everyone seated at the head table with their spouse or significant other but me and my husband were separated. I never would have noticed it if she had not made me aware of it.

Rezin was busier than ever. The International church meeting was nearing very fast. They were hoping that his mother would be elected at this meeting. Rezin was traveling everywhere with his mother to support her and make sure that they had everything in place.

We arrived two days before the meeting started. I made use of this opportunity to be as supportive as I possibly could. I was available to do whatever they required of me.

Niamke was fifteen months old. The day before the meeting was supposed to start I had Niamke in my arms and was descending the staircase at the motel where the volunteer campaign workers were staying. Suddenly I was not walking anymore. I had missed a step and was falling. All I could do was call on the Lord and make sure that Niamke would not get hurt in the process. When I landed at the bottom I could not move. Both my ankles were sprained and my head was hurting. I had fallen down fifteen stairs. Thank God Niamke was fine. God kept him.

They transported me to the hotel where we were staying. When I entered the suite, I was put down on the couch and for the next seven days was flat on my back looking at the ceiling for the entire meeting. A doctor came to see about me daily and a therapist came by whenever she had the opportunity. While I was lying there one day, the Lord spoke to me. He reminded me of the very first meeting I attended and showed me how he had granted my request. I was stunned.

Remember the closing of the first International church meeting which I attended in 1988? It was an extension of my honeymoon. I left imploring God never to allow me to attend another meeting like that again. I had missed the 1992 meeting which was held in Milwaukee, Wisconsin because I had just had a newborn baby and were unable to attend.

Here I was in Iowa, and God was still answering my prayer although I wished He had done it differently. The very last day of the meeting I was able to get up and walk as if nothing had happened to me. I thanked the Lord for the experience and asked him to be a little gentler on me the next time. His mother was not elected to the leadership position that she was seeking, and all I had to do was pack up our belongings and go home.

We were at the airport and Rezin was unusually quiet. I asked him to leave the meeting and all it's happenings behind and not to bring it home with him. Well he did not comply. He was so upset that his mother was not elected. Every time he spoke to her he would tell her that he was okay. She did not know how I had to suffer with this man's disappointment, hurt and disgust. He was very hurt and taking it out on me. I told him one day that I did not deserve this kind of treatment and that he should go stay with his mother until he had worked this out of his system. He followed my advice by taking a vacation by himself. When he returned he was acting a little better but still very bitter. I had to remind him often not to go there with me. I told him that he should give up being his mother's campaign manager if he could not deal with failure. He did not want to do that and responded, "I will get my mother elected."

Life continued as usual. It was the first week in August and it was Vacation Bible School time. I had volunteered to be the VBS Director that year. Instead of having it at the park, we were going to have it at the church. The attendance for VBS was great. We had more than one hundred and twenty persons attending, and of that eighty percent were children. The kids enjoyed VBS tremendously.

The church was located in an Asian neighborhood and we had a lot of the neighborhood children attending. I went to help out in the kitchen one night and the kitchen staff was amazed that the pastor's wife would come and help in the kitchen. The women expressed that the other first ladies always wanted to be waited on but that I was so different. One gentleman made a very unusual remark that night that stayed with me. He said, "I know who the spiritual one in our pastoral family is." I looked at him with my mouth hanging open, and he just shook his head up and down three times. People found it unbelievable for me to come to visit and pray with the sick and shut-in.

I remember Rezin and me being in bed one night when the phone rang. A lady that attended our church called, and asked me to pray for her mother who was ill. I prayed and after concluding the prayer, I asked her to say hello to her pastor. She did. When he hung up he was furious and told me that I had no right to pray with his parishioners. I explained to him that she did not call or ask for him, but that she called me, to ask me to pray for her mother and that I gave her the opportunity to speak to him. I could not understand the big deal and just went to sleep.

I was crossing the street at church one morning. For a while I had noticed that this gentleman would sit in his car in front of the church every Sunday morning while Sunday school was going on.

I decided to approach him that Sunday morning. I walked up to his car and greeted him. I asked him what the reason was for him sitting outside while he could be benefiting from the Word of God on the inside. His response was that nobody had ever invited him to come to the Sunday school class. His wife was a member of the Sunday school. I laughed and told him that I would like to invite him to come to the adult Sunday school class as my guest. He got out of the car and from that Sunday on he attended Sunday school every Sunday and made valuable contributions to the lesson. I learned a valuable lesson through this experience. Don't assume that everybody will freely enter in. They sometimes have to be asked.

On November 28, 1996, the children and I were on our way to Cape Town, South Africa. It was going to be the children's first time meeting their family in South Africa. We arrived in Cape Town after a wonderful fourteen hour direct flight from Miami to Cape Town. I received several compliments on my children's behavior. They were good, busy but good. I could not sleep because I had to watch them most of the time. I was very tired when we arrived in Cape Town. My dad and sisters and several preacher friends and their spouses were awaiting our arrival in Cape Town.

When we got through customs there was this loud noise and everyone was screaming, "Welcome Mary!" Imaan had met some of the folk who had visited the USA and stayed with me for extended periods. Imaan saw her Oupa for the first time and ran into his arms after I had greeted my dad. I had placed Niamke in my sister's arms and they acted as if they had known my family forever. God blessed me with two wonderful sociable children. We were on our way home to see my mom and the preachers and their spouses followed.

My parent's home is very small and everyone was all over the place. They were from the backyard to the front yard and from the kitchen to every room in the house. It is quite an affair when I get home to visit. My mother was sitting on her bed and I kissed her. She did not concentrate on me as much as she did her grandchildren.

Because of the size of our home, I had made arrangements to stay at an aunt's house so that the children could be comfortable. My mother had fixed my favorite dish, snoek - the best fish in the whole wide world, and salads. My sisters served everyone graciously and we fellowshipped for hours. My children were enjoying their environment and family tremendously and I was glad. Whenever I travel to South Africa, I always try to stay awake until it is bedtime.

We got to my aunt's house and it was not a few minutes later that I realized that I had made the biggest mistake in choosing to stay with her. She had a house and not a home. Her house was not child-friendly at all. I had to make Imaan and Niamke understand that they could not go into certain rooms at all and they could not touch anything in this woman's house. It was after six pm and I wanted to go and sleep but could not because I had to watch Imaan and Niamke. I ran their bath water and put them both in the tub and prayed that they'd be ready to go to sleep when I got through bathing them. This particular aunt had visited me several times in the USA. I opened my home to her freely for months at a time. She stayed with Rezin and me for six months one time, and I never made her feel unwelcome in my home. She was working my last nerve. She had access to everything.

God was teaching me a lesson again. I had judged my parent's home as uncomfortable for my children, but while they were there they were happy and cared for with so much love. Here I was in a comfortable facility but the children were not happy. The next day when we visited with my parents the children did not want to go back to her home. I had no problem leaving them with my family. They did not even miss me.

Whenever I visit South Africa I am treated like royalty. My sisters do not allow me to lift a finger. My friends avail themselves to take me places, to see old acquaintances and friends. My sisters act as my secretaries and schedule my appointments because everybody wants me to come and visit them. My preacher friends normally invites me to speak at their churches. They do my laundry and everything that needs to be done for the children without complaining. They cook and clean behind me. They just make me feel special. They spoil me to death. I always think back to our childhood days when they would call me lazy and now they were driving me to laziness. They pay for everything that is needed and do not want to accept me paying them back. They also know that whatever money I have left over belongs to them when I get ready to leave.

We were spending six weeks in South Africa and I had it made. As far as my children were concerned, they were safe and happy and I could come and go as I pleased. They spent most of their time with their grandparents who enjoyed and spoiled them tremendously. Niamke would lay on the bed with my mother and have conversations with her as if she was his counterpart. I laughed one day when he was climbing on my dad's head and every time he got on top my dad would purposely make him fall. He would start all over again and just laugh when he stayed on top.

Christmas that year was so interesting. In South Africa you go to church on Christmas no matter what day it is on, to thank God for giving us His Son Jesus Christ. Niamke was all over the altar and Imaan was trying to mother him. I did not have to move because everyone was taking care of them. When we came home from church that day we had a beautiful family dinner. After dinner we opened the gifts and Imaan blurted out, "Is this all the gifts we are getting?" She had four gifts under the little tree and so did Niamke. I saw that as a teaching moment and told Imaan how blessed she was to be a pastor's daughter who receives so many gifts from everyone in the church. I always felt so bad at Christmas time because of all the gifts Imaan and Niamke would receive for Christmas. I also told her that Christmas is not about gifts for us but that it is a joyous celebration where we should be thanking God for the enormous gift He gave us through his Son. I told her she must never forget how blessed she is living in the United States and that children in South Africa sometimes didn't receive gifts at Christmas. We went and visited several family members and friends that Christmas afternoon and it was just a wonderful experience.

New Years came and New Years went. It was time for us to get ready to go back to the USA. We left South Africa on January 8, 1997. The night when we got to the airport there were sixty four persons who had come to see us off. We made a joyful noise at the airport through singing, and soon we formed a big circle and the prayer was prayed petitioning God to attach seven billion angels to the aircraft and to carry it safely to our destination. After the prayer the South Africans lifted their beautiful harmonious voices up to God by singing, "God be with you till we meet again." I cried and greeted everyone in the circle and then my family.

Niamke was hungry and he was trying to get out my breast so he could be nursed. My mother's last words to me before I went through customs were that I should get back my figure I once had. I laughed and asked her if she was telling me that I was fat.

We boarded the airplane and it was full. It started out in Johannesburg and came down to Cape Town full. Niamke, Imaan and I were assigned to two seats. I knew we were going to be very uncomfortable. It was three of us, however God was working on my behalf. The head stewardess came to me during the flight and told me that she was going to put me in business class so that I could be more comfortable with the children. She did and I thanked her and God profoundly. As soon as we were seated, Niamke grabbed a hold of my breast and nursed him to sleep.

Niamke slept for ten hours.

Imaan was talking to everyone telling our business (just like her mother). An elderly lady who was sitting across from us was talking to Imaan. I told Imaan to go sit with her so that they would not have to scream across the aisle at one another. The lady took out some game and occupied Imaan with it.

The flight coming back always seems longer than going. I had taken a nap when Imaan tapped me on the shoulder and asked me to escort her to the bathroom. It was three hours later. I asked the lady to keep an eye on Niamke and that I would be right back. I was blessed and highly favored on this trip. God did it. We landed safely in Miami. I taught Imaan and Niamke, who had become professional flyers, to always thank the Lord whenever the plane touched ground. Imaan was stretching and saying out loud, "Thank you Jesus." Everyone around us started laughing and I said, "That's right Imaan, we don't take anything for granted. God is so good."

We were tired and we had a three hour lay over in Miami and then a five-hour flight back to California. We sat in the same spot for the three hours. Imaan slept most of the time and I had to keep Niamke in my arms so that he would not take off. We boarded again and all three of us slept all the way to our destination. We were all happy to be back home and called South Africa to let them know that we had made it safely. It took us seven days to get back on the Pacific Time Zone.

We stayed up all night and slept during the day. Imaan and Niamke were trying to tell their dad how wonderful their vacation was and that they wanted to go live with Ouma and Oupa. They had spent forty one days with my family. We had been in California for nearly two years. The children had not even spent five days yet with their family in California. God blessed us to be able to travel to South Africa once a year from that year on and we spent lots of quality time with my family in South Africa.

When we were settled in, I decided that it was time to wean Niamke. Niamke did not want to let go but I had other plans. I wanted to do the Phen-Fen diet and could not allow Niamke to be nursed while doing it. Niamke tried everything to hold on to nursing but I had put my foot down. It was not going to happen anymore. Niamke was twenty two months old and I had had enough.

I was sleeping one night and I thought that my husband was trying to make love to me. My nightdress was being lifted and I felt it being pulled up. I was getting excited when I realized something was not right. I felt this small figure crawling up on me. I thought to myself that Rezin must have shrunk. When I opened my eyes Niamke had awakened, and was crawling up my body to get to my breast. I jumped out of the bed and laughed so loud that it scared Rezin. He grabbed Niamke and told him that his mother was not letting him have her breast anymore. Niamke cried because of his daddy's loud and mad response but that was the last time he tried to get over. I went downstairs and got him a glass of milk.

I came back from South Africa weighing two hundred and twenty six pounds. I was very disgusted with myself. I started the Phen-Fen diet and in twenty one days I lost twenty eight pounds. I stayed on the diet for three more weeks and lost another twenty nine pounds. I was back in a size fourteen and was happy about it.

In May of 1997, Rezin was preaching a revival not too far from our home. If he had to travel everyday it would have taken him about an hour to get there. He chose to stay at the hotel and not come home while he did the revival. I called him one day and told him that the kids and I were coming to hear him preach that night. He asked me not to come. I was so perplexed at his request that I just hung up the phone without saying another word. I was excited to go and support him, and here he did not want me to come. I did not hear from him again.

The revival was over that Friday night. I asked him to please come home that night as I had to attend a prayer breakfast that Saturday morning at six. Once again he refused. I had to wake my babies at five that morning because I had to take them with me. I was so mad at this man.

I went to the prayer breakfast and we had a blessed time in the Lord. The breakfast was over at 8:50 a.m. I was tired and told Deborah, the beautician, that I was going home. She said, "Let me relieve you from Imaan. Let her go with me so that you can rest." She asked me if she could give Imaan a shampoo. I was thankful. Imaan left with Deborah, and Niamke and I were on our way home.

Rezin came home and I decided to ignore him to the utmost. I did. He tried to be polite but I was looking for some kind of an apology which I did not get. I had a beauty shop appointment for two that afternoon. I took a nap with Niamke and rested until 1:20 that afternoon. When I got up I was going to take Niamke with me, but Rezin decided to surprise me and keep Niamke. I took his car and left.

When I got to the beauty shop, I had a call from Imaan to find out how I was doing at the beauty shop. I laughed and thanked Imaan for her concern. I was in the beauty shop just wallowing in how this man had treated me that week. The more I thought about it the madder I became. I had made up my mind that I would not go home immediately after the beauty shop, but that I would go to the mall and stay out as late as I wanted to get back at him. When the beautician got through with me, she wished me happy birthday and I thanked her for being the only one wishing me that day.

I left for the mall. When I got to the mall my eye caught the status of the gas tank. It was empty. That poured more fuel on my already bad attitude. I wanted to scream. I sat there, counted to ten and decided to go home. Rezin called me several times on my cell which I ignored. When I got home he was standing outside waiting for me. He told me to get dressed as we had to be somewhere that evening. I said that I was not going anywhere. He went into the bathroom and said that we had to go get Imaan from Deborah.

I refused to change clothes and we left. Rezin drove straight to the church fellowship hall. I saw a lot of cars on the parking lot and wondered what was happening at the church. When I walked up the steps to the door I decided to peer into the window of the fellowship hall. Rezin and Niamke had gone ahead of me. As I peered through the window, I saw a banner saying "Happy Birthday Mary." I laughed and went inside and they screamed surprise. There were a lot of people present including my mother-in-law and her husband. Rezin was celebrating my fortieth birthday when it was my thirty ninth birthday.

I had a good time that night. I received wonderful gifts and Rezin had to show off with the ultimate gifts. He had found a picture of my brother, my sister and me when we were little and had it restored and presented it to me. He also gave me this beautiful two-carat diamond ring. I do not make a big deal about receiving gifts and do not like opening gifts in front of everyone. That night the church secretary told me to sit down and open the gifts because they all wanted to see what I had received. I had to sit another thirty minutes opening gifts.

Imaan was having a good time. She told me she had known all week about the affair. I said, "Imaan and you would not tell your mommy." She replied that Ms Deborah purposely took her to the beauty shop because they were afraid that Imaan would tell me that day. When I got up to thank everyone, I just broke down and cried. All the pent-up frustration of the week was being released in those tears, and I thanked Rezin for the wonderful evening although it was a year too early. We went home and had a good night's rest. It was mother's day the next day and the church was packed with CME (Christmas, Mothers Day and Easter) members.

Rezin received his Doctoral Degree in 1997. The church gave him a fabulous gift, a trip for seven days for the two of us to Fiji. They had made reservations for us at this first class hotel. I was excited. Sister Pearl had volunteered to keep the children and I was set to go. When we arrived in Fiji, I was awe struck by the beauty of the land. We had an ocean view room and were on the top floor. Every night I would leave the door to the patio wide open so I could hear the waves crashing and roaring. I slept like a baby.

For the first time since Niamke's conception, we made love. I had forgotten what it was like. I enjoyed every moment of our time together. I asked Rezin not to ruin the memory of a wonderful vacation. He was and still is a very grumpy person when he wakes up in the morning. I cannot understand how people wake up grumpy, especially after God had blessed them with a good night's rest and saw fit to allow them to see a new day.

We went swimming every morning. I am not a strong swimmer but I know how to hold my body above water. I was swimming one morning and a crab got a hold of my big toe. I was screaming like someone who was being murdered. Quite a few people rushed to my aid. This Fijian guy took it off my toe and I went and sat on the sand enjoying watching everyone else. I was more embarrassed than anything else. We enjoyed the sights and scenery of Fiji very much. Every morning I would check in with Sister Pearl to see how the children were doing. We returned from Fiji with pineapples and macadamia nuts that we shared with close friends and neighbors. The kids were happy to have us back home.

It was 1998 and we had been renting for nearly three years. I told Rezin one night that the Lord had told me we were going to become homeowners that year. He laughed and said, "You go ahead homeowner." I believed God. I calculated how much rent we had given to our landlord and at the end of the day we had nothing to show for it. Well, it was seventy thousand dollars. I told Rezin we could have been investing in a home for ourselves with that kind of money.

The spirit prompted me to start looking for a home. I did. Every time I went looking, I would ask Rezin to allow me to use his Jaguar. I was driving a Toyota. It made a difference. They were more courteous and polite towards me when they saw me driving up in a Jaguar rather than a Toyota. I was looking in Anaheim Hills and Irvine. The prices were much higher in these areas than what it was in Yorba Linda. I drove to Yorba Linda three to four times a week. The homes were beautiful and spacious and the price was right. I came upon some homes one day and asked the girl to write up what kind of down payment we needed and where we could apply for a loan. That night I went home and told the Lord that that was the house that I wanted. I asked him to speak some sense to my husband and have him to come into agreement with me for this house.

That same night when I got home, our landlord called us and asked us if we would like to buy the home from her. She would credit us all the rent we had paid towards the purchase of the home. She said the market has taken a turn for the good and she intended to put the house up for sale. She was giving us a month to think about it. We thought about it but we decided not to buy the house. I wanted a new home.

Life in the married lane was tough. I was married, but felt like I had no marriage. The situation was getting to me. He was married to himself and his mother. I was always by myself cooking, cleaning, teaching, doing homework, running to the library, doing projects for Imaan's school, volunteering time at school and church, running errands and always busy. There were nights when I would fall asleep in front of the television. When I woke up, it would be past my children's bedtime and Rezin would be nowhere around. I felt like a slave. He was doing church work and his mother's work. He gave us no quality time. He told me several times in the marriage that he was called by God to do ministry and not everything that I expected him to do. He also felt that I was acting like his mamma. The only weird thing was that he was doing everything his mamma wanted him to do for her.

Rezin came home one night and said that he had brought me a tape that he wanted me to listen to. It was a lady out of Nebraska talking about her marriage experience. She was sharing how her husband would always be busy. She emphasized how she would pray in the spirit whenever he was trying to affect her spirit negatively. She would watch the interaction he had with his daughter and how he spoiled her and not his wife. When I got through listening to the tape I prayed and was inspired to start a married couple's fellowship at our church. I thought that this way it would keep Rezin accountable to the marriage. I called and sent out invitations for couples to come and fellowship with us at our home.

A new couple my husband knew in his childhood came to visit our church one Sunday. His wife and I just clicked. She became my laughing buddy. Her husband used to pastor and was retired. I called them and asked them to share with us their life experience that Saturday as a married couple. They agreed. That Saturday evening we had twenty-two couples present. The couple who shared with us inspired us tremendously. Everyone left very excited looking forward to the next meeting. We met every third Saturday evening at a different couple's home. I was fighting for my marriage, but it seemed as if this was not working either. The interest and enthusiasm that I wanted Rezin to show was not present. I prayed and prayed. Every time we met I thought we would leave to do better. But we (my children and I) still remained at the bottom of the priority list. Life continued.

Since the day we left Austell, I would return every three months to see about grandma. A young lady was taking care of her business. I would go and check on her to make sure that the house was clean. It also allowed her to spend some quality time with her grandchildren. Grandma was the one who taught them their abcs and 123s. She sang songs with them and tried to teach Imaan how to play the piano. She taught them how to kneel down and pray. Grandma was blind but she always wore eye-glasses. She spoiled them, especially Imaan.

She would fly out to be with us at Christmas time and Easter. She normally stayed for a month. We were her only family. Whenever something happened at home that called for repairs, I had to fly down and make sure that what was being said to her was true. Grandma loved us as if we were her own.

Our tenth anniversary was approaching. I was still looking for a home. Grandma called me one day and said that we were going to receive a call from her attorney. She said that she did not give us a wedding gift (which she did) but she had decided to put it up and give it to us if we made it to our tenth anniversary. The tenth anniversary came, and Rezin flew to Austell and received a CD that grandma had placed with her attorney for us. The CD was twenty six thousand dollars and when Rezin cashed it at the bank it had matured to forty-four thousand dollars. I was ecstatic. I thanked God and grandma and told her we could now purchase a home.

We found a home and told the salesperson we would be back, not knowing how we were going to do it. Well God supplied and we had the down payment to buy the home. We returned to the office and were just in time to get the last house in that particular phase. It had twelve floor plans and it was the largest one at thirty- four-hundred square feet. It was going to be six months before the house would be completed.

Our landlord had placed the house we were renting on the market the day we signed for the purchase of this new home. It was on the market for three hours and the house was sold. The gentleman that bought the house complimented the agent who in turn complimented the landlord for the excellent upkeep of her home. She in turn called me and thanked me for having taken such good care of her home. She said that the buyer who was moving from New Jersey had asked the real estate agent whether we ever used the bathrooms in the home because they were meticulously clean. The kitchen and the bathrooms are the places where I place special care, because these rooms have a lot to do with our health and hygiene. The other news was that the new owner wanted to move in immediately. She said that she would forego the rent for that particular month and also refund the previous month's rent and the security deposit.

We moved into a three bedroom apartment close to where the house was being built, so that Imaan could enroll in school and not be interrupted in the middle of the school year again. We went from 2800 sq ft to 1800 sq ft and it was quite an adjustment. I only unpacked the necessities.

In July that year I flew to Austell and when I entered grandma's porch there were pink slips all over the gate. They were from the gas company, the water company, the electric company, all informing her that her utilities were being cut off that day. I knew that nobody had been by to see about grandma and when she opened the door for me she was so happy to see me and the children. I called the companies immediately and paid the utilities by phone. Grandma was very disgusted. Her lady who had been writing her bills had not shown for a few months. The refrigerator was bare. I asked her to get ready because we were going to the store. I had my two children and blind grandma. I took my time with them. Grandma always enjoyed the way I fixed lamb and she wanted me to get some lamb which I did. We got fresh fruits and vegetables and meats and everything that was needed for the house. We left the store and went home.

Grandma was sitting and listening to the baseball game that evening when Niamke climbed on her lap and played with the air conditioner above her head. I was cleaning and changing the linen in my bedroom when I suddenly realized it was very hot in the house. I asked grandma why it was so hot. Niamke had turned the thermostat up to 94 degrees and put it on heat. I opened the front door to allow the evening breeze to help cool down the house. Grandma just laughed. I had bathed Niamke and Imaan and it was bedtime. We prayed and they went to sleep that evening.

The children were fast asleep when grandma and I were still talking. She asked me if the promise that I made her years ago still stood. I asked her what she was talking about. She hesitantly reminded me of the time when she asked me not to allow anyone to put her in a nursing home when she became old. She said that I had promised her that she could come and stay with us when she was ready to do so. I said, "Yes grandma I meant every word that I said." I called Rezin and asked him if it would be okay for grandma to come and stay with us and he agreed.

Grandma moved with us in July, 1998. I thought that grandma was eighty-five because she always wrote her age as 12/12/12. The change and adjustment had an effect on grandma's breathing. She woke up one morning just wheezing. I took her to the hospital and they kept her overnight. We were still living in the apartment and it took a lot of adjustment.

We were nearing the end of October and the builder informed us that we might be able to move into our new home in November. I was happy because everyone would be able to have their own bedrooms. We also would have some more needed space.

In November I received a bill for the hospitalization of grandma that was refused payment by the Health Insurance Company. I called them and they in turn referred me to call Medicare. They asked me several questions and had grandma to talk to them. The lady asked grandma what her correct age was, as the payment was refused because it did not match the date of birth on her records. Grandma would not tell her age and we concluded to speak back to each other when we found the correct date of birth. Every time I asked grandma she would laugh and say 12/12/12.

The Lord directed my paths to a lady who worked for social security. I gave her the necessary information that I had and asked her to please find out what the correct date of birth was. When she got back to me I was so stunned. She said Mary I want you to sit down when I give you this information. Grandma was looking good and the only thing wrong health wise was that she was blind. She did not take any medication, (and still does not) and was in good health. She had a good mind and everything was working fine in her body. The lady told me she was born 12/12/03. She was a month away from turning ninety five. I laughed so loud and just thanked God for how He had kept her and especially the times when she was traveling those long distances by herself from Austell to California and back. God is awesome in all His Ways. When I told grandma she just smiled and said "do not tell anybody else." I laughed for days and sometimes just sat and stared at grandma, just marveling at her health and strength and fervor for life.

We moved into our new home on November 28, 1998. Grandma's room was on the main floor and the wall from her room led her to the bathroom. The laundry door was in between Grandma's bedroom and the bathroom. She adjusted very quickly and never needed my help in getting around in the new home. The house was beautifully decorated as God had blessed me with the gift of interior decorating. The master bedroom was at the top of the staircase and the children's bedrooms were connected to each other. I had the hardest time getting Niamke to sleep in his own bed and sometimes even Imaan. I did not care anymore about them sleeping in my bed because nothing was happening there. The house had six bedrooms of which four were used. The other two we turned into an office and an antique sitting room. It had three full baths, a large kitchen, a family room, a formal dining room and living room. We were blessed beyond great measure.

The church assisted me again with the move and by the end of the day, my house was in order. I could live. We had the house blessing. I requested that no gifts be brought as God had blessed us with so much. A church member catered the event and it was a wonderful afternoon of fellowship and thanksgiving.

It was our first Christmas that year in the new home and I invited the entire family for Christmas dinner that year. They all came on Christmas Eve and spent the night. We were up most of the night. We awakened the next morning to the smell of breakfast being cooked. I was so glad that I did not have to do it by myself. Rezin's twin brother started the breakfast and between him and my mother-in-law, the breakfast was being prepared. The office was filled with gifts for everyone.

That was the first Christmas that my children received gifts from their grandmother. It was a beautiful day and we had eaten plenty and were full and falling asleep all over the place.

It was about three thirty that afternoon when I came back downstairs and the house was sort of empty. People had left without saying goodbye or thank you for allowing them to come into our house and enjoy our food. They just left. I could not believe it. I was raised that you do not leave somebody's house without saying thank you for the good time they provided you and especially without greeting the hosts. I got over it.

The year 1999 was again a very busy year for Rezin. He had a lot of traveling to do on behalf of his mother's campaign. I found myself at home most of the time. I was so happy that I had grandma and the children.

Ever since we came to the church I was encouraging Rezin to have it cleaned, as I did not like living in a clean house and the house of the Lord was run down and dirty. Rezin could not find the time to put that in his schedule. Every Sunday after church, I would nag him about the church and how it looked. He ignored me so I incited another lady who would always talk to me about the appearance of the church. She started working on Rezin's nerves about it, and I concluded rather her than me.

The church had many fundraisers that year. Most of them were for his mother's campaign. The church people were talking all around me, but would not say anything to him about it. I decided to ignore them too.

My prayer life and walk with God had become very focused and intentional. I was reading more and spending more time than usual in the Word. I was trying so hard to let my walk be my talk not only at church but at home too. In my mind I had decided that things were not going to change as far as my marriage was concerned and had released it to the Lord.

It was May 8, 1999. We were to celebrate my forty-first birthday the next day. Rezin came home late that evening. I had fallen asleep in front of the television and Niamke was lying at my feet fast asleep. When Rezin entered he awakened Imaan. Earlier that day he asked me if he could use my car. I obliged and he was gone most of the day. He asked me whether I would get the mail out of the mailbox. I was stunned when I realized that it was after 11:30 p.m. I did not move.

He asked me if I would be so kind to go to the store and get him some red dye for the red velvet cake he wanted to make for my birthday. I was thinking to myself, "Now why can't you go?" But I replied "okay" seeing he wanted to do something nice for me. I asked him where my car was as it was not in the garage. He responded that he left it parked in the driveway. I left the house and Imaan followed me and said that she was going with me.

When I got to the driveway there was parked a brand new white SUV. I yelled in the house "Rezin whose SUV is sitting in our driveway?" He was standing in the window just laughing and Imaan said, "Happy Birthday Mommy." I turned around and there was Rezin standing and handing me the keys to my new vehicle. He wished me a happy birthday and said that I did not need to go to the store. He just wanted me to see my birthday gift.

I took the SUV for a spin around the block and Imaan wanted me to go and show our neighbors my new vehicle. I laughed and told her that we would do that the next day.

I thanked Rezin for the thoughtful gift and we (the children and I) went to bed. Rezin was still downstairs baking a red velvet cake. I awakened about 2 a.m. Rezin was still baking. I went downstairs to see what was taking him so long. The first red velvet cake he had baked had fallen and so he made another one. I looked up at the kitchen ceiling and there was red dye all over the ceiling. I asked him what had happened. He explained that when he opened the bottle it just flew all over the place.

I had a wonderful home-made dinner cooked by Chef Rezin that evening. We had our friends over and the dinner was wonderful. Rezin could really cook but he was lazy and all of the culinary gifts that he was blessed with just laid dormant. I thanked him for a wonderful evening and for making my birthday so special.

The year 2000 came. My Sunday school teacher had given each of us a postcard and asked us to write our new year's resolution on it and to keep it somewhere where we would always be reminded of it. I remember so well her asking us that we do not resolve to lose weight but to have something meaningful. I wrote out my resolution and asked God to give me wisdom, knowledge, counsel and might, but most of all understanding. Didn't I tell you before to be careful what you ask God for?

The year 2000 started with a bang. My brother, who is the only blood relative that I have in the USA, was found guilty of a crime which I believe he did not commit.

I had been in a season of fasting and praying. I was petitioning God on behalf of my brother day and night. I would pray the psalms and just cry out unto the Lord.

My brother and I loved each other but could never stand one another. He was very competitive as a child and always wanted to be right. I could not stand his arrogance. It was always I, I, I. It seemed like he never gave God credit, but that everything that happened in his life that was good was because of him. I sometimes looked at him talking and saw his lips moving but was not listening to a word he said. It seemed like he was always bragging. Sometimes I wanted to say something, but decided to hold my peace.

He is a very intellectual man however the intellect is not submissive to the Spirit of God in many ways. He came to the USA in 1976. I came in 1985. He had never returned back to his home and I assumed that he was ashamed of his heritage. I had been home so many times since my arrival, but he had not been home yet. My mother loved her son. He was her only son. He would call my mother and tell her that he was planning to come home. They would be all excited and he would never show. My aunt told my mother once that she should stop believing him and just wait and be surprised when he shows up one day. He never did.

He had been married for twenty years and had a fourteen year old son who had never had the pleasure of meeting his grandparents, or family in South Africa.

He was found guilty in early February 2000. I was left with the burden of having to tell the family back home. I cried as if my brother had died. The only thing that could not bring closure to this terrible event was that we could not get the body to lay it to rest. He was imprisoned.

As I look back on this situation, I ask myself the question over and over again, "Why didn't he call our family in South Africa himself, to inform them of this guilty verdict?" The judge himself was so surprised by the verdict, that he did not allow my brother to be sent to jail immediately. He gave him an opportunity to get his business taken care of and at sentencing, which would be twenty eight days. Then later he would be admitted to prison. When the jury was interviewed by the press that day, they were asked the question of how they came to a guilty verdict? Their response was that he was too arrogant. Arrogance determined his guilt!

Now look at God preparing me for this event. I was watching a documentary one night on A&E of innocent men that were in jail because of juries that made mistakes and judges who do not have the backbone to render a just verdict because of their fear of being re-elected. I sat there watching the entire program listening to the cries of men and their families who could not have their cases reopened, because they did not have the necessary resources to afford a good attorney to handle their cases. Men were interviewed who left their pregnant wives and had never seen their children because of the distance they were placed from them.

The next day I was in the bookstore and bought two new CD's. The one CD was "T. D. Jakes Live from The Potters House" and the other was Richard Smallwood's CD, "Healing." I loved track eight on Live from the Potter's House, "**This test is your storm**." I would replay it over and over again. On Richard Smallwood's CD I could not get past "**Healing**."

That Sunday when I got to Sunday School I was asked to lead the Adult class as the teacher would not be present. The Adult class was studying the book "**You Have To Face It To Fix It**," authored by Dr. Matthew Watley Sr. The chapter I had to lead was "**Facing public embarrassment**." God is Awesome in All His ways.

The day when I received the call that my brother was found guilty, I drove around for hours just crying. The tears were not so much for him but for my mother. I knew that this news could send her to her grave. I came home hours later and shared the news with my husband. He did not say anything. He just looked at me. I went upstairs and told the children that we needed to pray for their Uncle because he was found guilty of a crime that we believed he did not commit. My son who was five years old fell to his knees and started praying a prayer I will never forget. He said, "Now Lord You Yourself come down and pick up my uncle and place him on a cloud. Put Your hand beneath the cloud and don't allow my uncle to fall through. Please keep him safe." The prayer said it all and I went downstairs and sat listening to my CDs just crying. There was no one to console me but God.

I had finally calmed down enough to call home and tell my family the news about my brother. My mother answered the phone and asked me immediately what the verdict was. I paused for a moment and she said, "Oh Mary please don't tell me" and I could hear her fighting back some tears. I said to her that her son was found guilty and that he would be sentenced in twenty eight days. My mother was quiet. Not a word came from her, and I started praying for her. My mother must have passed the phone to my sister for she was the next voice that came on. We were just a few days away from celebrating my mother's eightieth birthday. The children and I were set to go to South Africa leaving February tenth and returning on February 24th. I was glad that I would be able to see her in a few days.

In the meanwhile, calls of concern were extended from everyone except my in-laws. My mother-in-law had just preached for my brother a few weeks before and not a word came from her or the family.

The church was talking about it. You can find the most hateful people in church. One pastor posted the fact that my brother was found guilty on the church website. There was nothing wrong with it, but it would have made a difference if he had asked the readers to pray for him. There were rumors and gossip all around me. Sometimes folk would make comments around me to get a response. I was tight-lipped. I ignored them. I was inspired to write a letter to the leadership of the church on the lack of their involvement in the case. I started drafting the letter. The letter was completed by the end of that week and I showed the letter to Rezin asking him for his opinion. The response was so sad, but I obeyed. He told me that you cannot send this letter to the church leadership because my mother will never be elected to the hierarchy of the church. I exploded. "Why does your mother always have to be considered in everything that I do? Are you married to her or married to me? You're always looking out for your darn mother, instead of looking out for your wife and children. She raised you for herself and you cannot let go of her apron strings. You need to make up your mind who you want to be with, your mother or me. She has been in my marriage since day one and I cannot take this anymore." I ran out the house and went for a drive.

The Sunday following the verdict I could do nothing but cry in church. At the time of invitation to Christian Discipleship, I found myself at the altar. I asked the church to pray for me and through snot and tears I confessed to the church that I had answered my call to ministry sixteen years ago and that I truly believed that everything that was happening to me was happening because I was running from God. I was standing before them broken to the utmost and so disheartened by the church, but I wanted to renew the commitment that I made in 1984 unto the Lord and fulfill the call to ministry.

In 1984, I had gone to my pastor, Rev. Messias and told him that I could not explain what was happening inside of me but that I knew that God had called me to ministry. Rev. Messias was very glad to be informed of this good news and told me to give it a year's thought and watch and listen to God very carefully and intently. He said to me that I would not be allowed to preach my trial sermon until the year was over. He advised me to work in the office of an Exhorter in the church.

It was not even a year later when the Lord opened the door for me to come to the USA. Rev. Messias immediately recognized this was an opportunity from God to help me in the process. He said that I could study in the USA and enjoy the process of seminary. He gave me his blessings and I came to the USA.

Worship was so different in the USA than what it was back home. Services were more uplifted and women were doing so much more than what I was exposed to in South Africa.

I remember asking my pastor in Austell, on several occasions if I could serve as a Sunday school teacher. He always answered that he would look into it, but he never got back to me. I was very conscious of my language and accent and became very intimidated by the process. I completed my undergraduate work but never advanced to seminary. I had told my husband on numerous occasions that I had promised the Lord to serve Him and that I felt that I had just walked away from it.

Rev. Messias visited the USA on several occasions. He always reminded me that I must never forget that I had answered the call of God. The church received my request joyfully that morning and I was scheduled to preach my trial sermon the first Sunday afternoon in February. I did. My scripture was from Psalms 24. My focus verse was verse 3. **"Who shall ascend into the hill of the Lord? Or who shall stand in His holy place?"** My sermon topic was "Climbing up the Mountain." The church was well attended that Sunday afternoon and they approved my request to enter ministry.

My children and I left for South Africa on February tenth and deplaned in Cape Town South Africa on the morning of the eleventh. We were happily greeted at the airport by family and friends and were on our way to see my mom. My sister shared with me while driving that the verdict had had a terrible effect on my mom. She said that she did not want anyone to know about it.

When I walked into the house I saw the same look on my mother's face that I had seen so many years ago when my father had abused her and we had found out about it. I also saw that look a second time when my youngest sister became pregnant outside of marriage. I greeted my mother and could hardly keep the tears back, but I had to be strong for her sake. The children kissed her and she hugged them as if she did not want to let go. Her first question was about my sister-in-law and nephew. She asked me whether I had seen her son. I told her that I would see him as soon as I got home for the sentencing process. I asked her not to be ashamed of this situation and that we must face it so that God could fix it. I reminded her that she was my faith role model and that she could not give up on God.

People always came to my mother to ask her to pray for them when they had problems. I implored her to call on others now to pray and intercede on behalf of the family and especially for her son. She agreed with me. When mom's brother and sister-in-law visited that evening, she told them through sobs and tears. I had to run in the bathroom to cry as I did not want to cry in front of my mother.

It was my mother's eightieth birthday celebration. A couple in her church did all the catering. It was a wonderful affair and my mother and her two living siblings and cousins were able to enjoy the afternoon with family and friends. There were about two hundred people at the party and we had the best singing group present who sang all my mother's favorite hymns. Friends told stories and experiences of old, and how my mother was their inspiration and motivation in so many ways. They truly encouraged my mother in the Lord that afternoon. I had to remind her to smile many times that afternoon.

When we got home that evening my mother asked me to close the door behind me and to sit down. She said, "Mary when I die I want you to ask Catherine and Iris to sing, How Great Thou Art at my funeral." I asked her if she knew something that we did not know. She grinned and said "Anything can happen Mary - you just don't know." I asked her not to give up on God. Her reply made me happy when she said that she could never give up on Him.

My local church in South Africa asked me to preach that first Sunday that I was home. I preached from Psalms 78. My sermon topic was "Moral amnesia." Before I preached, I informed the church of my brother's situation and asked them to pray and not gossip about it. I believed it was God who had put my brother in time out. My mother sat with her head bowed, tears streaming down her face as I made the request before the church on behalf of the family. After service one of the church members said to me, "that is what happens when you forget where you came from."

Imaan and Niamke were on vacation but had lots of homework to do daily. They did not like it a bit because it took away from their time of being spoiled by everybody.

I had a pleasant surprise visit from an ex-boyfriend that year who blessed my visit by paying for all the extra unnecessary expenses I had incurred. The car that I rented was paid for in full by him. He took my children shopping and bought some art for me to take back to the USA with me. My mother warned me not to start any mess. I told her that he was my friend and nothing more.

We left South Africa on the twenty fourth, winging our way back to the USA. As we were traveling the Lord showed me clearly how He had blessed me with times of refreshing every time we visited South Africa. Remember I told you how royally I am treated whenever I visited South Africa? I did not have to do anything, but everything was being done for me. The Lord granted me an opportunity on a yearly basis just to be spoiled by my family and friends. It was no coincidence, but it was all orchestrated by God. At home I would be doing so much all by myself. I prayed for a long time for God to give me a helping husband, but he was never available to help. I had grandma and the children to take care of twenty-four-seven and the house chores and church duties and school requirements. God made it so clear to me that every year that I was able to travel to South Africa, it was God giving me a time of resting and refreshing. I let out a shout of thanksgiving unto the Lord at that moment. God is so good and He is faithful.

I had called my husband before we left South Africa to make sure that we came home to a clean house. When we arrived in the USA we were glad to be home and the house was clean. Praise the Lord!

I had told everyone that I was not going to the International church meeting that summer. I was talking about it openly one day when a pastor took me aside and told me that I needed to go if for nothing else but to be supportive of my husband. He expressed that my mother-in-law had a very strong and forceful opponent to deal with and it was his understanding that this lady would be elected rather than my husband's mother. I asked him to pray about it and to let me know whether the Lord would allow me to go and not have anything bad to happen to me again. He said to me, "Go Mary, you do not have to attend the meetings, you can take the children sight-seeing and do whatever you want as long as you are there for your husband when the election is over." I went home and gave it a lot of thought and prayer and I decided to go for the last three days.

My children and I arrived in Chicago, Illinois on that Tuesday. I was looking forward to seeing my husband and staying with him. When we arrived in Illinois, he took us to a hotel where the children and I would be staying. I was shocked again. I asked him why the children and I could not stay with him. He answered that he did not want to be disturbed by me or the children and that he was very busy. I said to myself, "So much for support."

During our first year in California we attended the annual conference in Los Angeles. Rezin had gone two days ahead of me and I left on the opening day of the conference. When I got to the hotel I had to find Rezin to allow me to get in the hotel room. It turned out that he and one of his associate ministers were sharing a room. I was shocked when he informed me that he was going to stay with the minister and I could be in the other room with my children. I thought that he was kidding. He gave me the key and left saying that he did not want to be disturbed by me nor the children as he needed to be focused. When he walked out the room, I said to him that he should move in with his associate when the meeting was over. Niamke was four months old and Imaan was three-and-a-half years old. I had no help from this man who was my husband. We argued for a while and I decided to let it go because his mind was made up. I had my car and he had his car. We would see each other at conference and act as if nothing was wrong.

The children and I kept ourselves busy in the streets of Chicago and also in the malls. We would ride the bus from one side of town to the other and never get off until we reached the place where we boarded the bus. The children were excited about their grandmother's election, and they wanted to help campaigning. I spent time with my South African friends and never entered a meeting.

The election took place, and again my mother-in-law was not elected. I could not help but feel sorry for her, because she really believed that the church was going to elect her that time. The family was broken, especially Rezin. He had spent a lot of money, time and energy on the campaign. A CD of grandma was used for this event and here we were again leaving Illinois with her not being elected. His attitude was mean even before we left Illinois. When we got home, I asked him to go somewhere and shake this thing out of his system because I was not going to take it. The family walked around smiling, but on the inside they were hurting. One of Rezin's brothers left the church and another one just did not want to be bothered with the church anymore. The election of leadership in our denomination is a very painful and ugly process. People compete for a position and in many ways have to pay their way to make it to the top. When they are not elected, they still have to go back and smile and pretend that after all that fighting and competing, that it never happened.

Rezin was on the phone with his mother one afternoon. She informed him that she had decided to give it one more chance. This has been a childhood desire, and she believed that she had to get it. I asked her that day to let Rezin go as her campaign manager and her response blew my mind. She said, "Mary you raise your family and stay out of our business." I asked the question, "Does that mean that my husband is not a part of my family - does he belong to you?" I looked up toward heaven and said, "Lord you heard her." Rezin laughed and said, "My mother really told you." I did not think that it was funny, and let it go immediately. It was placed in God's hands.

We were blessed leaving that church meeting with new leadership for our district. I had fasted and prayed that God would bless us with this particular couple to become our leadership. I had watched them and admired them for a long time. They were deeply spiritual, and I thanked God that he had answered my prayers.

It was August, 2000. I was trimming the rose bushes when the phone rang. I ran in the house and answered. It was my sister calling from South Africa to inform me that mom was given six weeks at the most to live. She had developed stomach cancer. I cried and then concluded the phone call with my sister by saying that God is Able, and that we believed God. I called my mother and told her that she would live and not die. She replied that even in death she would live. I asked her, "How did it feel to know that you are dying?" She said that she had known all her life that one day she would go to meet her Maker and that she was satisfied and excited about it. My mother was in good spirits and I prayed with her and hung up after the prayer as I was about to break down. I called her three to four times a week just to hear her voice and tell her how much I loved her and how grateful I was that she was my mother.

At our local church, Rezin was really home. His presence was being felt and seen. He had decided to refurbish the sanctuary. I was so happy. His mind was off his mother's work and finally he was doing what God had called him to do at this particular church. He was ministering to the needs of the people and the community. We had church services held in the fellowship hall for more than two months. When the church was finished, it looked beautiful. Rezin's spirit and attitude had changed a lot. He was more pleasant to deal and live with.

I was on my way to Charles Schwab in Ontario,California one morning. I ran into one of the choir members of a church in Ontario. I had seen this lady before but had never really spoken to her. She greeted me with so much enthusiasm. I stopped and spoke to her for a few minutes. She said that she had seen my husband a few nights ago coming out of a place that he should not be in. I looked at her and asked her, "Where?" She said that she saw him coming out of a pornography shop. I said, "No, it could not have been my husband. You must have mistaken him with someone else." I asked her for her phone number.

My mind went back to the last few Fridays when I had been cleaning. I was cleaning out Rezin's pockets and throwing away papers he left laying behind. I came across some receipts which I looked at but did not pay them much attention. I had put it in my drawer just in case he needed the receipts. I was so naïve and thought that it was from a lingerie shop that he had made some surprise purchase for me.

I rushed back home and took a closer look at the receipts. I called the number on the receipt. When they answered I asked what kind of a shop this was. The lady said that it was a pornography shop. I asked her what the numbers on the ticket meant. She said that it was for a private room. I asked her where it was located. It was the place where the lady had seen him.

All kinds of questions were going through my head. What was he looking for at this place? Why look for naked bodies to turn you on when you have a wife at home? He is definitely not looking for God but for a sexual thrill.

G. K. Chesterton wrote, "Every man who knocks on the door of a brothel is looking for God. That is not what the man is consciously thinking at the time - but that's what he's really doing. He is looking to fill a huge craving; an irresistible urge. He may think that this urge is simply a sexual desire, but it's not. He's looking for God."

I felt like an inanimate substance. I was benumbed. I sat on my bedroom floor for hours just staring at the ceiling. When I finally came to my senses I called the lady and lied to her. I told her that Rezin was at the pornography shop on behalf of one of the church members who had called him for help.

I went to the denomination's webite, and posted a question. How can you trust a man who is a pastor and is addicted to pornography? I ended the question by asking whether you can trust having your daughter around him. I gave more details than what I am giving you right now.

He was a regular visitor to the church website. When he came home I pretended as if nothing was wrong. I was in bed asleep that night when he came and awakened me. He was crying. He said that he knew that I had posted the question on the church site. I was ready for him. I told him that he disgusted me and humiliated me all the time. I said that if I ever made him look bad it would be justifiable, but I never did. I told him that his heart was not made for marriage and that he was looking for the things of God in the wrong places. I suggested to him to seek help for himself. He apologized and promised me that he would never go there again.

I am glad I was designed for a love relationship with God.

In December, 2000 I received an invitation from my Bishop's wife, Rev. Helga Christian to become a mentee of hers. I accepted joyfully and what an on-time invitation it was. My new year's resolution that year was to be more consistent in all my ways and to receive wisdom, knowledge, counsel and might, but most of all understanding from the Lord. She had outlined the itinerary for the year and we were assigned a lot of reading. I was so happy that I had someone to call upon and ask to explain to me the deeper things of God. It was all God-orchestrated.

That same month the Lord placed upon my heart two numbers. It was as if God was trying to tell me something but I could not connect it. The numbers fourteen and twenty three kept on appearing in my mind's eye. I asked the Lord one day whether I was supposed to play the lotto and use those numbers. I was driving behind a car one day and the license plate number was 14M23. I wrote those numbers down in my Bible and asked the Lord to give me understanding as to what these numbers were supposed to mean.

It was February 3, 2001. My sister called to say that if I wanted to see mom for the last time I would have to come immediately. Without thinking I said to her we will leave on the fourteenth and return on the twenty third. My sister who is a registered nurse said that she doubted whether mom would make it through the next few days. I realized then that the dates I gave her were the numbers the Lord had placed in my spirit. I was at peace. I said to her that we would be there on the fifteenth and that mom would still be here. I called the travel agent and made arrangements for Rezin, myself and the children to travel to South Africa on the fourteenth of February and return on the twenty-third.

I called my sister-in-law who had never met my mother and asked her if she and my nephew would travel with us. She told me she had to think about it. I said whatever, and gave her my travel agent's phone number. Two days later she called me and said that they would be traveling with us. I was so happy that my mother would have the opportunity to see her grandson for the first time and enjoy her last few moments on earth getting to know him.

I called my mother's pastor and told him that my sister-in-law and her son would be traveling with us to South Africa. My mother's pastor was really there for my mom during her illness and he privately shared with my mother that her daughter-in-law and grandson were coming. My sister wanted it to be a surprise for mom, but I believe that the thought of meeting her daughter-in-law and grandson kept her alive a little longer. "Thank you God. You are awesome in all Your ways." I asked her pastor if he would invite some of the church people to come out to celebrate my mom's birthday with her for the last time.

I had informed my Bishop and supervisor and they prayed us through the experience. We left the shores of America on Valentines Day and arrived in South Africa on my mother's birthday. When we got to the house, everybody had come out to greet us, and I was not in the mood for all the people who were present. My mother's face lit up when she saw her grandson who looks just like her son. She was happy to meet her daughter-in-law and grandson for the first time.

My family was not staying at my mom's house, so I took advantage of the opportunity to have their hosts take them home. I asked everyone else to leave because I wanted to work on my mother's home-going celebration with her. People were offended and asked me not to say that in front of my mother. My mother responded that she has been waiting for me to come and work out her home-going celebration and that she knew that I was the only one who would do what she had asked for. People left and mom and I worked out the details of her home-going celebration. Mom had asked us all through our lives not to wear black at her funeral and not to cry. I asked her if she would be okay with the people coming over that evening to celebrate her birthday with her. She said she was fine. My mother was smiling and looked so radiant. When we got through, I went with my sister to the store to pick up some cakes to serve that evening.

Everybody was back at 7 p.m. and the house was packed. We sang all my mother's favorite hymns that night and I thanked God for my mother who introduced me to Jesus at a very early age. I honored my mother by reading Proverbs 31. My friend preached a powerful word that night and we closed by singing "How Great Thou Art." My children sang "I almost let go," and mom just laid there smiling, looking so contented. Everyone in the neighborhood was standing outside and listening. I was tired that night and when we got to our place of abode, I went straight to bed and rested till 11am the next morning.

Everyone was trying to invite us to come and share a meal with their family. I accepted with the understanding that we might be able to or not. It seemed as if my mother was getting stronger and stronger each day.

It was February eighteenth when my sister came to me and apologized. She said, "Mary you know I told you that mom was dying. It seems like she is getting stronger and stronger each day. If she does not die before you have to leave we will understand if you go back and not make it for the funeral." I looked at my sister and said to her, "Don't worry about God's business. It's all in his Hands. Let's watch Him together these next few days." She said "Okay. I just wanted you to understand that we were okay if you have to go back and cannot make it back." I said, "Thank you for your concern. Now let's allow God to have His way."

We had several invitations and I allowed my family, my sister-in-law, my nephew, my husband and children to enjoy them while I stayed home. I was gone most of the day on February 20th. I got home that evening. Mom was sleeping and sounding like a train. My youngest sister was reading several scriptures to my mom. We had a dinner invitation for 6pm that evening. We were all standing around the bed when Niamke got onto the bed and laid his head on my mother's chest and just laid there. We sang a hymn and went out.

We had a beautiful dinner at my friend's home. At 8:22pm the call came that mom had gone to be with the Lord. I let out a cry and that was it. My friend prayed with us and we left. When we got home the house was filled with people. My mom's pastor was there and the associates and some of the officers of the church.

We could hardly get in.

When we entered the room my sister-in-law just broke down, and cried so loud as we all stood around the bed. My mom's pastor asked me about the program and I promised him that I would get one to him the next day. He wanted to know who was going to do the eulogy. I informed him that he was her pastor and he would be doing it. Someone had told him that my husband was going to preach the eulogy. He seemed relieved to know that he was doing it. I could not allow anyone else to do it but him. He was such a good pastor to my mom. He visited her regularly and prayed with her on the phone when he was away from home. My sisters and I agreed that we would not come across as a confused people and not cause any chaos. We were together. Everyone had their assignment.

My dad was walking around the house as if he was lost. I took him with me the next day to make the final arrangements at the funeral home and ran some errands with him.

My sister had my mother wearing blue, and mom's request was to wear white. I wanted to buy her something white but my sister insisted that she was not going to allow me to change her clothes. She was very adamant about it and I left it alone. Mom was laid to rest that Friday morning February 23rd at 10am. It was a joyous celebration. I was seated between my dad and my husband. I kept my promise that I had made to my mom and did not cry. To tell you the truth, I did not deem it necessary to cry because I knew that mom was in a better place. I kept my promise to my mom that I would not wear black. I wore the brightest and boldest colors that day, and my dad was the only other person who wore grey and not black. My sisters were dressed in black and white. Rezin extended the invitation to Christian discipleship after the eulogy. Two men accepted Christ as their Lord and Savior that day. I did not know who they were as I had my eyes closed.

Mom was laid to rest and we departed from the cemetery asking the people to please return to their homes as we just wanted the family to be present at the repast. It was done at my request and that caused a lot of talk, but it did not affect me because I knew that we had entertained all week long. We needed some time as a family just to share with one another the last few hours we had left in South Africa.

In South Africa people do not bring food to your home when you experience sickness or death. Those who come to visit you have to be fed and entertained. It can be quite costly. We went home and enjoyed the company of each other for the next few hours. My sister-in-law and I left the house at about 3pm and went and bought twelve parcels of Snoek (the best fish in the whole wide world) and chips. That was our last favorite meal that we had to have before we left South Africa.

When we got to the airport, there were so many of my friends and family awaiting us. I left my family with the friends and checked in our luggage and got the boarding passes for us. I went back and joined the more than seventy persons who had come to see us off. We sang and prayed and then it was time for us to go through customs. When we entered the door to customs, I heard my sister calling me, but I could not retrieve my steps.

They slept most of the way back. I was watching my kids and their dad sleep. When they woke up hours later I tried to take a nap.

When we got back to the United States, I had a message from my sister to call her immediately as soon as I got her message. I did. My sister said that just as we were entering customs a couple who belonged to our church in South Africa came at the last minute to greet me. The wife, Mrs. Colley came to show me her new born husband. This lady had been married to this man forever. Her husband was an alcoholic for as long as I can remember. He became saved that day at mom's home going celebration. She wanted me to know that God finally had answered her prayers.

I'll never forget. I was fifteen years old when Mrs. Colley asked me to come and assist her one evening at her home. It was a Friday night and her husband had started a pattern of bringing men into her home and making her home the place where they would get drunk. She had children, three boys and one girl and did not want them to see this ungodly witness. She said to me that she could not tell me what she was about to do but she needed for me to be present that night. She knew that her husband had the greatest respect for me and that he would not act ugly in my presence toward her.

I went over early that Friday evening. Mrs. Colley had rubbed down her entire body from head to toe with Vaseline. She was shining. Now Mrs. Colley had an unusual shade of black (we used to call it midnight black). That night Mrs. Colley undressed herself while her husband and his friends were drinking in the front room. She was naked. She put on a white apron to cover her front and tied it in the back. She was covered in the front but her rear was showing. Mrs. Colley took a tray and put some refreshments on it. She went in and served these drunk men. When she entered she received a smile from her husband who probably thought she was being nice. When she turned around all they could see was her black behind. Her husband started yelling some curse words and told the men to get the hell out. He approached her and she purposely called me to come help her get the glasses out of the room. Her husband looked at me and he too left. We laughed so hard that night and every time we thought about it. Her mission was accomplished. Those men never set foot in her house again. "Thank you Jesus." So it was important for her to let me know that he became saved that day at mom's home-going celebration. I called her and we praised God together. We had to go back twenty-eight years to recall and laugh about that event one more

147

time.

Look at God. He gave me the numbers fourteen and twenty three. We left on the fourteenth and on the twenty third mom was laid to rest and that night at 8pm we were on our way back to America. Everything took place in God's time.

We got back on a Saturday. That Sunday we were celebrating the church anniversary. We hardly had any sleep that night as our bodies were still on South African time. I got to church late that Sunday morning. Bishop Philo was the preacher. When I walked in the church they were singing my mother's favorite hymn "Great is Thy Faithfulness." I had to remind myself that I had come to worship God and not to reminesce mom's home going. So I wiped my tears and focused on worship. Service was long. Every presentation that could be made that Sunday was made and every song that could be sung was sung that Sunday. Bishop preached that Sunday on "God's Property." His sermon was so appropriate and inspiring, and he took his time for which I was glad that the Word was not shorter than everything else that was taking place in worship that morning. We went home, and dinner was served. We enjoyed good fellowship and while doing so my children and I fell asleep on the guest. We awakened that morning at 2 a.m. and were up for the rest of the night. I took the children to school the next morning and that kept them awake all day. We placed ourselves intentionally on the Pacific Time Zone and waited till after eight to go to sleep. My mother-in-law and her family never called me to express condolences to me.

Chapter 9

Sometimes if you know the
purpose of a thing, why it is
put where it is, you will recognize
it as a clue to something much bigger.
Anonymous

"And they shall be of Thee
They shall build up the old waste places;
Thou shalt raise up the foundation of many
Generations, and thou shalt be called the
Repairer of the breach, the restorer of
paths to dwell in."
Isaiah 58:12 NIV

Evaluating My Life

Parishioners sometimes assume that because you are the pastor's spouse you should know more of Christ than they do. They will approach you with questions and expect you to give them a satisfying answer. Some folks are seeking and hungering for the deeper things of God and looking to you to lead them to it. Some folk study for information and not for formation.

I have been in church all my life. If I have missed three Sundays in my entire life of attending church it is a lot. My mother forced my brother and myself to go to church. My two other siblings could stay home, but Kenneth and I had to make it to church. It did not make a difference to her whether it was raining, lightning, thundering or flooding. We had to go. I tried to act grown one Sunday by showing my mom that she was not going to force me to go to church. So I stayed home. The consequences of my behavior that week taught me to never miss church again. My mother gave me the cold shoulder all week long. Whenever I spoke to her she would just ignore me and not say a word. I did not like my mother treating me that way, so I decided to do the right thing. I never understood it until I became an adult.

As a child, the Sunday morning schedule started at 8:30 at the Lutheran Sunday school. From there, we had to leave for the 9:45 Sunday school at our church. Then we had to stay for the 11am morning worship. We would leave church at 11:55am to go to the Full Gospel Sunday school which would end at 1pm. We would arrive home tired and hungry. After enjoying a beautiful Sunday dinner, we then had to make it to wayside Sunday school at 3pm. That lasted for an hour. At 5:30 p.m. we would be on our way with our mom back to evening service at our church. So Sundays were truly the Lord's day. I loved going to church. It was a place of escape. At 12 years of age, I was asked to teach Sunday school in the absentia of an adult. From there on, I became a part of the Sunday school staff.

I love church. Most of my best friendships were formed in church. Church had become the place for me where I was motivated and encouraged to keep on keeping on. It was at church that I got my training for public speaking. Church was a place of peace and tranquility and oftentimes a place of rest. Church was the place where I met the love of God and later came to experience the God of Love.

In 1998 I found myself evaluating my life spiritually. I decided that there was more to life than what I was receiving. I felt that my life was stuck in the same place and that I was going nowhere. Sometimes I felt that I was not moving forward at all, but that I was going backwards. I felt an emptiness in my life that was unexplainable. I had been studying the Bible for so long but felt that God was only real to me in my head. There were moments in my times of study where the Presence of God was nowhere to be found. I prayed and it seemed as if my prayers did not get any results. Sometimes I was led to feel guilty about not praying enough. I would become so confused and frustrated about not being able to read or identify the signs when my life was in so much chaos. My interest in church work was on a decline. I was hungering for a greater sense of the Lord's presence and wanting to find fulfillment in Him. My prayer became daily that God would send me a Spiritual mentor to help me understand the deeper things of God. My desire was to get to know God to the utmost.

Since 1998 my life has been bombarded with devastation and destruction. I did not understand it then, but I do now. I was forty years old and my prayer request became for God to send us Godly leaders to our district. In the year 2000, I left the international church conference arena satisfied and rejoicing in the fact that God had answered my prayers in the persons of Bishop Philo Christian and his wife Rev. Helga Christian. Despite the fact that my mother-in-law was not elected to the hierarchy of the church, I was contented that God had placed the district in the hands of these spiritual leaders. It was all God.

I have known of the Christian family since I was six years old. Bishop Philo's dad, Bishop Harris Christian became our Bishop in South Africa in 1964. I believe that because we were amongst the darker skinned people in the colored church that we attended, they were attracted to us. I also know that it went much deeper than that. The relationship that was established with our family will forever be recorded in my memory.

Bishop Harrris was a unique leader. Our church was located in District Six. Drunks would always gather outside the church at church time. They would sometimes be so loud that we could hardly hear anything that was going on in service. One night Bishop Harris went from the pulpit to the street and invited all the drunks to come in for worship. They had the most beautiful voices and knew every hymn and the harmony that would come forth in service would be so beautiful, it still rings in my ears. It was often difficult to control their behavior during the entire worship. However, Bishop Harris never allowed the ushers to put them out.

We as children had a good time with them being present because we had a lot to laugh about during service. I'll never forget one service while the offering was being received. One of the inebriated attendees got up and took an offering plate. When he had finished taking up the offering, he went right out the door. The brothers went flying after him, and again it was a joke to us as children. My mother would pinch me so hard during those services that I was navy blue by the time I got home.

Bishop Harris was also responsible for my dad giving up alcohol and becoming saved. Every time Bishop Harris and his wife Mother Topaz would be in town they would get in touch with our family. Bishop Harris took my dad aside one day and asked him if he realized what the effect of his alcoholism was having on his children. Shortly thereafter, my dad stopped drinking. He was very patient with my dad in helping him turn his life around. My father became saved under the direction and coercion of Bishop Harris. I am forever thankful to God.

I will never forget the prophesy that was spoken into my brother's life. He prophesied that he would be a great vehicle for God if he remained humble. He always spoke life into our lives and blessed us with spiritual blessings in Christ Jesus. I did not understand it then but I do now.

Mother Topaz saw something in my mother and decided to nurture it. My mother was a very well-spoken person. She had a command of the English language and knew the Bible very well. However, my mother was very shy and had low self esteem. Mother Topaz always brought mom spiritual books when she came from the USA to South Africa. Mother Topaz would have my mother prepare and lead devotions. Whenever my mother hesitated, mother Topaz would say, "You can do it Sophia" and my mom would just show out. My mother became so confident in speaking in front of people that she started accepting speaking engagements outside of her local church. Everywhere she spoke, I was with there cheering her on. My mother's prayer life and faith increased, and she shared it freely with other women.

In 1966, Bishop Harris and Mother Topaz came to South Africa with a big delegation. Mother Topaz had an American beautician traveling with the delegation. My sister and I had long thick coarse hair. I will never forget the experience with the hair stylist. Mother Topaz had watched my mother taking care of our hair. It would take mom hours to do our hair, especially if it had to be washed. She suggested to my mother that the beautician show her how to do black hair. The beautician decided to do my sister Joyce's hair first. Thank you Jesus! She washed and hot combed my sister's hair. After spending nearly a whole day doing it, it was beautiful. Joyce had the most beautiful long sleek pony tails kept up by two red ribbons in her hair. Her hair was hot combed so well that it was down to Joyce's waist. I could not wait for my hair to be done the next day. However, when Joyce woke up the next morning, she lifted her head from the pillow but her hair did not rise with her. Joyce cried so hard and we treated it as a joke. We did not know any better. After Joyce got through crying we laughed and joked about it. Joyce's hair did not grow for years but it was beautiful for that few hours. My mother did not allow the hair stylist to touch my hair.

A college dean and his wife were also in the delegation. They wanted to adopt me, and I was ready to go but mom would not allow it. My mouth spoke words to my mother that have come to pass, "I will live in America one day."

Another experience that I had as a child and credit the Christian's for is the fact that I know most of the hymns of the church by heart. The church services were always packed with children. There were not enough hymnals in the church for everyone. The adults were able to participate in the singing of hymns but not the children. Bishop Harris changed that. He called for all the children of the church to be at the church on Saturday afternoons from one to four. We had to learn and memorize the hymns for Sunday. We never sang the same hymn twice a month. We had to learn the hymns every Saturday so that we could participate in worship through singing.

I sang in the junior choir. I would always sing above the choir and had to be silenced and toned down many times. I was put out of the choir as I sang too loud for our choir director. I was a loud alto and was sick and tired of being pinched for singing too loud. Well I sadly accepted the dismissal from the choir. When Bishop Harris learned about it, he took me back to the choir and asked the rest of the choir to sing as loud as I was singing. Soon we had a spirited choir and we were all sounding good for the glory of God. I was back in the choir and even got a solo.

The impact that the Christian's had on my life will forever be remembered and revered.

Bishop Philo and Rev. Helga were now on the scene. I had admired this couple for a long time. During spring break, (while we were in college) Rezin and his friends would hit the road to Baltimore to go and worship at Bethel. They went to be blessed through the great preaching of Bishop Philo.

The first time I heard Rev. Helga preaching her focus was on missionaries wearing white dresses. She preached how the missionary dresses remained white because their missionary apparel did not compel them to become dirty. I'll never forget leaving that place so convicted that I refused to wear white for a while. She was the first woman that I heard praying a prayer of praise and thanksgiving. She did not ask God for anything but just adored His Holiness, His Righteousness and Faithfulness. She took her time praying, and I wished silently that I could pray like her. She always impressed me whether it was through remarks she made, through teaching, praying, or preaching. She always had a smile on her face.

In 1993, we attended the church leadership council meeting in Detroit, Michigan where Bishop Philo and Rev. Helga were the hosts. I walked into the conference hotel booths area one day when Rev. Helga saw me coming through the door with sixteen month old Imaan. I knew who she was, but she did not know me. She greeted me with a smile, hugged me and said she had to take me to this particular booth. It was called Tea Cakes. She bought Imaan her first African outfit that day and told me to buy Imaan's cute clothes from Tea Cakes.

Rev. Helga was now my supervisor and was I glad. Bishop and Rev. Helga were always surrounded by a lot of people the first few months of their arrival in our district. I decided to wait until the greetings had calmed down before I went and welcomed them.

It was at Missionary night during annual conference that I introduced myself. I welcomed Rev. Helga to our district. I formally introduced myself to Bishop at the first Lay Banquet in Los Angeles that year.

We attended our first annual conference under the new leadership of Bishop and Rev. Helga. It was wonderfully refreshing. I wanted to be a part of ministry again. Rev. Helga recognized the pain I had within me because of my brother's incarceration and would always encourage me in the Lord. Bishop wrote a book called. "God Can" and gave me a copy to send to my brother in prison.

In February 2001, when my mother went to be with the Lord, Rev. Helga was the one who prayed me up and through the experience. She constantly encouraged my walk in the Lord. She taught me how to become intentional.

On March 24, 2001, I received an invitation from Rev. Helga to become one of her mentees as a clergy spouse. She had a five point code which was compassion, integrity, confidentiality, enthusiasm and humor. God had answered my prayer, and I accepted. It was a ten-month journey with six other sisters. We were required to present the given subject from her by recommending a book, an article, a CD, or a film that would enrich the circle in an one hour conference call each month. It was enriching and refreshing. I was one of the first presenters. We covered topics such as prayer, self-care (health development), marriage, interior decorating, music, current events, women's issues, parenting, financial health, congregational life and leadership development. The topics I presented were on prayer and congregational life.

We had to read, and I enjoyed it because by accepting the invitation I was now being held accountable and responsible to do as it was required of me. I felt she was the hardest on me during the ten month tenure but I grew so much. My entire spirit changed and I felt I was being led closer to God. "I thank you Rev. Helga for being obedient to the Holy Spirit and for including me." The ten months went by so fast, and soon we were approaching our closing retreat. Before we got there, I had another drastic change taking place in my life.

It was annual conference 2001. The sidewalk talk was that my husband was being moved to another conference. We had been in California for over six years and now we faced being moved again. Bishop finally told my husband that we were being moved to Columbus, Missouri. I never complained but accepted it. When it was confirmed at conference publicly in October of 2001, I asked the Lord prayerfully to strengthen me for this journey. I did not know then what I was asking of Him, but God is faithful. When I shared the news with grandma (who was a month away from her ninety-ninth birthday) she said the following words which I will never forget, "Oh Mary, I pray for you because Columbus is a wicked city." I asked her to explain, but that was all she said and she would not elaborate. She was talking to me in the spirit. I recanted, "Grandma whether it is wicked or not, God is still God."

We began ministry at our new church that first Sunday in November. The people received us graciously. That Sunday morning my husband formally introduced me at the end of worship and asked me to come and pray with him for marriages and families. He expressed to the church that God had blessed me to start a very successful marriage ministry at our former church. He told them he was looking forward to seeing me operate in that capacity with married couples at the new church. We prayed and satan even heard us. I stayed in Columbus until that Tuesday after the first Sunday. I then returned to California with the children, leaving Rezin behind.

We had decided that we would allow the children to finish out the school semester in California. The children were very receptive of this move. In the meantime, it was left up to me to pack up 3400 square feet of house and make the necessary arrangements to get us to Columbus. The members of our former church were so kind and helpful in making this transition.

I was sitting with Esther (a member of our church in California) who was my main helper during this time of transition when she expressed to me how blessed Rezin was to have me as his wife. She said that she would never allow him to get away with the things I allowed him to get away with. She felt that when he came home for the few days he did, that he could have been doing something more constructive by helping me get the house in order to make the move to Columbus as pleasant as possible.

He came home and did absolutely nothing. He always wanted me to understand how tired he was. I did not complain, but quietly I felt that I was the one who was tired, as I was the one seeing about the children, seeing about grandma and getting the house packed and ready for sale. We had lived in the house for three years and it was a brand-new house. I had kept it up very well. I wanted him to lease the house, but he did not want to do that. The real estate market had skyrocketed and he wanted to sell. I'm forever thankful to the people of our church in Orange who helped me and eternally grateful to Esther, who helped me into the wee hours of the early morning.

I encouraged her and her husband to buy a house in the same vicinity where we were building. They were blessed to get a new house that fell out of escrow and were able to move in before our home was completed. I gave a lot of things away but still had a lot to transport to Columbus. On December 21st, 2001 we were on our way to Columbus, our new place of residence.

We moved into an 1800 square-foot town home. It had three levels. On the lower level, we used the family room as a storage area. Grandma was in a new environment and because she was blind, I had to do everything for her. I did not want her to fall or trip over the boxes stored outside her bedroom. The bathroom was not on the same wall as her bedroom, and this confused and frustrated her. I availed myself to grandma's every need, but in the process I took away her independence.

It was a few days before Christmas and I was trying my best to get the house in order so that it would look like a home when Christmas arrived. We had very few groceries in the house. It did not occur to me to go and shop so that we could have a decent Christmas meal. The thought did cross my mind that someone in the church would probably invite us for Christmas dinner, seeing we had just moved to town but nobody did. I did not get to the store on Christmas Eve, and that Christmas was the first Christmas that we had no Christmas dinner. I did not get the children any gifts. It was Christmas the way it is supposed to be celebrated. My children however did not feel that way. They were gracious and kind to accept the situation for what it was.

It was cold in Columbus, and we all needed thermal underwear. On New Years Eve, I rushed to Wal-Mart and bought us more than a hundred dollars worth of thermals and promised the kids that we would have a wonderful New Years dinner. On New Years day, I got up and prepared rack of lamb, baked potatoes, broccoli casserole, corn, salad and bread. I made it a fun time for the kids and asked them to be our waiters. Imaan and Niamke went upstairs, and when they came down they were ready to serve us. They had changed into black pants and white shirts and each of them had a white towel over their arm. They ushered their dad and me to the table and we sat down. They served us with glee. At the end of the dinner, they gave us a tip bill. We laughed and complied. I was monitoring them very closely to see what the effect this move had on them.

The holidays were now over and I had to get them enrolled in school. The new school was a block away from us and both of them were enrolled and able to start school. Our new life had now begun in Columbus.

The mentoring circle was having its closing "Women Aglow" Retreat in San Diego, California in January 2002. Our theme scripture was taken from Philippians 3:10-12. **"Now I have given up everything else - I have found it to be the only way to really know Christ and to experience the mighty power that brought Him back to life again, and to find out what it means to suffer and to die with him. So, whatever it takes, I will be one who lives in the fresh newness of life of those who are alive from the dead. I don't mean to say I am perfect. I have not learned all I should even yet, but I keep working toward that day when I will finally be all that Christ saved me for and wants me to be."**

By the time we got to it, it was much needed for me. I had so much anger within me towards my husband because of how he had treated this move. He did not participate in helping to get things organized the way they were supposed to be and then had the nerve to criticize the hard work that I had put into it. I thanked God that I could get away for a time of refreshing.

I flew into Ontario Airport, and went by our previous home which was still on the market. I drove to San Diego. I was late for the retreat. I greeted everyone and plopped myself down in a chair.

My sister Doris and I were sharing a room. I was glad because Doris had such a peaceful Christ-like spirit that helped to place me in a different frame of mind. I enjoyed our times of praying and sharing honestly with each other. The weekend schedule was hectic, but it was good.

When I left that weekend, I was crying all the way back to Yorba Linda. I implored God not to let this wonderful feeling leave me and to strengthen me to implement the things that I had learned that weekend. I visited with Esther and her husband for a few hours and then Esther took me to the airport. A feeling of sadness came over me. I knew when I left California that time that I would not be back for a while. For the first time, I realized that the move had actually taken place. I sat on the plane looking out of the window and cried myself to sleep.

I deplaned in a happy mood and thanked God for traveling mercies. We concluded our mentoring circle with a conference call on Ash Wednesday, February 13, 2002. God was preparing me for what was yet to come.

If Rev. Helga, my spiritual mentor did not get a hold of me when she did, I believe I would have been stuck on the staircase of life. I was very comfortable with my Spiritual Mentor. I had many defenses against the changes she recommended me to make, but she patiently and lovingly helped me to achieve them. She dealt with my personality differences so effectively and was able to stretch my views to a new level of understanding. There were times when I was not completely honest with her. She never pressured me or forced her thoughts on me. The mentoring helped me to grow in a new way of relating to God. My spiritual mentor understood my personal journey so well that I was able to grow. God blessed me with a teachable spirit and I received everything that came my way. This season was short but intense and very fruitful. My spiritual mentor instructed, taught, admonished, rebuked, encouraged, and prayed with me. God placed her at the right time in my life. Everything I learned I had to go and implement for what was still ahead.

Through this mentoring event my relationship with God became my top priority again. Through the mentoring circle something that I had lost was found again. I was encouraged to live in the now and to enjoy God to the utmost. I left San Diego knowing that I had experienced the presence of God. I had a deeper understanding of the things of God. I left blessed and ready for a new beginning. We sisters had developed a relationship that was so real that to this day we still care about each other with great concern and love.

Columbus was not a very pretty city. It had a lot of run-down homes which were boarded up. It just had a very depressing look to it. The church was having a new parsonage built for us in the city of Columbus.

We were living in Creve Port. I do not know how you feel about light coming into your home, but it is very important to me. We did not have a lot of sunlight coming into the town home, and sometimes I felt so down because it seemed so dark in the house. My mother used to get up in the morning and say, "Open the windows and let the blessed sunshine in." So I opened the blinds daily but there was hardly any sunshine coming in. Darkness has a very negative effect on my spirit.

I was anxious about the parsonage getting done. I would go to the site daily to see how much progress was being made. We had a groundbreaking blessing ceremony when they started building the house. Rezin anointed the foundation after it was dug out. I was so happy that God was being made the foundation of this new home for us.

My children attended school in Creve Port. Through my daughter's school projects, we were able to learn the city of Columbus. Columbus had a lot to offer, and I finally came to the conclusion that Columbus was a great city for raising children. Another good thing about it was that not only was it fun and entertaining, it was also very educational and free of charge. I started adjusting. Niamke had his first black teacher, and she worked with him and challenged him to the utmost. Imaan was enjoying her new friends and loved the environment. She did a project on Brown verses The Board of Education. She received an "A" for her presentation.

We had two other clergy families to be moved to Columbus with us from California. For the first six months the Lucius family were our friends. Mrs. Lucius and I would drive around Columbus just to familiarize ourselves with the area. We would stop at every store and find out what they had to offer. We ran into so many sales and good food places. Very soon we knew how to get around and get to the places where we could find what we needed at very economical prices. God is good.

Once a month, Mrs. Lucius and I would make our way to Costco and just enjoy the outing. Our families would have dinner together regularly. We would enjoy the time at their home. Mrs. Lucius had all these games for us to play. For the first time in my life I felt like Rezin, the children and I were actually spending quality time together as a family. Those were wonderful memories because the children actually had fun with their dad playing these games with them, which he never did.

We celebrated my birthday in May and the Lucius' accompanied us to Morton's restaurant in Clayton. It was a beautiful evening and I received a book from the Rev. and Mrs. Lucius called "Prayers That Avail Much" compiled by Word Ministries, Inc. This book would forever change my life.

It was June 2002, and we were traveling to the minister's conference in Hampton, Virginia. Rezin was the coordinator of this trip and there were about twenty two going from Columbus. Everyone was excited because Rev. Jackie McCullough, Bishop Jakes and Bishop Jones were the speakers for the minister's conference that year. We arrived, and the Word of God was awesomely ministered to us at this conference.

The first day when Bishop Jones preached I personally could not understand a word he was saying. He was preaching the series "Liberating the Liberator." It was my first time hearing him preach and seeing him in person. I was told that everyone around me could understand what he was saying. I was so frustrated and just sat there. Bishop Jones made reference in his sermon to the pain of divorce. Immediately my ears opened and I could understand what he was saying. As soon as he completed the reference I could not understand him anymore. So I sat and waited for it to be over. I remember telling a friend that I could not understand what he was preaching about but that I did hear him speaking on the pain of divorce. I left that day saying that I would like to meet his wife to hear her side of the story. I heard someone saying so clearly to me that I would not have to meet her as I would have my own story.

The rest of the week we enjoyed God to the utmost and for the next two days, I clearly understood Bishop Jones.

We were back in Columbus and my husband had now become friends with another minister in the city. His name was Tabeal. Tabeal was married but was hardly ever seen with his wife. I am a very friendly person and will talk to anyone. Tabeal was (and still is) a very talented musician. I always complimented him for the fine musical presentations that he made. When we first came to the district, my husband did not approve of me speaking to Tabeal. He bluntly told me to stay away from him because he was gay. Well, I do not believe everything people say about other folk unless they know and have experienced the person in that capacity. I said to my husband that he should not say bad things about people just because everyone else were saying them. I kept on speaking to him, and he and my husband eventually became best friends.

For a brief moment I was glad. He lived about twenty minutes away from us. He was the leader of the conference. His church was about five minutes away from our church. He and my husband would meet for lunch in the city on a regular basis. Fellowship with the Lucius family ended when Rezin became Tabeal's friend.

In August we moved into our new home. I had to pack that which needed to be packed and moved to the new house. We moved in to the new home less than a week before the new school year started.

Rezin had purchased a ticket to Los Angeles and left the very next day, leaving me with all the unpacking once again and also relocating the children into new schools. I was furious. This man had no consideration for anyone but himself. So he left.

The people of the church came and helped me unpack and I kept going until the wee hours of the morning. I would sleep for a few hours and get up and unpack again. I cannot stand an untidy place. It depresses my spirit, and I do not have room for depression in my life. He was gone for four days and when he returned, there was but one day left to get the children ready for school. I ignored him and kept going. I was the one who needed a break, not him.

We were now living in the city, and our children were attending the schools in the city.

I was very impressed with Imaan's teacher but had great concerns for Niamke's class. Every time I entered his classroom, children would be in time-out in the four corners of the class and it was very hard for Niamke to concentrate. Niamke was there for three days when I enrolled him at another school. This was another experience. Niamke was nearly beat up twice and his teacher had absolutely no control over the class. I was praying. I went to sit in Niamke's class one day, and the teacher asked me to step out so that she could tell the class what she expected of them while I was in class. I was so mad. I asked her to dismiss Niamke and he was gone. It was the fifth day of school and Niamke was being enrolled into the third school. It was a private Christian school and Niamke seemed okay.

I got to Niamke's school unexpected one day and the teacher had her baby running freely in the class. I said, "Lord Help." I went to the principal's office and asked him whether the teachers were allowed to keep their babies in class while teaching. The principal informed me that the secretary, who was the baby's grandmother and baby-sitter, were out sick that day and that the baby was not in class on a daily basis. That afternoon I rallied parents together and asked them to help me get a signed petition to the principal's office stating that we did not pay for teachers to baby sit their children at school, but that we paid so that our children may get a good education.

Niamke did not want to leave that school, and I decided to keep him there and monitor the situation very closely. On a daily basis, I spent two to three hours a day at his school until I felt satisfied with the situation. Imaan was doing well. Her teacher was a well-seasoned teacher and she called me every time she needed me to be of assistance to her in class.

I asked the ministerial alliance to become involved in the school system and to show their presence in the classrooms for the sake of the man-child. I found out that so many of the boys had no fathers present in their homes and came to school mad at the female teacher, not wanting to cooperate with her because of the frustration they experienced at home with their mothers. They always referred to me as being old because their mothers were thirteen, fourteen years older than them.

Between Niamke's and Imaan's school, I was kept busy and not forgetting about grandma. Grandma had a bedroom on the upper floor right next to the steps. I had to keep grandma's door locked as I did not want her to wander and fall down the stairs and hurt herself. We turned the door lock inside out. Whenever I was gone, I was at peace that nothing would happen to grandma. God even provided me with a lady to take care of grandma with the greatest tender love and care. She came from 9 in the morning and stayed until 1:30 p.m.

I went to the church one day to surprise my husband with a picnic lunch basket. When I got there, he had gone and no one knew where he was. I called his cell phone several times but there was no response. So I concluded that that was what I got for wanting to surprise him. I felt that he was spending too much time away from the home and blaming it on the church. He wanted us to move into the city so that he could be close to home. He said that he would be able to come home for lunch and be there for the children and their homework, but it was not quite working out that way.

In November 2002, I wrote him a letter and told him that he was neglecting the family and that we were becoming strangers in the same home. He was busy all the time. The letter did get a positive response from him. He apologized and tried to do better, but I made the biggest mistake the next month. It was December and the children and I left for South Africa for three weeks. I completely lost him in that time. I believe that he took ill while I was gone and that "nurse" Tabeal took care of him.

It was January 30th and we were celebrating Rezin's birthday. I had asked Tabeal to find us a restaurant to celebrate Rezin's birthday. We had our children, the Lucius family, the Rodgers family, Tabeal and his wife. We went to a Japanese restaurant and had a wonderful time. At dinner that night when drinks were being ordered, I noticed that Rezin and Tabeal were both ordering the same drinks, long island teas. My daughter Imaan paid close attention to the order as well. When the drinks came she wanted to taste her daddy's drink. I gave him one blank stare because I was learning something new too. I waited until we got home that night and told him not to order those kinds of drinks in the presence of my children again and to be mindful of the example he was setting to them.

In February for Valentines Day, I prepared a beautiful Valentines Candlelight dinner. He was present in person but not present in mind. So again, I felt that I was eating by myself. I started paying very close attention to his presence at home. He and Tabeal were spending all this time supposedly doing church work. When he got home, he would get on the phone and talk to Tabeal for the rest of the night. He would make the call in my presence and move to the basement, talking for hours. Whenever I came in his presence the call would be terminated. I would go back upstairs and he would remake the phone call to Tabeal.

Tabeal had now become a part of his mother's campaign committee. Tabeal was dictating Rezin's schedule and life. I did not feel good anymore about this relationship between Rezin and Tabeal. Tabeal was the "leading" pastor in our conference, but would always be so negative of our leaders. He always opposed Rev. Helga's programs that she presented to us.

I would invite Tabeal to my home just to observe the interaction between the two of them. I did not know what I was looking for, but something about this relationship was not right.

Tabeal's wife Hedda had left for California and was gone for months. I thought that she had gone to see about her family when someone told me that she had made a remark before she left. She told the person that her husband had more time for another man than for her, and that she was gone permanently.

It was summer and a lot of church meetings were taking place. Tabeal and Rezin had to travel to every meeting. They saw themselves as leading pastors. They were more political than spiritual.

I was in a deep sleep in July of 2003. It was about 2 a.m. in the morning when the phone rang. I answered very politely and the person asked me how I was doing. I answered, "Good." He then said to me that I should check on the status of my husband and hung up. I immediately called the hotel in Philadelphia where Rezin was staying. The front desk informed me that Rezin had checked out. I did not understand but I knew that his mother was in the same hotel, and that she would know about his whereabouts.

I called her. She told me that Rezin and Tabeal were sharing a room, to call back and ask the front desk to put me through to Tabeal. I was shocked. I did not call because I knew he was okay, however my mind was running 1,000 miles an hour. I looked at the phone monitor and the person that called was registered as

Unknown name. I asked the Lord to remove this from my mind and to allow me to sleep in peace.

The next morning I called Rezin and told him of the night's experience. He was more interested in knowing who had called than anything else. When he returned I asked him why he did not inform me that he was sharing a room with his friend and that I was shocked to learn it from his mother. He said that that was his business and that I was not his mother and he did not need my permission to do what he wanted to do. I told him that we needed counseling. His reply was that I was the one who needed it; not him.

In July, 2003 we were suppose to celebrate our fifteenth anniversary. I got up gave him his card and wished him happy anniversary. We had friends from Cape Town, visiting with us. The children - especially my daughter were excited when they gave us our anniversary gift. They gave us a book called, "How to love each other." I wanted to scream so loud but could not, because she was watching me. All I could do was give her a big hug and say, "Thank you." She had been watching us for a long time now. She beckoned my girlfriend to take her to the store so she could buy us this book. She told my friend that she saw it when she was with me at the store, but could not get it then as I would have known what she was getting us for our annivrsary.

My girlfriend took her and while they were out, my daughter shared with her that ever since we had moved to Columbus it has just not been the same. She said that she wished she could move back to California and maybe things will get better again. She also expressed that she was so sick and tired of hearing us arguing and fighting over things that were not important. She said that she heard us at night when we thought that she and her brother were asleep.

On the evening of our anniversary, I was out and when I finally got home it was after eight. I noticed driving up to the house that it

169

was very dark inside. My daughter had switched off all the lights in the house and had lit every candle that I had in the house. She placed two wine glasses in the formal living room and filled them with coke soda. She told her dad to propose a toast to her mother when she entered. I was met by my daughter when I came in and she ushered me to the living room where her father was sitting. She said to both of us, "Now you all be nice to each other and enjoy your anniversary. You will not have any interruptions from us." She took her brother upstairs and slammed the door close behind her so that we could hear that they were now behind close doors.

I sat on the couch in the living room with my heart crying, because my child was indirectly saying to us that she wanted to see us do better. She wanted her parents to love each other as they were supposed to. I sat there for forty minutes and Rezin did not say a word. I drank the coke, got up and went to bed. The next morning my daughter wanted to know from me how it went. I said to her, "Thank you so much for planning a wonderful, romantic evening for your mom and dad. Forgive us for the bad example that we are setting, but just continue to pray for mommy and daddy."

I had to run for the bathroom, because I did not want to break out in tears in front of my daughter. I sat and cried in the bathroom while the shower was running.

The end of that month we decided to take a family vacation and introduce the children to the place of their father's birth. We went to Tuscaloosa, Alabama. We stayed at the Hyatt Hotel. Everyday we traveled to his aunt's home where we ate most of our meals and then went on several excursions. This aunt was referred to as the crazy aunt in Rezin's family. She was not as educated as the rest of the family, but to me she had the most common sense.

His aunt and I had talked, and she planned a trip to the zoo. We had a good time. Rezin was there with us and seemed to be enjoying himself tremendously. He was a completely different person. It was nice being with him, and he was peaceful. Everyday when we left the hotel someone would walk up to us and compliment us on being such a beautiful family. In my heart I would cry, "Lord make us beautiful indeed." His aunt took us to the park one afternoon, and for the first time in my life I observed the father of my children pushing our children in a swing and chasing them around the park. They were enjoying him to the utmost.

We had our best vacation that week in Tuscaloosa, Alabama, despite all the chaos that was going on in our lives. Rezin did not have the pressure of Tabeal, his mother, or the church. He was so relaxed and nice to have around. We looked at buying some property in Alabama around a beautiful lake and having a home built down there. We visited his dad's grave. The family took us out and informed us about the family tree. Everyone in the graveyard was related to his family. My children were excited to know how many cousins they had and how big the family was on their dad's side. At night, Rezin and I would sleep so close together that I just knew that this was the beginning of something new!

We returned to Columbus, and the next day he left for Florida. He and Tabeal were together again. The whole time he was in Florida we hardly heard from him and when he returned it was back to the old way of life.

I received a phone call from the church one morning asking me to make my way to the emergency room, as Rezin had fallen down a flight of marble steps and had hurt himself. When I got to the hospital, I walked in the same time as Tabeal. When Tabeal saw Rezin, he cried and I could not understand the tears. As far as I was concerned he was still alive, so why was he crying? Tabeal saw my facial expression and asked me if I did not feel my husband's pain. I was too mad to feel any pain and just glared at him. Rezin had a gash in the forehead, he had hurt his knees and twisted his wrists and sprained his ankles. Tonka, Rezin's armor

171

bearer, entered the room and he started crying too. I was too outdone and just looked at these men crying over someone who had just had a fall.

The nurse entered and said that there were only three persons allowed to the room. She asked one of us to leave. No one was moving and Rezin asked me to leave. I was furious and took the walk to the waiting room and then returned immediately. I told them that I was back and someone else had to leave. Tonka left and I stayed for a while. It was time to go and meet the children at school, and I left Tabeal with Rezin. He was in good hands. I did not go back to the hospital again and helped the kids with their homework. It was late that night when Rezin was released and sent home. Tabeal brought him home and said that he would take him the next morning as he had to see a specialist.

Tabeal was at the house at 7 a.m. He and Rezin were on their way to the doctor's office. I went about my day and did whatever I had to do.

The rest of that week Tabeal would make his way to my home every morning at 7 to see about Rezin. He had a chair placed in my bedroom. I would still be in bed and he would sit in that chair giving Rezin the necessary exercises and therapy he needed for the improvement of his wrists. I was not pleased at all with this man in my bedroom so early every morning, but I endured.

I was on my way to Costco's one Saturday afternoon. The children refused to go with me. Their dad was still experiencing a lot of pain and "nurse" Tabeal was visiting. I had left and was about four minutes away from Costco's when my phone rang. It was my daughter calling me. She complained that their dad had told them to stay in the basement and not to come out of it. I felt like I was being stabbed through my heart. I called home and asked Rezin what was the reason for confining the kids to the basement. I made him understand that if anyone should be confined to one area of the house, it was Tabeal and not our children. They were in their home but Tabeal was visiting our house. He immediately told me that Imaan was listening in to their conversation and the consequences were for them to play in the basement.

I went back home and took the children with me to Costco's. I was frantic. I decided to go to the movies afterwards. We went back to the house, put up the groceries and went to the movies. From the movies, I went to my friend's home and stayed until after eleven that night. We went home, took a bath and went to bed. I had absolutely nothing to say to Rezin. Tabeal's wife was still gone. I could not make up my mind or try to understand what was going on, but I was praying without ceasing.

There was absolutely no relationship between Rezin and me anymore. I felt like I have always felt since three months of marriage; that we were nothing else but roommates. In August of that year, I called his mother to ask her to encourage him to go to counseling with me. She asked Pekah, her oldest son who is the psychologist, to come and visit with us.

He came on a Sunday morning. Worship had started when an usher asked me to move over so that my brother-in-law could be seated next to me. I looked back and there he was coming down the isle. He sat with me and the kids. We enjoyed worship together. After worship, I asked Rezin if we were going out to eat together as a family. His reply was that we were going to his supervisor's appreciation that afternoon and that we would have dinner at this event. He furthermore asked me not to wait for him as he wanted to speak with his brother before he came home.

When they arrived home about ninety minutes later, I was sitting and watching the Word Channel. Pekah came and sat down with me, and soon Rezin joined us too. His brother told me that there was never only one crazy person in the relationship but that it took two crazy persons to mess up something good. I did not appreciate him calling me crazy, but I endured for the sake of my sanity. He then told us that if his dad was alive, he would say that this family does not believe in divorce and that we should find a way to work it out. However, because dad was not alive anymore and we were living in a different time and age, that the least thing that Rezin should do was to go for counseling. He said, "Go for counseling so that when you get to divorce court, you can at least tell the judge that you have tried to reconcile this marriage, and it just has not been able to work out."

It felt like a knife was being pierced through my heart. How dare this man encourage his brother to go for counseling so that when he gets to divorce court.....? I was too through. That evening, Rezin said that we would go for counseling and that he would find us a counselor the next day.

He did. I was looking for an African-American counselor but he found us a Caucasian counselor. I personally felt that a White counselor would not understand the depth of our situation (socially and culturally) as well as an African-American counselor would. I called to find out the status of this counselor and whether she was a Christian counselor. She was very polite and informed me that she was a Christian counselor.

At our first visit we made the friendly introductions and then we got started. I expressed to the Counselor that I had become very frustrated in this relationship, and that I felt he was married to his mother and Tabeal more than he was married to me. I told her that I felt that he was taking care of his mother and Tabeal financially and that they were his top priority. I also informed her of the unbalanced relationship that he had with Tabeal - the person whom he at one time wanted to convince me was gay.

I am not going to lie, I was disappointed when I learned that the counselor was Caucasian. But when I met her in person and when she opened her mouth, my spirit was at peace and connected with her immediately. Rezin did not have a willingness to open himself up and share sensitive and personal information. She made him understand that it was very imperative if he was looking for favorable results for his relationship with me and that she had an understanding heart.

She encouraged us to buy the book "Getting The Love You Want" written by J Hendrix and to read the first few chapters in the book before we had our next meeting with her. I went and purchased the book and started reading immediately. I did my assignment and when we got back to Counseling, she was ready for us. Our answers differed as the night differs from day. She told Rezin that he should let go of his mother and her dreams and start paying closer attention to his wife and children. She said that she could not understand how he could have a bank account and credit card with his mother when he did not have any financial association with his wife. She also asked him to take the time that he spent daily with Tabeal at lunch and spend it with his wife.

The next session would call for us to come with a written marriage vision which we would present to her at the next counseling session. That was the most interesting session to me. I learned that day how far removed this man was from me and my children.

Writing the marriage vision required us to each write a series of short sentences in the present tense describing our personal vision of a deeply satisfying love relationship. We had to rank the sentences from 1 to 5 according to its importance, 1 indicating "very important" and 5 indicating "not so important." This was our Marriage relationship vision.

Rezin	Sentences	Mary
3	We pray together	1
1	We communicate well with each other	1
5	We eat dinner together	2
4	We share with one another	1
1	We trust each other	1
3	We put each other first	1
1	We are honest with each other	1
1	We work well together as parents	1
4	We have daily private time together	1
4	We share important decisions	1
2	We speak respectfully to each other	1
4	We make love	1
5	We bank together	1
1	We respect each other's view point	2
1	We listen to each other	1
1	We settle our grievances peacefully	1
5	We have fun together	1
2	We seek God' direction for our lives	1
1	We raise happy and secure children	1
4	We have mutual romance	1
2	We have self control	1
2	We have an active faith	1
3	We have good conversation	1
4	We live within our means	1
5	We save together	1
1	We respect each others friends	2
5	We encourage each other to use our gifts	1
2	We give each other great patience	1
3	We study the Word of God together	1

The Counselor was astonished. She asked us to review it and to discuss it at home so that we could understand why each of us thought that it would be difficult to achieve those things that we ranked 3 and above.

The next week, we both had to attend an annual conference meeting before we were to attend our next counseling session. I left the meeting twenty minutes before our scheduled Counseling session time. I noticed Rezin not moving.

I was sitting in the waiting room, and it was eight minutes past the scheduled time when I went downstairs and asked where the counselor was. Rezin was not there either. When I got to the receptionist, the Counselor just walked in and asked me what was I doing there? I said that I did not understand. She informed me then that Rezin had cancelled the session. I told her that the both of us just attended a meeting together and he did not say a word to me about postponing the session. Tears welled up in my eyes, and she said for me to come to her office.

She spoke to me that day as a mother who loved her daughter so much and just wanted the best for her. I left her office contented and at peace. I received everything she said to me that day in confidence. Needless to say we never made it back to counseling again.

It was the last Sunday in October, and Bishop Philo was preaching that morning at our church. Rev. Helga had accompanied him and he brought an awesome word to us that day. After service, Rezin and I accompanied Bishop Philo and Rev. Helga to lunch. During our time of fellowship Rev. Helga asked the question of us, "How has Columbus changed your life?" Rezin replied that he was much busier now than he was in California, and that the responsibilities were much greater.

My reply was that I had become a very lonely person and that Rezin has no time for me and the children. I further stated that he blamed the church, but I did not think it was the church keeping him as busy as he wanted them to believe. Bishop Philo and Rev. Helga spoke to both of us at length of the importance of balance in the work environment and the marriage relationship. We ended the conversation in prayer and left for our various destinations.

That night at home Rezin was very quiet. He sat there staring at the ceiling. I knew he was mad at me for being honest that afternoon over lunch, however it did not bother me. He later told me that I insulted him that afternoon. I said let's pray and discuss it. He left and that was good enough for me. I was not going to get into a heated debate with him.

It was the week of annual conference. I went before the Board of Examiners that week and the recommendation was made that I be ordained an itinerant deacon in the church. I was humbly excited in the Lord. All through the worship, I just cried in thankfulness to God for having brought me thus far by faith. After the ordination, we all had to line up across the front of the church and people were allowed to congratulate us. I saw Bishop whispering in Rezin's ear and he came and congratulated me by giving me a peck on the cheek and then he left. I knew that Bishop had reminded him to come and congratulate me.

I left the scene of the conference and went to the missionary meeting. Rev. Helga congratulated me and we had our business session.

Rezin's mother was in town. She never got around to congratulating me. I later learned from Tabeal that she suggested that they should take me out for dinner or something to celebrate my ordination with me. Tabeal said that Rezin objected. God is good and worthy of all praise. I did not need to be around anyone fake.

That Sunday morning at church, Rezin was trying to act glad about the ordination because the church was glad and excited that their pastor's wife was now an ordained minister. He tried his best, but

I knew that he had so much difficulty in expressing himself that morning and especially presenting me to the church as Reverend. The pulpit was filled with visiting preachers and I sat on the lower level of the pulpit across from Rezin.

The next Sunday, one of the associate preachers said that he should allow his wife to sit next to him in the pulpit. He said no that I would be a hindrance to him. For the next few Sundays, the congregation started questioning him as to why he had placed me on the complete opposite end in the pulpit, and why I was not seated next to him. He handled that problem very effectively that next week. He moved the chair that was next to his in the pulpit so no one could be seated next to him. I was okay with wherever I was seated. I was not there to be seen sitting next to him but to worship God. Whenever we were granted the opportunity to sit together at a worship service, he always found himself a seat away from me.

I found myself weeping a lot in worship and people would always come after service and ask me if everything was okay. My response would be, "Just pray for me." I came home one afternoon and Rezin told me not to cry in his pulpit anymore and that I was a distraction and hindrance. I obeyed. Every Sunday morning I would pray to God to strengthen me so that I would make it through service without crying, and God sustained me.

In December we celebrated Grandma's hundredth birthday. I had invited the church to come and celebrate with us in praise and thanksgiving to God for grandma's one-hundredth birthday. I asked Tabeal to provide us with the music for that evening. Grandma looked so beautiful that evening. Her silver hair was beautifully done by Ms. Sophie and she was dressed to the tee. We had visitors who came to celebrate with us from California, Illinois and Georgia. I had the most beautiful cake made for grandma at a French Bakery. It was beautifully decorated in fresh glazed fruit with a white chocolate scroll on top of it wishing grandma a very happy birthday.

I realized how blessed I was to still have grandma in my life. I honored her that night and thanked God for placing her in my life the way He did. I said that grandma was (and still is) my children's real and only grandma. I said that my mother was blessed to spend some time with my children, but that she had gone to be with the Lord.

Grandma was blessed to spend the most time with the children. It was grandma who taught my children their 123s and abcs. It was also her that taught them how to kneel down and pray. She did not teach them the Lord's prayer or Now I lay me down to sleep. No, she asked them to think of three things that God had done for them that day and to thank Him for that. Then to think of people who needed God's assistance and to pray for them, and then she told them to ask for forgiveness for any sins that they had committed and then to ask God to bless family and friends.

She modeled faith, hope, love, and holy living to all of us. I celebrated her for being a godly grandparent. She was the real grandma supplied to us by God Himself. I also said that Rezin's mother was too busy to spend time with her grandchildren as she was a career woman following her dreams.

Grandma however has been in my children's life since they were born and did so much for them on a daily basis. My son and daughter honored grandma and then it was Rezin's turn. He did not have much to say, but expressed his thanks to grandma. We sang all of grandma's favorite hymns and read her favorite scripture. It was a wonderful evening in the Lord. Everyone seemed to have had a wonderful time.

While people were leaving, I found Rezin and Tabeal sitting in the formal dining room by themselves. Rezin was crying. Tabeal was consoling him. I asked him what was the matter and why he could not talk to me about whatever it was that was upsetting him. I asked him what is really going on between him and Tabeal. He said that he could not talk to me about his problems; he could only share them with Tabeal. I left the room and went and sat in the kitchen, physically and emotionally exhausted.

He came in later and told me not to ever insult his mother like that again. I responded, "How did I do that?" He replied that his mother is their grandmother. I was ready for a fight. I responded "Your mother is their biological grandmother and that is all she is. She never sends them a birthday card, she never buys them a Christmas gift, she never calls them to congratulate them on their achievements, and when she is in town she never attempts to do anything with them or for them. All she is to them is their biological grandmother. My family in South Africa has spent more time with our children than your family has tried to." I said, "It is a shame."

My God-given mother from California, Sister Pearl, motioned me with her eyes to be still, and I stopped. We went to bed that night tired and not speaking to each other. My thoughts were why he would be crying on this man's shoulder when he had a wife to cry to.

The next day was Saturday, and the children and I spent the day with our guest coming in and out. I had to go and get my sister-in-law from a meeting at the airport Hilton Hotel. We came home and watched a movie and then went to bed.

We went to church the next day. I had invited Tabeal to come and have dinner with us that Sunday afternoon. His wife was still gone. We were seated at the table and the dinner was delicious.

After dinner I started cleaning up, and again left Tabeal and Rezin in the dining room by themselves. I was working in the kitchen and decided to check for the last time to make sure that everything that needed to go in the dishwasher was in it. When I walked in, Tabeal was trying to hold Rezin's hand. Rezin pulled away immediately and I just looked. My mind started wondering all kinds of things. I finally had to shut my mind down because it was upsetting me.

Chapter 10

Grant us the will to fashion as we feel,
Grant us the strength to labor as we know,
Grant us the purpose, ribbed and edged with steel,
to strike the blow.
JOHN DRINKWATER

"I humbled my soul with fasting."
PSALM 69:10 NIV

Fasting

I grew up in a very diverse religious community. We lived in the second house from the corner at 47 Francis Street, Cape Town, Republic of South Africa. There were five brick homes attached to each other. On the left of our home lived Christians, and on the right lived Muslims. The street was about forty-eight percent Christians, forty-eight percent Muslims, and the rest of the population on the street were Indians and Jews. I was never attracted to the Muslim faith because the women could not go to mosque (church).

I always admired how the family would get together as soon as the sound went forth from the mosque to call them to prayer. I remember the month of Ramadan very well. The Muslims fasted for forty days. They would fast from sun-up to sun-down. During Ramadan, they would have a feast every night. They would share with the neighbors by giving them a beautiful plate of the best tasting deserts wrapped in brightly colored saran wrap. It would look so pretty that you did not want to touch it, but it had to be eaten.

I had a friend named Farieda who would always ask me to help her fast. I would say to her, "Girl I don't know how I can go without eating all day but I will try." And I did try until I saw one of my Christian friends eating something good. By the way, my friend Farieda converted to the Christian faith later in years. Praise the Lord! My experience with Farieda inspired and stimulated my interest in fasting.

The church that I grew up in as a child did not preach or teach about fasting as far as I can remember. It was not until I came to the United States, that I heard preaching and teaching on fasting and praying. I remember a girlfriend in college told me one day that she was fasting. My first response to her was that I did not know Christians fasted. She replied, "No Mary, we do fast and that is the only way that you can get a breakthrough when you are going through something and you need the Lord's favor." She was a preacher's daughter, so she must have known what she was talking about.

I started reading Scriptures pertaining to praying and fasting. However, when I tried to do it, I would always fail. Years later, I was sitting in service and the preacher referred to a time in his life that he went through an extremely difficult situation. He went into a period of fasting and praying. He went on to say something that would stick with me for the rest of my life. He said that in times of fasting and praying the presence of the Lord was so real to him that he could hear God speaking as if He was standing right next to him. I fasted a lot of times but never got through the fast. I never felt that I was doing it correctly.

In October 2003, my life seemed so out of control that God called me to a time of fasting. God placed so much literature obout fasting in my hands that year, in preparation for the fast He was calling me to. I accepted the invitation. My fast was going to be to the honor and glory of God. I committed my fast unto the Lord. I told God what areas of my life needed spiritual improvement, although this was not my top priority for fasting. I committed my times of fasting unto the Lord. I asked God to teach me how to discipline myself and my thoughts according to His will. This fast was intended for forty days. My hours of fasting were from 10 at night to 5:00 p.m. the next day. During the forty days, I only ate vegetables and fruit, and drank juices and lots of water. Seven days before my fast I would continually ask the Lord to bless me with the necessary strength and determination that was needed for the duration of the fast.

I started my fast and successfully made it through the first day. Thank You, God. The second and third day seemed to be even better than the first day, and so was the rest of my fast until the completion of the forty days. I thought that it would be a challenge because I still had to cook and prepare meals for my family.

The experience was so exhilarating that it jarred me on to do another fast after seven days of eating regular meals again. I felt the presence of God so strong in my life during the forty days that when the fast was over, I felt like I had lost God. I did another forty-day fast. This time I sacrificed something that I enjoyed while I was fasting the first forty days.

I was so strengthened by the power of God that I was able to go to restaurants with my friends and sit and watch them, unaffected by their eating. When they asked me why I was not eating, I would tell them that I was not hungry. By the end of the second fast, I saw that the hand of God had moved in some of the situations that I had laid before the Lord. The best surprise that I had was one morning when I passed the mirror and did not recognize the person in it. I turned back and looked in the mirror again and said "Hi gorgeous." I stood in front of the mirror smiling and thanking God for this extra benefit of fasting. I was a former shadow of myself.

People were very curious about how I was losing the weight. They did not accept or respond to me very nicely for giving God the credit. I replied, "God has decided to give me a new makeover, a new body, a new mind, and a new spirit. Hallelujah!" One lady said to me, "Stop being so selfish Mary, and share the information. We all can see that it is working." I said, "Yes, fasting and praying." Someone else responded, "She is crazy." And I responded back to them, that I was okay with being crazy for Jesus. Very soon the Lord would show me why He would give me the latter response. I love God with all my heart and with all my soul and with all my strength and with all my expectancies.

In December, 2003, three days before we were to leave for California for our Christmas vacation with my husband's family, Rezin came home and told me that he did not love me anymore. I was devastated. I cried and cried and cried. I called my mother-in-law and told her that I did not feel like coming to California, pretending around their family that everything was okay when in reality it was not. She encouraged me to come and assured me that we would sit down and talk when we got there. She also told me that whatever I do, not to move out of the house and that Rezin was probably just going through something.

My children were looking forward to this trip, and they knew that if mommy was not going, nothing much as far as fun was going to happen for them. I decided that I would not disappoint them. This was going to be the family vacation and I was going to make the best of it.

We left for California and checked into the Wyndham Airport Hotel in Los Angeles. We rented a SUV from Enterprise and we were on our way to my mother-in-law's house. When we got there, we greeted and sat around talking about nothing until my son said the he was ready to go to be with his first friend in life, Peter. I asked Rezin for the key, and we trotted our way down Interstate 405 to Costa Mesa, California where the Isaacs family lives.

I met the Isaacs family in November, 1996. We had boarded the airplane in Atlanta, on our way to Cape Town. We had an eighteen-hour flight ahead of us. Jacob and Linda Isaacs had four beautiful children, Deidre, Lee, Nellie and Peter. I was traveling with my daughter, Imaan, and my son, Niamke. Niamke was eighteen months old and Imaan was four years old.

I was seated in the last row on the airplane. Linda approached me and asked me whether she could sit with me for a few minutes so that she could nurse her thirteen-month-old son. Both of us were still nursing these boys. I said, "Certainly," and at that moment Niamke was reaching for my breast. So we sat nursing and talking. We became acquainted with each other and learned that we only lived a few blocks away from each other. We lived in

Irvine. Linda lived in Costa Mesa. Linda and I became sisters in the real sense of the word from that day on. Niamke and Peter refer to each other as first friends in life. Nellie and Imaan are one year and one day apart in age.

When we returned from South Africa that year, we visited each other daily and did things together for the sake of the children. We were able to freely express and practice our South African upbringing and culture and also practice speaking the language for the children's sake. We felt like family. The children refer to each other as cousins, and to me and Linda as aunt and to Jacob as uncle. Sometimes Linda and I just laughed when our children introduced us to their friends. Yes we were family. Linda became my support system and my sister whom I could speak to during the difficult times of my life. We would do for each other without expecting anything in return.

We reached the Isaacs residence. The children greeted each other joyfully and then disappeared. Linda and I went for a ride, and we just cried together all the way to the mall. When the children saw us again, we had forgotten about the crying. One of them asked, "Why are your eyes so red? Have you been crying?" Linda and I looked at each other and together we answered, "Allergies." We both laughed. I spent the rest of the day with Linda until late that night. I knew that Rezin was waiting for me at his mother's home, but I was not rushing to get back. I did not feel like going back, but I had to. The children were spending the next two days with my sister, Linda.

I reluctantly left and took my time getting back to Los Angeles. God must have been driving, because I cried most of the way back. God took me safely. When I arrived, Rezin gave me one ugly look and we left for the hotel. He chose to sleep in one of the beds and went to sleep. I wanted to talk about what was happening in our lives, but we ended up screaming and insulting and hurting each other. Hurting people hurt people. We both went to sleep. I was feeling so much pain that I cried myself to sleep. I will never forget the experience of the hotel.

The Lord awakened me the morning of December 22, 2003 at five. He instructed me to go to the window and write down everything I saw. The first thing I saw was the empty parking lot. I saw planes ascending and descending. I saw a sea of lights. I saw that every robot or light in the street was amber. In the far distance, I saw the mountains. It looked as if they surrounded Los Angeles. On a billboard I saw five Cs written in white on a blue background. I wrote it down in my diary and went back to sleep.

That next day my girlfriend was supposed to pick me up to take me to the beauty shop. I waited for her most of the day. When she did show up, it was too late to go to anybody's beauty shop. So I spent the day by myself crying in the hotel.

Rezin came back from his visit with his mother. We had dinner together, and we ate without speaking a word. I endured his presence. On Christmas Eve I went to get my children in Costa Mesa and spent the day with Linda, Jacob and the children. Linda had Imaan and Niamke to open their Christmas gifts that she had gotten them. After they had opened their gifts, we went to the mall to allow Linda and the children to get their gifts from us. The children pleaded with me to stay in Costa Mesa instead of going back to their grandma's house in Los Angeles, but I would not agree to it. My flesh was tempted but the spirit took control. My children, I thought, were unaware of what was happening between their dad and me.

We were on our way back to Los Angeles singing and telling jokes, and laughing and just having a good time. I had spoken to my spiritual mentor, and she asked me to create as much joy for the children as I possibly could. So with that in mind, we drove back to Los Angeles. All of the in-laws were there. We greeted them and the children disappeared.

I found myself sitting on a couch alone with my eyes closed. I called a friend, and she told me that they were having service on Christmas. I told her that I would see her there.

Later when we got back to the hotel, Rezin told our son to share the bed with him. My daughter shared the bed with me. My daughter asked him why he was not sleeping in the bed with mommy. He ignored the question.

It was Christmas, three days later when the Lord awakened me at five again. He told me to go to the window and look out and to record what I saw. When I looked out, the parking lot was full and there was no room for cars to park anymore. The Lord whispered in my spirit, "As empty as your cup might seem to you now, it will become full and overflow again." It was very cloudy that morning. I could not see the mountains, but I knew they were there. The Lord said to me, "You cannot see the mountains, but you know that they are there, so it is with me. Just as you cannot see me, just know that I am with you always." My favorite Scripture came to mind; **"As the mountains surround Jerusalem so God surrounds His children both now and forever."** (Psalm 125: 2) Some lights in the city were green and in my spirit I heard God saying, "Sometimes we have to come to a "stop" in life, but remember the "go ahead" follows." I saw planes ascending and descending. The word from the Lord came, "In our lives we will have tribulations, but be of good cheer for I have overcome the world." I saw the blue billboard again, and the Lord brought to my remembrance my wedding day sermon, "The five Cs of life, Christ-likeness, Compassion, Communication, Consistency, and Commitment." Well, the Lord had spoken. I prayed and thanked God for the Word and went to the bathroom. I did my devotions and went back to bed and laid there just tearing to myself.

We got up that Christmas morning and left for the in-laws. I dropped my family off and was on my way to church. Rezin's twin brother was serving brunch that day, and I was expected to meet them at his home. Worship was awesome and Rev. Sherman Gordon preached from Mark 12:41-44. His sermon topic was "God Is Watching Us." Verse 44 says **"they all gave out of their wealth but she, out of her poverty, put in everything all she had to live on."** I could identify with her. The sermon he preached was for me, and while he was preaching, tears just flowed because the message had encouraged my soul tremendously. I left refreshed and asked God to give me the strength to make it through the rest of the afternoon.

When I reached the house, there was hardly any parking space on the street, so I just kept circling the house, not wanting to go in. About ten minutes later, someone left and I parked and went inside. They had started eating already. My stomach was tied in knots. I really did not want to eat, but I knew it would be interpreted that I was "acting evil." I ate a little, and the food was good. I sat around trying to be cordial and friendly to everyone present. My mother-in-law, Rezin and Pekah (the psychologist) went into a room. I was waiting for them to call me, but they never did. They came out laughing and I closed my eyes in the chair and fell asleep.

A man's voice awakened me. It was the voice of my husband's uncle who was standing in the bedroom door, telling him how selfish he was to lay sleeping on a comfortable bed while his wife sat sleeping in an uncomfortable chair. Rezin responded, "She made it here all the way from South Africa by herself, and if she wanted to, she could find her way to the bedroom." His uncle was looking for a response from me but there was none. I just wanted to get away from them but had to wait until Rezin was ready to go, since we were spending Christmas with his family.

They finally got to the opening of the Christmas gifts and had gifts for everyone except me. That was the first Christmas that I did not receive a gift in my life, not even from the man I was still married to. He gave his mother a stack of $100 bills, and she got what she asked for. I did not get anything, but I had already decided that I was not going to have a pity party for myself. I had purchased myself a devotional book and wrote in it:

To Mary
I love you. Let God bless you through this journal and
do likewise.
Love ya
From Grandma Elizabeth
"It is God who holds all things together
and by Him all things consist."

That was my Christmas gift. It was the best Christmas gift that I had ever gotten. It was a devotional journal. "Daily in Your Presence" written by Rebecca Barlow Jordan. So I did get a gift that Christmas, didn't I? That journal would be the mouthpiece of God Himself to me for the next year. Hallelujah!

We left Los Angeles a few days later. All his mother said was "goodbye." I wanted to hear her say that she would pray for us or at least some word of encouragement. We left. The only person I could turn to was God and God alone. I should have turned to Him in the first place. Only God could fix what was wrong and not Rezin's mother. Get the lesson Mary-get the lesson. Turn it over to Jesus.

Whenever my life was out of control, I would become a slave of the stomach. I was oblivious to my bondage to food and my leakage of spiritual power. I have never really looked at what caused this lust for food until God had called me to abstain. I was a size 6 when I came to the United States 20 years ago in 1985. I noticed that every time I was faced with spiritual warfare, and most of the time I did not see it as spiritual warfare but a problem that took it's time to go away, I would feed my face uncontrollably.

In 2003, I was a size 20W. I was still looking like 20 pounds of potatoes forced into a 5-pound bag. I gained so much weight not facing the problem and most of all not yielding it to God. The apostle Paul insisted on the importance of disciplining the bodily appetites and not making provision for the flesh to gratify its desires.

Whenever I was overweight, I had low self-esteem, no confidence, was tired, very self conscious, depressed and sometimes just plain, old mean. I read somewhere that, "satan is a stubborn foe, and he will not relinquish his grasp on the spirit and souls, minds and bodies of men unless compelled to do so." Fasting seems to provide that force. God prepared me way back as a little girl to admire Muslims fasting around me and pricked my interest to want to know more about fasting.

Back in October of 2003, God knew what was coming, and he provided me with a way of escape. Obedience is better than sacrifice. I would probably have been as big as a house and hiding somewhere now. God directed me to fast and pray and strengthened me to maintain pressure until the enemy was compelled to loosen his grip on the captive (me). Fasting is not a command or an option but it is a passion.

The benefits that I experienced through fasting, were so awesome. Isaiah 58 tells us about it. I experienced it personally according to the Word of God:

1. Revelation Knowledge
2. Healing Power
3. God's Protection
4. The Lord's Presence
5. Deliverance
6. Guidance
7. Anointing
8. Revival

I became more disciplined in my everyday life, but most of all in the things of God. Every time I completed a fast I would feel so complete. I communed with Jesus 24/7. I would wake up out of my sleep and find myself talking to God. There were days when I questioned God and He would answer me right there and then. I became a very quiet person. I would be on the phone for hours at a time, but fasting took me away from the phone and television unless it was the Word being preached. I spent more time reading, not only the Bible, but all kinds of spiritual material. My prayer life changed completely. My girlfriend honked at me in the busy traffic one day, and pulled up beside me asking, "Who are you having such an intense conversation with?" I hollered back "Jesus." She laughed and drove off.

I had purpose in my life again, despite what was happening around me. I could not wallow in my situations but faced them boldly. I became completely free in Christ Jesus. People started moving in church when they saw me coming, because I was just too loud for them.

I started laying hands on the sick and claiming newborn babies for the Kingdom. I went to the hospital one day to visit a sick person. As I entered the long hallway to the elevators, the Lord focused my eyes on a scene appearing about 50 feet ahead of me. A young lady had just given birth to the most handsome baby boy. The mother who was being escorted to the door in a wheelchair was about 13 years old. There were four generations of women beside her. No man in sight. Her mother who looked no older than 28, her grandmother could have been about 42, her great-grandmother who was about 55 and then the great-great-grandmother who was about 70. The mother was holding the baby up as a showpiece and everyone that passed her "oohed and aahed" about this baby.

When I got to the family, I laid my hands on the baby and started praying aloud. "Father in the Name of Jesus, I claim that this baby will be a showpiece for the Kingdom here on earth. I plead the blood of Jesus over his life and that through him every generational curse in this baby's lineage will be broken. I pray for this mother that she will now realize the God responsibility that is ahead of her, and that You will empower and equip her to train him to become the best reference found in all the earth. I pray that you will now raise up a man of God to give spiritual leadership to this man-child that he may know You, and know that he is made in the image of God. I pray for this young mother that You will now cover her vagina with the blood of Jesus that she will remain pure until marriage. We claim it done in Jesus' Name."

My daughter and son were so embarrassed and warned me that if I did that again they were going to pretend they were not my children. The seventy-year-old mother thanked me with tears in her eyes, and the others looked at me as if I was crazy. I kept going. I am free and I am so grateful. I do not care what other people say or think about me. I am me and express myself freely. Hallelujah!

Fasting also gave me an unusual sense of enduring power, inner strength and outer strength. I had power to stand face to face with the enemy and not flinch. I had the power to rebuke the enemy and the power to say "no." I cannot live without fasting now. Oh what peace! The peace of God that surpasses all understanding keeps my heart and mind in the knowledge of Christ Jesus.

Although crying is sometimes seen as a sign of weakness, emotional instability, or lack of faith and hope, I have always given myself freedom to cry. I cried a lot during this period. My car radio was always on the gospel station 1800 AM. I remember getting off the airplane in Columbus and receiving a call from my girlfriend Nona inviting us to dinner. I told her we had just arrived, and that I would call her when I got home. We got home and Rezin told me, "I am going to a banquet at the Holiday Inn or Marriott or Hilton Hotel." He would not tell me exactly at which hotel it was, because he said that it was none of my business.

When we got home, we put the luggage in the house, and we left for Nona's home. They were ready too. I was driving when the hymn, "Be not dismayed whatever betide God will take care of you" was playing. I tried to be cool but could not contain it. Tears were pouring out of my eyes as if a faucet had been opened. My daughter was sitting in the front seat of the car with me. She had been observing me crying for a while. She said, "Stop the car mommy," and tears were streaming down her face too. I lost it and just sobbed. She said, "Mommy, what is wrong?" My response was "nothing." Then she said, "You always force us to tell you why we cry but now you won't tell us why you are crying so much." Through uncontrollable sobs I said, "Ask your daddy." I regretted it immediately. She said, "Mommy, please stop crying." I tried, but was not very successful that day. My son sat and just observed us. He did not say a word about the current events.

We got to Nona's home and I went into the bathroom. Nona followed and we both sat and wept. She continuously said to me, "God is going to make everything alright."

We had met Nona and her husband Lonnie twelve years before. Rezin was a pastor in Lenexa. Nona and I were both pregnant at the same time although we had not yet met. Imaan was born two months before Lonnie Neville, who is Nona and Lonnie's first born. Nona, Lonnie and little Lonnie Neville, whom we called by the middle name Neville, joined our church when Imaan was about six months old.

I immediately took to Nona. She was and still is a very genuine, kind, generous and loving person. Nona's home is the one that everyone in the neighborhood knows that you can always walk in without having to call and have a scrumptious meal awaiting you. The one thing that I admired about Lonnie and Nona's relationship was their togetherness and outward expression of love for each other. When Nona was doing something around the house, her husband, would be right there helping her. They would play sports together and always exhibited a spirit of unity and harmony. I have never heard her husband raise his voice at her publicly. I said to her that I wished my husband was like hers. He was always so helpful and there for her. I started comparing. I did not know about the golden rule; don't compare, don't compete and don't complain.

When Imaan was four months old, she spoke her first word. At one year of age, Imaan was speaking in full, grammatically correct sentences. Imaan had a lot of sense. She called me "mommy" and my husband, "daddy." She called Nona, "Mamom" and Lonnie she called "dada." We had friends named Frankie and Toliver. Imaan called Frankie "Mom" and Toliver "dad." Whenever I had any obligations or meetings to attend, I was comfortable leaving my child with either of these couples. Neville and Imaan, however, got to spend a lot of time together. They loved each other and whenever Nona's parents would visit, Imaan would be spoiled by grandpa as if she was his own flesh and blood.

Nona always looked out for me. I never asked her to, but she would always give me time to take care of Mary. She would call me and tell me to have Imaan ready and get her up and have her for the whole day and sometimes even for weekends. Nona must have known that I felt like a single parent most of the time. Rezin was so busy doing church work and God's work that he forgot that he had work and a family at home. Well, he told me that he was called by God to preach and not for all the other stuff that I expected him to do at home and with the family. Nona gave me times of refreshing, and I enjoyed them very much. We became good friends for the next three years that we lived in Lenexa.

Nona became pregnant in 1994. The Saturday when she told us that she was pregnant, my husband came home and made love to me that night very urgently. I had to be pregnant too. Well I did become pregnant. Nona was due January and I was due in April. Nona gave birth to a beautiful girl in January of 1995.

We were moved from Lenexa to Orange, California in February 1995. However, we vowed that we would stay in touch and remain friends. It was about a year later that Nona and Lonnie moved from Lenexa, to Columbus, Missouri. In December 2001, we were moved to Columbus, Missouri. It was good to have Nona and Lonnie in Columbus. I had a place where I knew I could leave my children and they would be safe. It was all God orchestrated. Our friendship had remained solid and rooted in Christ Jesus. I was blessed by God to have a sister who would do and do and do some more for me whenever it was needed. I do not know where I would be today if it were not for the presence of Nona and Lonnie here in Columbus for such a time as this. God had this set-up wonderfully orchestrated on my behalf and I cannot thank Him enough.

I was tired that evening and left Nona's home at 6:00. The banquet was supposed to start at 7:00 p.m. and I decided to be home before Rezin left. We got home and he had left already. I called him and told him that I was feeling sick and was going to take myself to the emergency room. I asked him to come home. He was mad and it took him an hour and twenty minutes later to get home. By then I had taken two Tylenol tablets and was feeling better. I had to get out of the house to relieve myself from the pain that had erupted my inner being with such intensity in order to keep my sanity. I left and drove by several hospitals but did not go in. I ended up at the mall and sat in the mall by myself until it closed. About twenty minutes before the mall closed, a middle aged white man came and sat beside me. He greeted me with the words, "God is so beautiful just close your eyes and listen to God through the water and allow Him to minister to you." Tears started rolling again. When I opened my eyes the man was gone, and I decided to leave. I did not even feel the presence of the gentleman leaving, he was just gone.

On my way home, I stopped in front of the church where Rezin pastored. I prayed that the spirit of divorce would not touch the congregation. I pleaded the blood of Jesus over the sanctuary for everyone that would enter in. I also prayed that the spirit of confusion would not come forth in the church as it was coming forth from the leader. I prayed for God to keep the people focused on Him and not on what was happening in the life of the pastor and his wife. I asked God to shield him from the fiery darts of the devil and that God would keep him safe and not allow the devil to touch him. I asked God to protect the portals of my mind. I left and went home to sleep.

December 29, 2003

I woke up this morning and my spirit was singing "Be still and know that I am God." My spirit would not let go of it and soon I was singing out loud, "Be still and know that I am God." I sang it over and over in English then in Afrikaans. I must have sung it for more than an hour and received it as a message from God. The phone rang and it was a newlywed calling from Texas. She was crying and told me that she and her husband of nearly three years were separating. I was still for a moment and then started ministering to her. My pain was so great that as I was ministering to her I was really ministering to myself. I concluded the conversation about forty-eight minutes later with prayer. I asked God, "Why are you doing this to me? Don't send me any more women to call me about their marital problems, because I am still trying to figure out my own." Well God is God. He is Sovereign. He can do whatever He wants to when He wants to and how He wants to.

For the next few months I would have so many women in my care experiencing marital problems. A girl whom I had not spoken to for years called me out of the blue one day. She said, "Mary I need you to pray for me. My husband and I are thinking about separating." Another girlfriend called me one day telling me that she just got through sleeping with another man and that she was feeling so bad that she needed prayer right then. A couple that was joined in holy matrimony by Rezin called me one day for prayer as she and her husband were going through some difficult financial times. She felt she was bringing home the best salary and he was just wasting money. Another woman had just been married for four months called me to ask me to pray for her and her husband because he was just acting a fool. My neighbor called me one day and asked me to come down to her house immediately because she had just called the police on her husband whom she hit first and he hit her back. "Lord, what are you doing?" Oh my goodness. I watched God in awe giving me the strength to encourage and pray women through their situations and believing in my heart that God would even cure mine. All of these couples stayed together, except for the one who committed adultery. She and her husband are contemplating divorce.

My niece e-mailed me a petition from the Atheist population. The petition requested all devil worshippers to fast and pray that clergy marriages would be destroyed. I stood in awe. We Christians do not want to fast and pray all the while the devil is fasting and praying and being very effective. Forgive us Lord for we have sinned in thought, word, and in deed. We take God for granted too much. We will not do what the Word of God commands us to do, so we must suffer the consequences.

There is great value and blessing in fasting. I regret being so old in life before I learned this lesson, but I am thankful still to be able to learn and implement it in my life. I have fasted many times in life, but I now realize that I did not really know what I was doing. I fasted for short periods, not more than seven days at a time and also long periods. I came to enjoy the longer periods of fasting like forty days at a time. It taught me discipline to the utmost.

I have come to learn that the length of the fast is not what is important, but that the purpose of the fast is to glorify God. The fast must be God-directed and not circumstantially directed. It must be exercised with a pure heart and right motives. Fasting is worshipping. Fasting is not starving or dieting. Fasting is enjoying intimacy with God to the utmost. Fasting is being strengthened in the things of God. Fasting is mentally, spiritually and physically healthy. It has nothing to do with the physical but is deeply rooted in the spiritual. Fasting is physically beneficial to you. Daniel 1:15 says "they were better in appearance..."

Fasting is self-denial. Fasting opens us to receive and obey fresh light about God and allows us to grow in the knowledge of truth. Fasting allows the power and gifts of the spirit to be exalted. Fasting intensifies your prayer life. Fasting is a matter between the individual and God. Fasting is a God-appointed means for the flowing of His grace and power that we cannot afford to neglect any longer. Fasting teaches us contentment. Fasting is spiritual renewal.

Fasting must be done unto God and the basic motive being the glory of God. Fasting must be God-initiated and God-ordained. Fasting is intense focusing. Fasting is financially rewarding. Fasting is a powerful weapon to our spiritual armory. Fasting is preparation. Fasting is peace.

It is important to understand the effects of fasting on the spirit, soul and body. Before committing to a fast, I encourage you to study the Word of God and read books that provide important and effective information about fasting. Do not boast or talk about your fast.

Whenever I went to the restaurant with friends, I would tell them I was not hungry. At home, I was still preparing meals for my family and dinner was normally served an hour after I broke my fast. Wear festive clothing. Humble yourself before the Most High God and people. Listen to God and not to impressions and voices which are not from God. Remember satan knows you are fasting. Pray at least seven times a day. Be joyous and not moody. Thank God for His faithfulness. Eat to appease your hunger and not to satisfy your appetite. Do not weigh yourself. Remember it is not a diet. It is a fast committed to the glory of God. God is preparing you for the next level.

Today I cannot live without fasting. It is a part of my lifestyle. Every opportunity I get to get someone else involved or excited about fasting, I take it. I walk by people today who do not even recognize me anymore because of this new body God has given me. So when friends tell me that I look good (as if I am not supposed to) I humbly respond, "What did you expect? I serve a Good God and He has given me a new mind, a new spirit a new attitude and a new body." All praises be unto Him. I cannot say it enough. I love God with all my heart, and with all my soul, and with all my mind, and with all my strength, and with all my expectancies. I am God's favorite daughter.

Psalm 69:10 says "when I weep and fast, I must endure scorn."

Chapter 11

God will never shield you from

the requirements of being His son or daughter.

ANONYMOUS

"….that ye may know what

is the hope of His calling….."

EPHESIANS 1:18 KJV

Stand

December 30, 2003

I had a call from my spiritual mentor early this morning encouraging me in the Lord. I shared with her that I was hosting the Ministerial Alliance Christmas party that night. The Word of the Lord to me for the day was to be still and know that He is God. My prayer that day was that Tabeal would not show up at the Christmas party.

The evening started out fairly slow. Everyone was running late. Tabeal showed up, walked into my home and did not greet me. I was cool. I decided to ignore him too. However, Rezin and Tabeal started ridiculing and mocking me.

I was standing with my back to them looking in the window that showed their reflections, when Tabeal stuck his tongue out at me and Rezin just laughed.

Tabeal sent text messages to Rezin across the room, and they both looked at me and just laughed. He finally motioned for Rezin to go downstairs to the basement and they made sure that I noticed them going downstairs.

We were playing dominoes, and Tabeal was sitting to my left. Every time I had to make a move he would look at Rezin and give him a big smile. My spirit was getting weak, and I was just about to submit to the flesh when the Scripture came to mind:

"Blessed is the man that walketh not in the counsel of the ungodly, nor sitteth in the seat of the scornful, for his delight is in the law of the Lord and in His law doth he meditate day and night." (Psalm 1.1)

Earlier that day a girlfriend called and told me to be still and know that God is God. My flesh retreated, and the spirit became strong again. I just continued to ignore them.

Rezin put in a movie and quite a few of us sat watching it. Tabeal said that he felt so depressed. He got up and said he was going home. Rezin saw him to the car. They spent another forty minutes standing outside consoling each other. He came in and went straight to the bedroom. I noticed that night that both of them were wearing the same rings on their wedding finger.

Most of the night, I was in the company of other people, but never a part of what was going on. My body was there but not my mind. I was by myself with my own thoughts, feelings and hurts. I thanked God that night for allowing me to make it through another day.

December 31, 2003

Today, I awoke and realized that this was the last day of the old year. I looked back over the past year and thought about the times that I wondered whether I would make it to the next day. I thanked God and decided to celebrate the unbelievable year that I had made it through.

I celebrated the many blessings God had poured into my life. I celebrated most of all that God had protected the portals of my mind. I celebrated my accomplishments and my hardships because they had served to make me stronger. I decreed and declared that I would go through this day with a spirit of humility, but with my head held high and a happy heart.

I stood in the window marveling at the beauty of the earth and confirmed within my spirit that God and His divine plan ensures me that everything will be all right.

I had a call from my neighbor who was experiencing marital problems and asked me to come down and pray with her. I did. I stayed for a long time until Rezin called and told me to come and see about the children. I prayed with her and gave her a devotional guide, then left.

When I got home, Rezin was wearing a blue shirt with black pants. I told him he looked nice. He rolled his eyes at me and said, "You don't." He left, and my daughter came to me and shared that Tabeal was taking them out on Saturday. I lost it. How dare this man make arrangements with my children without consulting me about it! I was enraged. I felt this man had already stolen my husband and was about to steal my children too! Oh no, it was not going to happen!

I called Tabeal and told him he needed to talk to me first and ask my permission to take my children out. His reply to me was that I should not take my frustrations out on him because I was experiencing marital problems. "Calm me down God. Calm me down. Spirit where are you? Take control. Take control." No answer. No response.

Tabeal told me that he wanted to meet with me because I was defaming his character. My reply was, "When I wanted to meet with you, you did not want to. You also lied to me and played me for your fool." I realized then that the declaration I had made earlier that morning was being destroyed, and I hung up on Tabeal.

I questioned myself, "Why is it so easy for you to worship at the feet of satan? Didn't God tell you to be still and know that He is God?" I went into the closet and prayed, asking God to forgive me and to give me strength to operate effectively in the power of the Most High. I read Isaiah 52 and 2 Corinthians 1. I then left for the beauty shop.

Rezin came home at 8:30 p.m. that night. I was getting ready for Watch Night service. He saw that our dance clothes were on the bed. He wanted to know who had given me permission to have the dancers participate in worship that night. I told him that the pastor was not available to speak to nor would he speak to me. He told me that I was out of order, and that God was going to get me. I told him that I would call the group and inform them that we would not be dancing, but I did not.

I went downstairs to the computer room. As I turned on the computer, the Lord told me to open my Memorial Day book. I started weeping again because in my mind's eye, the Lord showed me where he had brought me from - over hills, through the valleys, through the sunshine and the rain. He showed me how He delivered me from death and rape. He showed me how He had provided for me all these years, how He had kept me and sustained me despite everything that was happening to me.

I asked God that night to let it be the night of reconciliation between Rezin and me. I was still fighting for my marriage. Well?

I left for worship at 10:00 p.m. I had forgotten that the kids had not had dinner that night. On the way, they reminded me. Every fast-food place was closed. I went down Queenshighway and Popeye's was open, but the line was very long and I was not going to be late for worship. My son started whining, and I stopped and waited my turn. "Patience Mary, patience!"

We got to church and the dancers were rehearsing. We prayed and took our places in the sanctuary. Service must have been going on for more than forty minutes before Rezin came in. Tabeal was on the program, but he was not there. Rezin went to the front pew in the church and sat down. The dancers ministered, and I went back downstairs to get dressed.

I came upstairs and stood in the foyer contemplating whether or not I should go and sit next to Rezin or just sit anywhere in the sanctuary. I walked down the isle to the front pew and sat down beside him because after all, this was Watch-Night service. This was where we made New Year's resolutions, and just maybe Rezin's would be for God to restore our relationship.

As I sat down, he was text-messaging Tabeal during worship! I was so disgusted. I knew then that I had made a mistake by sitting down next to him. No one knew what was going on between him and me. So I remained seated.

That night the preacher preached the sermon "Transformed for Your Purpose." At 11:50 p.m. Rezin was called upon to pray us into the New Year. "Help us Jesus." I listened very intently to what he was praying for that night. He prayed for finances, health, miracles, children, and for the release of the Holy Spirit. No prayer for marriage and relationships. He concluded his prayer with thanksgiving. He asked everyone to hug someone and to wish them a Happy New Year. He acknowledged everyone except me. I went to him and wished him a Happy New Year and went home.

Chapter 12

DRAW ME CLOSE, LORD JESUS

"Draw near to God and He will draw near to thee."
JAMES 4:8 ALF

Drawing Close to God

God has many names and attributes. We know His names and attributes well, but have we experienced Him in spirit and in truth by name?

Each of God's names in the Bible represents a way He wants us to trust Him. His names have so much power and when spoken and called on in faith, they bring blessings and increase our awareness and closeness to God.

Most people who have been victorious in their struggles have come to a deeper revelation of God's nature and character. In the most desperate and darkest hours of my life, God revealed His names to me as I needed them.

I came to the realization and understanding that in order to know God by name, I must experience Him. The experience normally is very painful and comes in the form of destruction, death, divorce, devastation or in simple terms, trials and tribulations. Through my own experience, I learned and met God by name. He was using my difficult situations as the best way to draw me closer to Him. It is not until the names of God and the awesome power of His attributes saturate our spirits and is applied to our daily lives that we have power.

This is much easier said than done. I have been convinced that I would always trust the Lord, no matter what. But then I would be hit with a time of unexplainable testing, and old doubts would set in again. Many a night I cried unto the Lord, "Lord, I believe; help Thou my unbelief."

Every time I graduate to the next level, I am met there by a greater devil. I would panic, try to work things out, have sleepless nights brainstorming, worry and scheme. I thank God that He did not give up on me. But I have learned to trust in Jesus. I have learned to trust in God.

The one best thing that happened to me was that I did not turn from God, and He did not turn from me. I sought Him more intensely. The world does not have the answers. I went through the valley of the shadow of death and I feared no evil, because I knew that I knew that I knew that I knew that God was with me. His rod and His staff they comforted me.

Remember my Christmas gift? It was now being put into practice. It was the first day of the New Year and God's name is Alpha And Omega.

The month of January came with bitter tears. It seemed as if the temperature had been turned up in the firey furnace. Thank God for Jesus who was in the firey furnace with me. If I ever needed the Lord before, I sure needed Him in January. Could it get any worse? Would I be found steadfast, unmovable, always abounding in the Lord? Could I still love God with all my heart and all my soul and my entire mind and all my strength and all my expectancies? The names of God is awesome and it is true.

God never allows us to go through something, without also offering us the promise of His presence. I increased my knowledge about God, but could I be found obedient and faithful at all times? It was January 1, 2004 and I was about to embark on a journey that will blow your mind.

I am now starting on a new journey with my Daily Devotional written by Rebecca Barlow Jordan. God's name is: "Alpha and Omega." *"I am Alpha and Omega, the Beginning and the End."* (Revelation 21:6).

From the Father's Heart...
My child, you are often confused about who I am and where you are going. When you arise in the morning, I am with you. When you work through the day, you will find me close by. From the time you open your eyes until I close them in sleep at night, I am always with you, ready to guide you. Do not worry about knowing

how you fit into my plans. Be concerned only with knowing Me and spending time together. Your future is in My hands.

A Grateful Response…

In your time, Lord every step is ordered and every thought recorded. You know the past, present and future. You have planned every day of my life with purpose and love. Gently, but firmly, You are preparing a glorious ending for me in heaven. I give my life into Your safekeeping. How marvelous is Your wisdom.

I received that message as straight from the mouth of God. Through tears, I started journaling my response: God, Thank You for the true Word for such a time as this. Thank You for assuring me of Your presence and that You are God and God alone. I trust You Lord and whatever You do is always for my good. I am so thankful that I am journeying with You at this time. Keep me consistent in all my ways. I honor You. I bless You. I love You forever and ever. Amen.

After church that Sunday, I came home and rested for a few minutes. Soon we had to leave again to go to a ministerial installation service. Rezin allowed me to ride with him. Rezin and Tabeal were seated next to each other in the pulpit. His assignment that evening for worship was to read the Scriptures. He chose I Timothy 4: 1-15. It was a Scripture so appropriate for him. "Don't you get it Rezin? God is speaking to you. Listen."

Oh, well. Remember that I told you that they were wearing the same rings? Every time I looked at them sitting next to each other, they would turn the ring on their finger, smile, look at me and then at each other. Service was over and I was ready to go home. Tabeal decided to call a meeting to evaluate the service.

When I got home that night, I had a message waiting for me on the answering service from a lady in South Africa. I had not spoken to her for years. Her message said that she had great concern for me and had been praying for me that past week intensely and hoped that everything was all right with me. She wanted me to read Ephesians 3:17. I took out my Bible and it read: *"So that Christ may dwell in your hearts through faith. And I pray that you being rooted and established in love may have power together with all the saints to grasp how wide, how long and how high and how deep is the love of Christ."*

This lady nearly became my mother-in-law years ago. Who but God could have placed me on her heart? At a time when I felt so unloved, she encouraged me not to lose sight of how great the love of God was and is for me. "Thank You God for ending my day on this high note." Rezin then informed me that he was leaving for Las Vegas the next morning. I asked him why he would do that, knowing that I was scheduled to have outpatient surgery the next day. As I finished the question and listened to his rude response, I heard God saying, "Be still and know that I am God." So I let go.

It was January 5, 2004 and God's Name was, "Wonderful Counselor." I woke up singing in my spirit the anthem "Lift up your heads O ye gates." Very soon, I was singing out loud. At 5:20 a.m., my daughter was getting ready for school. At 5:40 a.m. Rezin said "goodbye" and I just kept singing. The spirit said stop, and say goodbye. He had gone out the door already, so I opened the door to the garage and said "Goodbye, the Lord grant you traveling mercies." He did not say a word. He left.

After the children got off to school, I did my devotions. Normally I do not answer the phone when I am busy doing my devotions, but that particular morning the phone was ringing and the Spirit whispered for me to answer it. I could not concentrate on my devotions, so I answered it. Guess what? I was scheduled to have outpatient surgery that day. The call was to inform me that my doctor was sick and that they were going to have to reschedule surgery. I praised God and thanked Him for telling me the night before, "To Be Still and know that He is God" because He had already worked it out. I joyfully restarted my devotions. Surgery was rescheduled for January 14th at 11:00 a.m. Thank You God!

My children were still unaware (at least so I think) of what was happening between their dad and me. However, they knew that everything was not OK. I noticed that my son was expressing his love for me at least seven times a day. He would walk up to me and just hug me and say "I love you mommy." My daughter was being so helpful around the house, and every time her daddy raised his voice at me or said something ugly to me in her presence, she would sign-language for me to be quiet and just smile.

The one thing I hated about this process was that Rezin was so disrespectful to me in the presence of our children. My daughter was sitting on the kitchen counter one evening watching me cook. He came in, and I informed him that the surgery had been rescheduled for January 14th at 11:00 a.m. and that I needed him to be there for the children. His response was so outrageous. He said, "Don't tell me how to schedule my time and do not demand me to be here for the children." I started responding back in the flesh when I felt someone pinching me. My daughter mumbled under her breath, "Just ignore him mommy," and I did.

Through the Word of God, God prepared me for battle. Every Scripture I heard and every sermon that was preached was from Isaiah 4:17. I got into my car one morning and the song "No weapon formed against you shall prosper" was playing. Spiritual warfare is real. I have experienced it to the utmost and it was just getting worse. When godly men do ungodly things and do not even realize it, the Word of God teaches us how to fight victoriously. However, the problem was that all the equipment is spiritual in nature and when you are not used to using it consistently, you do find yourself in trouble.

My heart desires to have godly thoughts; ones that would please God and be in keeping with His identity in Christ. It is much easier said than done. It is an intense battle. The flesh wars against the spirit. The head against the heart. The intellect against faith. My emotions against doctrine. Fact against truth. The world against the Word of God. How do you do it? **"We walk by faith and not by sight"** is a Scripture that we recite so easily. Sometimes we forget to connect it with **"faith comes by hearing and hearing through the Word of God."**

I dressed for battle daily. I put on the helmet of salvation, the breastplate of righteousness, the belt of truth, sandals and the sword of the Spirit. There were times when I came out victoriously, and then there were times when I flunked big time.

The flesh loves to elevate itself. The flesh loves to be in control. The flesh loves to have the last word. The flesh wants its way. The flesh becomes indignant when others do not agree with it. The flesh plots and plans. The flesh maintains a sin-filled life. The flesh wants to be in control. It is independent.

Everyday the enemy and his forces try to take advantage of my weaknesses and get in the proper position, ready to carry out their commander's orders. I do not know how many times I told the Lord that I was laying down my independent ways and that from here on in, I acknowledge my absolute dependence on Him. I found God to be more than faithful to me no matter how I would disappoint Him. He saw me through to the very end. He is still faithful.

On the morning of January 12th, I was playing my praise music and doing my devotions when Rezin came into the room. He kicked the CD player and told me that he did not want to hear or see me being spiritual around him. He said, "I am sick of this shit." He was looking like someone who was being tormented and did not know what to do. I felt so sorry for him. I prayed silently for God to forgive him, for he knew not what he was doing. When I reached for my prayer book, I noticed that he had torn out a stack of pages (all the prayers pertaining to marriage). I prayed for him in the spirit and waited till he had left and continued my devotions.

My son prayed that morning for me, asking God to strengthen me and for God Himself to take me through while I was going through. I wanted to scream and cry but contained myself. I had asked Rezin to please talk to the children, as they had a lot of questions. His response was for me not to worry how he handled his business with his children. When the children came home that day, I asked them whether their dad had spoken to them. My daughter replied that at the bus stop that morning, he had asked her how she would feel if daddy lived in the house and mommy lived in another house. I looked at her without asking for her response. She looked so sad, and I just wanted to go somewhere and cry some more.

On January fourteenth the children were off from school, and this was the day that I was supposed to have outpatient surgery. Rezin left for Florida without even telling me. A sister from the church had volunteered to go with me and to take the children to the mall while I was having my surgery. Surgery was supposed to last for ninety minutes but it lasted for two hours and ten minutes. When the volunteer came to pick me up, I was hurting and tired and looking forward to getting to bed.

We were on our way home when my daughter let out a loud cry. She shocked me and would not stop screaming, "Mommy help me." She was crying uncontrollably. I asked her what was wrong and she said that she had a pain in her back which she could not endure. We went straight to the Emergency room, and when the doctor entered we both were lying on the bed. The doctor asked who the patient was, and I explained to him that I had just had outpatient surgery and that my daughter needed his attention. I could not move and he was kind enough to let me use the bed. He examined my daughter and then sent her for some x-rays.

I was lying on the bed while they were doing all this, and the lady who accompanied us went and got her and my son something to eat. I felt so helpless not being able to move around the hospital with my daughter. I prayed and cried in the spirit before the Lord to allow the doctors to find out quickly what the problem was, as I was so cold and not feeling good at all. We spent two- and-a-half hours at the hospital, and most of that time I slept. When we got home my daughter called her dad to inform him of her mishap. He asked her to put her mother on the phone and started cursing me out for not informing him immediately. I did not allow myself to listen to him because of the vulgar language he was using and hung up. He had no idea that if he had been at home where he was supposed to be, he would have been able to be of help. We went to sleep that night and all of them got in the bed with me.

On January 18th, we had come back from church, and I had to run an errand on my way home. When we got home, Rezin had been to the house. I went into the kitchen for a drink of water when my daughter came out of the bedroom with a note her father had left for me on the bed. The note read:

> To my big mouth wife
> From your ex-husband

I was so disappointed that my daughter had gotten a hold of the note, and she asked me what did daddy mean by saying, "He is your ex." I called her and her brother together and told the children that their daddy was contemplating separation. I told them that daddy was going through a very troublesome time and he needed our prayers. My daughter wanted to know whether Tabeal had anything to do with it. I said that I did not know, and that she would have to talk to her daddy about it. I felt so tired and needed some space, so I decided to go to my girlfriend's home and spend the afternoon with her and her family.

On our way there, I asked my son how he would feel if his daddy decided to divorce his mommy. He said to me, "Mommy daddy loves you too much. He will never ask you to divorce him." I knew then that he was the one with whom I will have to work with. I was so mad at this man for acting so cowardly by not wanting to inform the children about what was happening in our lives but leaving me nasty letters around the house. I sat with Nona and just cried in her bathroom. I was blessed to have her to hear me out. The children had a lot of fun at her house because there is always something to do. We left for home. That evening I told him that I had to tell the children what was going on because of the note he left for me on the bed.

I decided that it was time for me to check up on the status of the kids at school and also to inform the counselors of what was going on at home. When I entered my daughter's school, her counselor was walking down the hallway, and she walked up to me and just put her arms around me. I knew then that she knew something. She took me to her office and informed me that my daughter had spent the last two-and-a-half weeks in her office every morning before school crying because she was so hurt at what was happening at home. She was encouraging my daughter. She was a Christian and would pray privately with my daughter before class. I could not contain it anymore and just thankfully sat and wept for the blessing of this counselor.

This was so unfair to the kids. My daughter was trying her best to be there for me. She tried her best not to shed a tear in front of me because she wanted to be strong for me. I waited until after school so that I could give my daughter a hug and tell her that it was okay to cry, and that I was available for her. I asked my daughter whether this event had affected her in the classroom. She replied that she was okay for the rest of the day after her counselor had prayed with her. I could not thank God enough for providing my daughter with a way of escape and for placing the right person in her pathway.

I left for my son's school. His counselor said that he seemed unaffected, and that he was doing very well but that she would keep a close eye on him. I spoke to my spiritual mentor and she again reminded me to create as much joy for the children as I possibly could. For a moment I thought that creating joy meant for them not to be disciplined. I found myself feeling sorry for them and allowing them to do whatever they wanted. I was reminded by the Spirit that I had to train up the child in the way they should go. I sat both of them down one afternoon and told them that the rules still existed and that they would be disciplined. I thank God that I came to my senses.

My daughter was learning how to cook. She loved cooking and soon my son wanted to cook too. They helped me with the preparations of meals. They still had their chores. I would sit and tell them about my childhood which they enjoyed very much. My daughter would always get a movie out, and we would watch a humorous movie together. They would tell jokes that I did not understand sometimes, but laughed anyway. My son is an artist and he would sit and have me pose for a picture. He always messed up his sister because he loved to tease her.

Our prayer life was always in tact. I would pray with the children individually each morning, and at night we would pray collectively together. We were praying one evening when Rezin came in the house and pulled my daughter out of the prayer circle. I was so mad but started praying in the spirit for this uncouth man. I said, "Father forgive him for he knows not what he is doing." In the morning when I saw them out the door, I would say to them, "Remember who you represent and make sure that you will be the best reference found in all the earth. Have a blessed day in Jesus." Rezin responded in front of my children, "You are crazy just like your daddy. Ooh Jesus, ooh Jesus help her, hahaha." I prayed for him because he truly did not know what he was doing. There were many other times when he was just plain rude and disrespectful of our prayer times.

I was discussing Generational curses with the children one evening when Rezin came up the stairs and said that there was no such thing and just laughed. In my spirit I prayed that they would not pay him any attention. They were screaming at each other and I told them that it was a generational curse that we had to pray out and ask God to remove it from continuing in our family. God showed me the next morning how it penetrated my son's heart. I had asked him to get up and to get ready for school. He would not move. When I said it the fourth time, I raised my voice. He got up and said, "I thought we prayed out this curse of screaming at each other last night." My heart rejoiced and I thanked God that he did not listen to the voice of his dad. I responded, "Please forgive me for raising my voice, but I just thought you did not hear me as it was the fourth time I was calling you." He gave me a smile teasingly, and said, "I love you mommy."

On January 20th, Rezin asked me to come by his office at 2pm. I went. When I got there his secretary told me to go into the main office where he was. I entered his office without knocking. He wanted to know why I did not knock. I responded that your secretary told me to go straight in. He said, "Next time, you be sure to knock before you enter." I just looked at him. I remained standing and was waiting for him to ask me to sit down. He informed me that day that he really wanted us to separate, and that I should start looking for a place. He said that the Lord had told him to get rid of me so that his ministry could start flourishing. He also told me that Tabeal was giving him a birthday party and that I was invited. It became very quiet and I asked him whether there was anything else we needed to discuss. He said, "No you can go now and look for a place for yourself." I looked at him and said that I was not going anywhere. I left his office. When I got in the car the song was playing, "Be not dismayed whatever betide God will take care of you." I started sobbing so bitterly and drove down the street and just thanked God for reassuring me that He was with me.

Prayer time was very important to me. Since the first three months of marriage, I had been praying by myself. When God blessed me with children, I prayed on a daily basis with them. I try and live in an attitude of prayer. It gives me energy, persistence and hope for the future. Prayer sustains me. Prayer keeps me intimately in contact with Jesus and consciously in touch with the Father.

Rezin had no respect for prayer time. He would sit and make fun of the kids when we got through praying and tell them that they were so prayed up that he could feel the Holy Ghost and just laughed. We were praying on January 21st, when he came upstairs and pulled my daughter out of the prayer circle. My spirit was vexed and I decided to remain quiet. My daughter looked at me not knowing whether to go or stay in the prayer circle. I told her to go with her daddy and that he must have something very important to discuss with her. She left and I stayed with my son and concluded the prayer time. I went downstairs, and on the Word Channel, James Robison had a lady discussing the book "When Godly men do Ungodly Things." It seemed as if every time Rezin would do something grievous, the Lord would give me a word to encourage me. It was as if He was telling me that he sits high and looks low and sees everything under the heavens. It was no coincidence that the title of the book exactly matched the situation in my house.

On January 23rd, I received an invitation to the birthday party of my husband from Tabeal. Tabeal's so-called wife had returned that day. The invitation read that Tabeal and his wife Hedda along with three other pastors in the city were giving him this party. I called the pastors and asked them why were they disrespecting me along with Tabeal. They informed me that they did not know anything about it, and that they would not even be in attendance. Hedda was back after disappearing for nine months.

Despite all the chaos that was occurring in my home, I was still fighting and believing God for my marriage. I was still cooking and cleaning and doing his laundry. I had planned a surprise birthday party for Rezin, as it was his fortieth birthday. A Jamaican caterer was reserved, and I had invited friends from college to come and surprise Rezin.

Tabeal however had the last word. The children could not attend their own dad's birthday party. When I received the invitation, I called off the plans that were made for Rezin and decided to have the clergy spouses meeting on the thirtieth of January which was Rezin's birthday.

That night when Rezin came home, I knew that nothing was going to be able to contain my peace. I was in a fighting mode and as hard as I prayed, asking God to keep me from going down the wrong road - I could feel my flesh ready for the attack. My kids were in bed and Rezin entered. I asked him why he and his girlfriend Tabeal thought it necessary to send me, his wife an invitation. I said that if anyone ever gave you a party I was automatically invited. He did not have to send the spouse an invitation. He responded that I was not his spouse. I said he'd better go and have an Aids test taken. It had become loud in the house, and I heard movement upstairs. My daughter Imaan was crying. I went upstairs, and she had taken our wedding picture off the wall. When I saw her tears, I could not do anything else but cry and apologize to her. She told me that night that she was sick and tired of our fussing, and that she wanted to move back to California, because we never acted like this when we were living in California. I promised her that night that I would do better. I kissed her and she laid down, still crying. I asked the Lord that night to kill my husband. I was so mad at him. Everything that I was doing was benefiting him and making him look good. How could he have the nerve to keep on humiliating me the way he was. I went for a drive that night and came home after midnight. I thank God for His hand of protection on me that night. When I came to my senses, I repented and asked God to forgive me. I asked God to keep the devil from touching Rezin. I did not want to but did apologize to Rezin as well.

Rezin and Tabeal had done everything possible to attack my spirit, and because they were having such a hard time killing it they kept on mentally abusing, harassing, ridiculing and threatening me. They thought that they were the accountants of my worth. They called me little Helga, saying that I was trying to be like Rev. Helga. I had decided that I was not going to give the devil the satisfaction of stealing my joy.

Before going to bed, my eye caught the following words from an open book. "My child don't be so gloomy and discouraged, but continue to trust in me. Worship and Praise me for I will not fail you. As you fill your heart with my Word think upon my promises. Your heart will overflow with joy." I cried because that was straight from the mouth of God. I went to sleep.

January 30th was his birthday, and what an interesting day it was. My son called me from school at 8:20 that morning. He had forgotten to give me his class notes. He was performing with his class at 9:30 in a Suzuki recital. He asked me to call his dad, and please ask him to come, as he had not seen him play the violin yet. I said that I would. I called Rezin, and then rushed to get to his school. The performance was beautiful. At the end of the performance, students had to give lessons to the parents on whichever instrument the students played. Again, I was the only parent present. Rezin did not show.

I had so much to do that day. My time with God was cut short, in order to accommodate everything else that I had to do. I had scheduled a clergy spouses meeting at my home at 7:00 p.m. that evening. My mind was made up; I would not be present for Rezin's 40th birthday. At five that afternoon, I could feel a pity party coming on. I immediately stopped and started praying, however I could not utter any words. The spirit prayed for me. I could feel my spirit rising. I concluded my prayer, by asking God to strengthen me and to allow me to overflow with hope by the power of the Holy Spirit.

That evening it started snowing. I was so surprised when the clergy spouses showed up for the meeting. I thought that they might all be at the party.

There were nine of us that met that night. At the conclusion, I asked for prayer request. One sister said that she wanted the group to pray for me. She started opening up about how she was saddened by these so-called godly men, who did such ungodly things without any fear. She said that she could not go to the party because she could not believe how Rezin and Tabeal had been openly humiliating me. We prayed that evening and sat and shared with one another until after 11:30 that night. I was blessed by that meeting, especially with the prayers that went up for Rezin and me. They left, and I cleaned up and went to bed.

My phone rang at 12:07 a.m. I answered the phone. The reports of the party started coming in. One person said that she could not believe that Rezin and Tabeal would invite church folk to a party where there was liquor flowing the way it was. The phone kept on ringing until after 3:34 a.m., when I decided that I had heard enough. Rezin's mother and brother had flown in to be his support. Have mercy! Rezin came home in the early morning hours making a lot of noise, as if no one was sleeping in the house.

The children were not invited to their dad's birthday party. My son was with Nona and her family. My daughter had attended a sleepover. I left that morning to go and get Imaan and Niamke. We spent time with Nona and her family. I got home that afternoon at five. Rezin's mother and brother were at our home waiting for us. I then wished that I had stayed away longer. They were ready now to celebrate the belated birthday with the children. I forced myself to go. We got to the Chinese restaurant. I purposely ordered much more food than I could eat. His mother asked me whether I was sure I could eat all of that food. I said that I ordered it, and if I did not eat all of it, I would take it home. When the food came, I was privately ashamed, but just looked at them. I ate three scoops and could not eat anymore. I did not take the leftovers with me.

The evening was very strained, and the focus was mostly on the children. We left and Rezin took his mother and brother to the hotel, and the children and I went home. When I got home there were nine messages for me on the answering machine. Every message had a comment about the liquor that was served at the party, but one message got my attention. The message was, "We have made the biggest mistake. Before you and pastor came to our church, we were praying twenty four hours a day for you. We stopped praying when God answered our prayers. See me after worship tomorrow." I cried and asked God to forgive us for the witness that we were making.

Chapter 13

It is My love that draws men to repentance,
and My love lives in your heart.
You have the ability to show My love
to those who have hurt you.
My love in you does not dwell in
the sins of others;
it pays no attention to a suffered wrong.
So do not be overcome by evil but overcome evil with good.
WOMEN'S DAILY DEVOTIONAL

"Never let evil get the better of you;
get the better of evil by doing good."
ROMANS 12:21 Mof

He's Jehovah Shamaa

We were still married, husband and wife, but we had discontinued the marriage long ago. There was no way that our relationship was pleasing to God, but I kept on trusting Him. I had started a journey a long time ago that could not be traveled in any other way but by a growing faith. Faith in God carried me through my daily experiences. Hebrews 10: 35-38 says, **"Therefore do not cast away your confidence, which has great reward. For you have need of endurance, so that after you have done the will of God, you may receive the promise. For yet a little while, and He who is coming will come and will not tarry. Now the just shall live by faith; But if anyone draws back, my soul has no pleasure in Him."**

Every morning when I open my eyes I decree and declare unto the Lord, "To You O Lord do I lift up my soul. For All I Trust Him. I invoke blessings from the God of truth upon me this day. O that You would bless me indeed and enlarge my territory. Keep Your hand upon me so that no harm will come against me and that I may not sin against Thee." I set out everyday believing that the trials I faced were an opportunity to trust God.

The month of February proved to me that faith in God gives us the power to be sustained in our trials, but you have to obey in the face of great opposition to receive the blessing.

It was February 2nd and I did not feel like getting out of bed. I was feeling at my lowest ebb. My spirit kept on urging me to get up and do my devotions. I did not feel like it and just laid there. At 10:46 a.m. I got out of bed went into the bathroom and stood looking at myself in the mirror. I was feeling downhearted and said to myself that I would not become depressed.

I went back into my bedroom, turned on my praise music and started my devotions. God's Name for that day was Empathy. The scripture was Psalms 34:18: **"The Lord is close to the brokenhearted and saves those who are crushed in spirit."** I screamed, "God you know my every hurt. Thank you for speaking so clearly to my situation this morning." I laid prostrate before the Lord and went into a Praise litany and started feeling better. When I got through with my devotions I was ready to face the rest of the day knowing that I was in the hollow of God's Hand.

That night Rezin preached at Tabeal's church. I had the kids with me. It was a weeknight, and the children had school the next day. Rezin did not get up to preach till 9:28 p.m. I was watching the clock closely as the children had school the next day. Rezin's opening remarks were the acknowledgement of his friend Tabeal. He thanked him for the invitation and vowing before the congregation that Tabeal would be his friend until the last dog dies. He said that Tabeal was an angel sent from God. He acknowledged the first lady of Emanuel church Hedda, (Tabeal's so-called wife) and the first lady of Shiloh Temple, me. He prayed and asked God to bless the Word he was about to preach.

His sermon topic was "Don't hate, just wait." It was 9:43 when he started preaching. My mind was made up that at ten I was leaving for the children's sake. I left, and while walking out Rezin said from the pulpit, "It is a shame when your own family walks out on you while you are preaching" calling attention to us leaving. I smiled and kept going. I asked God to forgive me for leaving, but I knew that he understood that the children had to get their rest.

When I got home, the children and I prayed and they went to bed. I saw a stack of birthday cards lying on the floor in the closet. I picked it up and started reading the messages written in the cards. The third card that I read had a very interesting message in it.

It was from one of the associate ministers at the church Rezin pastored. The handwritten message read, "You have to treat forty like a bitchy woman. Stop fighting her and just embrace her and she will treat you right." I thought how disrespectful. The card upset me, and I decided not to read anymore. I spent my time with God and went to sleep.

Two days later, I received a call from Rezin while he was at work. He asked me whether I had made a purchase on his credit card that he shared with his mother. I answered, "Yes, I had made an airplane ticket purchase a few days ago." He said, "I thought you did not like the credit card that belonged to me and my mother." I answered, "You are right I do not like it, but if you can spend twenty-thousand dollars a month on a card for things I do not know about, I might as well put a hundred and forty three dollars on it for my benefit." He hung up on me and I continued my day peacefully.

That afternoon I had three persons to call me. All of them were experiencing marital problems and asked me to pray for them. As I prayed for them, I felt a burden being lifted from me.

It was a dark and cold night. I was on my way home from a prayer meeting. I was crossing a very dark bridge when I heard an unfamiliar sound coming from my car. I turned down the radio and listened. I then realized that I had a flat tire. At first I did not want to stop. I looked around and saw three homeless men pushing their carts. I asked God to give me some direction when my ears tuned in to the radio and Yolanda Adams was singing, "No weapon formed against you shall prosper." I had just passed the homeless men and stopped. The one brother looked in my car and told me that I had a flat. He asked me how far I still had to go. I answered that I had about a mile left. The other homeless brother said that he had everything in his cart to change my tire. I trusted God and got out. The three gentleman changed the tire. I hugged and thanked them and was on my way again. I thanked God for sending me his angels in the form of these homeless men and for His protection.

The next day I took the car to the shop and was told that the tire could not be fixed. I purchased a new tire and thanked the gentleman for his assistance.

That was the first of four new tires being purchased between the month of February and September. When I got to the shop for the fourth tire change, the gentleman whom God ordained to be the same person every time came out and sat next to me. He asked me if I was okay. I looked at him confusingly and said yes. He asked, "Is everything all right at home?" My mind started racing and I just stared at him. He said, "I do not want to scare you, but I want to show you something." I followed him and he showed me the tire. The tire was stabbed with a knife. He looked at me and tears were welling up in my eyes. I looked at him and said that I was going through some marital problems and asked him to give me the old tire. He said that that was the fourth tire he had changed and all of them were cut. I stood there just staring up at God and said, "Thank you God for protecting me no matter how hard the enemy was trying to destroy me." The gentleman squeezed my hand and told me to take care of myself. I took the tire home and measured it against a knife to make sure that this was happening at home. The knife fit.

That night when Rezin came home, I purposely rolled the tire to the trash can. I did not say a word. Every morning when he left, I would stand in the door and make sure that he did not touch my car. When he went into the garage, I would go out and check my tires while he was in the garage. I could not understand this man's behavior, after all, he was not only placing my life in danger but also our children who were with me most of the time.

On February 8, Rezin called for a ministerial meeting following morning worship. I was expecting to meet away from the crowd, but we met right in the midst of the crowd. The meeting had no agenda, and Rezin decided to talk about the sick-and-shut-in. It was very loud all around us, and we could hardly hear each other speak. Every one was eating around me. I was sitting there praying quietly that the Lord would strengthen me and keep me from temptation. I asked Rezin a question and he ignored me as if I did not exist. He had just preached on how men should treat their wives and children with respect and the love of God. I responded in the flesh and said that he needed to start practicing what he preached. He was the only one that I was speaking to and the only one that could hear me. He raised his voice and asked me not to insult him in the presence of his staff. Every one looked at him with a "What are you talking about?" look. I asked if the meeting was over and excused myself. I had fixed myself a vegetable plate and asked him to take it home for grandma and myself. I had to go to a baby shower and then to a women in ministry service.

That night when I got home it was close to 9:30. I was looking for the food, as I had not eaten at all that day and had thirty minutes left to eat. My daughter informed me that her father had thrown the food in the trash after he had fed grandma. Grandma's plate was separate from mine. I asked God to zip my lips and He did.

That Monday night at prayer chamber we had forty women present. We had a wonderful time in the Lord praying and praising God. The ministry was about eighteen months old. Women came together on Monday nights to learn how to pray. Women were testifying about breakthroughs that they have experienced in God through answered prayer. Samuel Chadwick says and I quote, "satan dreads nothing but prayer. The church that lost its Christ was full of good works. Activities are multiplied that meditation may be ousted and organizations are increased that prayer may have no chance. Souls may be lost in good works, as surely as in evil ways. The one concern of the Devil is to keep the saints from praying. He fears nothing from prayerless studies, prayerless work, and prayerless religion. He laughs at our toil, mocks at our wisdom, but trembles when we pray."

Prayer chamber produced many miracles. Women who could not pray specifically were now equipped to pray effectively. They were no longer shy but would boldly and courageously cast out demons in Jesus' name. They would lay hands on the sick. In our prayer times, we would anoint the entrances of the church and every pew. We would offer prayers on behalf of the pastor, his administrative abilities and staff. We embraced through prayer those things which we thought were impossible. Praying was not just mere sentiment or eloquent speech to us, but it became a part of life that we could not live without. We had a prayer habit going that was not done by force. Our hearts were gripped with the passion of prayer.

When I got home that Monday night, Rezin was sitting on the couch awaiting my arrival. The phone rang as I walked into the door. It was one of the sisters who attended prayer chamber just thanking me for encouraging her in the Lord. I Praised God. I was about to enter my bedroom when Rezin gave me a letter. The letter suspended me from all ministries and from sitting in the pulpit. It also brought charges against me that I had to answer before the steward board at a later date. He asked me to find myself a seat in the congregation. I could not respond. The Lord had assured me that He was Elohim. **"For the Lord your God is God of gods and the Lord of lords, the great God, mighty and awesome."** (Deuteronomy 10:17) I went to bed that night thanking God for creating me for His Glory.

I left the following day for an executive board meeting held in Phoenix. I was running late. Southwest Airlines was my carrier. I hate being late as it affects my spirit. I was the last to enter and the plane was full. I was looking for a seat. The only seat I could see was between an Indian man and a black heavy set lady. I asked the Lord to show me another seat because I did not want anybody's body touching mine that day, and did not want to smell Indian spices all the way to Phoenix. I was reacting to my foul spirit.

The Lord would not even hear my cry, and I was approached by the stewardess who asked me to sit down.

I greeted the gentleman politely and the lady too. I asked her how she was doing. She answered, "Jehovah is good." The plane started moving back from the gate. The lady started telling her story and did not stop until we were thirty minutes outside of Phoenix. It was all God. He Himself assigned me that seat.

She said that she had been married for thirty seven years. She continued her story, saying that they had just returned from a wonderful cruise where they celebrated their thirty-seventh anniversary. She said a week later, he was gone. I thought that he had died. So I responded, "Oh, I am so sorry to hear that." She continued saying that she could not believe him walking out on her after another woman, but she accepted it. She said that she found strength in daily standing on the promises of Jehovah coming from Isaiah 41:10,13. **"Fear thou not. Do not be dismayed. I am your God. I will strengthen you; I will help you, I will uphold you with my right hand of righteousness. I am holding you by the right hand, I am the Lord your God and I say to you, don't be afraid I am here to help you."**

She told me that all her children were grown and she had fallen on hard times, but everyday God came through for her. She said, "Baby a year later he found himself on the bed of affliction. I knew my children were watching me, and I was on my best behavior. Everyday I would be at the hospital. I would clean him and feed him and do whatever I could to make him as comfortable as possible." I asked God at that point what was the meaning of all this. She continued, "He died and my children are now the greatest blessing that I have because of how they saw me treating their dad with so much love and respect even though he treated me like a dog." She said that she travelled at least three to four times a month visiting her children in the respective states in which they live. "Baby, God's word is true. He will never leave you nor forsake you. Just trust Jehovah." I knew God was responsible for this conversation and I thanked Him.

I told her that I had to apologize to her because I did not want to sit next to her that day. I informed her that the conversation was no coincidence, for my marriage was in trouble. She encouraged me again and said, "Just trust Him and remember your children are watching. He will do it. Accept whatever comes your way."

The pilot came on at that moment and informed us that we were thirty minutes away from landing. I closed my eyes and tears just rolled down my cheeks. When we left Phoenix airport, the lady had her son to give me a ride to the hotel. I was very grateful. We exchanged numbers and departed in peace. The lady's last name was Mrs. Morgan.

The meeting was a time of refreshing for me. I met another Dr. Morgan who blessed me with two powerful books written by her: "Raising Children Of Destiny" and "The Battle For The Seed." The Morgan's - unrelated to each other, blessed me with tremendous spiritual gifts for the journey which was still ahead.

A week later, I was on my way to Chicago. The time in Chicago was well spent and whilst there, God placed two women in my care to encourage in the Lord. One lady was pregnant and was experiencing severe complications. She was just informed that they might have to abort the baby. She was praying for a full term pregnancy and hoping for a healthy baby. I said to her God is Able. I testified to her about my miracle and encouraged her to trust God. I laid hands on her stomach and prayed with her. We both shed some tears and then gave each other a hug. The other lady was experiencing marital problems. I was amazed at how many people were having marital problems. I started looking at the statistics and thanked God for making me aware that I was not the only person having marriage problems. I encouraged the sister and kept going.

When I boarded the plane, it was empty. I had a three-row seat to myself. We had about fifteen minutes before take off when I noticed this lady entering the plane. She passed all the empty seats and decided to come and sit next to me. I had the aisle seat and she took the window.

I really wanted to move but decided to remain seated. The lady sat there with her eyes closed and when the plane took off, she turned to me. In my spirit I started praying, "Father please give me a break and let it be good news." She introduced herself. I very selfishly not looking at her (hoping that she would get the message that I did not want to be bothered) told her my name. She asked if I knew anything about African traditions. I looked up and answered gleefully that I was from South Africa. She said that she just got through divorce after having been married to an African for fourteen years. She believed that she had a wonderful marriage. A year ago she was informed that she was married to man who was also married to an African woman in his native land for more than 23 years. I asked her, "So what do you want to know about Africa." She said, "I just want to know about the traditions and how they can use people to get them where they want to be and then throw them away like a piece of trash. They come here pretending to be so rich. Then when they have you find out they have nothing and that you have to support them and their families back home." I laughed quietly. I responded that all Africans were not like that and it was a little too late for her to do all that investigation as she was divorced. She said, "I know but I just cannot let go." My response to her was to let go and let God do it for you. I prayed with her and she sat there staring at me. I opened my book and kept reading.

When we landed in Columbus, I turned on my cell phone. I had four calls from my son's school. Every message was marked urgent. I called the school immediately, and they put me through to the principal. She informed me that they had called Rezin seven times that day and he did not respond to any of the calls. My son was very sick at school and was kept in the sick bay all day. The principal was trying to have him avoid taking the bus home. It was 3:05 when the plane landed, and when they checked the bus had just left. My flesh was imploring me to call Rezin and just cuss him out, but the spirit reigned. I tracked down the bus and met them as they exited the freeway.

When Niamke got off the bus he just cried. The only thing I could do was to hold him and tell him that I loved him very much. The principal called me later that day to apologize for putting my sick son on the bus. I thanked her for caring, and told her that it was not her fault. I gave him a warm bath and rubbed his body down with eucalyptus oil, prayed and put him to bed. He stayed home the next day.

This was also going to be a very special day for me. It was Ash Wednesday and Rezin had cancelled Ash Wednesday service. Something "greater" than the beginning of the Lenten season, was taking place. It was the day assigned for me to go before the church board and answer the charges that Rezin had brought against me. I did not like what was happening at all.

In my time with God that morning, He informed me that His Name is Advocate. **"And if any ...sin, we have an advocate with the Father, Jesus Christ the righteous."** (I John 2:1) God is so awesome. I can never repay Him for how wonderfully he has been treating me despite my inconsistent behavior.

From the "Daily in Your Presence" devotional journal, written by Rebecca Barlow Jordan, she pins the following words which suited my need.

From the Father's Heart
My child relax. No court in the
land can separate you
from My presence. No matter
how deep your sin or

how black your heart has been.
I paid for your past.
I was tried and convicted.
I served your sentence.
When the enemy accuses you daily,

I take the proof

of your innocence,

the DNA-Does Not Apply- to My Father's Court.

My own blood

covered your guilt and
sets your spirit free.

I laid before the Lord for forty minutes when my son entered and
came to recite his memory verse to me. **"In all thy ways
acknowledge Him, and He shall direct your paths."**
(Proverbs 3:6) He came and sat in the nook of my arm and told me
that he knew why he was so sick at school the previous day. He
said, "I was sick because you were out of town." I gave Niamke
some tender, loving care, and then I asked him to pray for me. He
asked God to bless me with peace and to not let satan come near to
my heart. I got ready to face the day.

I called Rev. Faith at 5:30 that evening. She asked me to go before
the Board with a spirit of humility. She encouraged me to take the
next few moments to get myself mentally, spiritually and
physically ready for this outrageous, uncalled meeting. She prayed
with me at length.

When I turned on the television, a preacher was preaching about
the outer court and the inner court where the enemy still has reign.
She said that he cannot come into the third dimension. It is behind
the veil where the enemy cannot touch your anointing. She went
on further to say that when God has given you a word and it seems
that everything is turned upside down, that is when you know that

you are in the third dimension. She said that you have to hold on because He is about to make that Word come to life. That was a good word for me to leave on and to go and face the Church board, watching this man embarrass his wife and mother of his children in front of the church.

God had prepared me all day long for that evening. I knew and could feel that people were praying for me. My spirit was good but I was very nervous. I had a debate with the devil just as I was walking out the door. He wanted to bring on a pity party and also show me all the options that I had available to me to bring this man down. I pleaded the blood of Jesus over my mind and kept going.

I took my children and we were on our way to church. In the car, my daughter wanted to know why I was not sitting in the pulpit anymore. She also inquired why I was going to church that evening. I tried to ignore her and asked her just to pray for mommy. Tears were close and I tried to be strong. I wanted to look brave when I faced Rezin and these people. My insides were hurting. My soul was crying. The spirit of God tried His best to console me.

One of the officers informed the other offices to please not allow the children to come near the room where I was going to be interrogated. He took the children upstairs to Rezin's office. My daughter heard this officer giving instructions pertaining to them and their mother. This challenged their curiosity. While I was in that room, my daughter and son made their way downstairs and stood listening at the window to what was being discussed about their mother.

The charges were as follows:

1. She feels she has the right to tell me (Rezin) to practice what I preach in front of my ministerial staff.
2. I caused dissension amongst the preachers
3. I hijacked ministries
4. I constantly speak to church members about our marriage

5. I make reference about our relationship at public functions
6. I criticize his pastoral performance
7. I have spoken to several of his colleagues across the district
8. I have misled the children about our relationship.

My flesh was rising as they started questioning me. Before I answered, I asked if we could have a word of prayer and then continue. I did not give anyone an opportunity to pray but prayed myself for all present. I asked God to bless us that night with the spirit of discernment. Also to allow us to be led not by power nor by might but by God's spirit. I was mentally, physically and spiritually exhausted. This man had tried every trick in the book to kill the spirit within me but had not been successful. As much as I wanted to throw in the towel, the Spirit would not allow me to.

One of the officers raised her hand and said that she felt that this was petty and that it should be handled at home. Rezin immediately spoke up and reminded them that they were the spiritual leaders of the church. They were not supposed to allow anyone to treat their pastor this way. They asked me to speak.

This was my response:

"I come in the spirit of humility before you tonight. I ask you to refer this situation back to the pastor so that he can handle his personal business at home and not embarrass the mother of his children in front of the church. We were in counseling where he attended three sessions adhering to his brother's advise, and refused to go back. Please make a recommendation tonight that he should go and continue the counseling for his own sake, as the church is watching the witness we are making."

Rezin interrupted and asked me to respond to the charges. Another officer implored that I do so.

I was starting to fight back on my own strength. I denied all the charges. I said any wife has the right to tell her husband to practice what he preaches. I did not cause any dissension amongst the preachers. They asked him to explain. He said that I was accusing an associate preacher of calling me a bitch. I responded that the associate should be standing here right now for using that kind of language with her pastor. What kind of relationship do they have for her to even open her mouth like that and not be reprimanded? This was all about the birthday card that the associate minister gave him for his birthday.

My strength was leaking like an open faucet. I asked the board if they had seen me hijacking any ministries. He interjected that every ministry that I have started I would not allow anyone to handle. I responded that it was a lie. If that was true, I would not allow others to teach when I am present or not. Whenever I am out of town I allow someone else to take over. I had been noticing at prayer chamber that Rezin would stand behind doors and hide while I was teaching and praying. I am very transparent in my teaching, testifying and praying and he interpreted that as speaking about our marriage to church folk. Maybe if he was home to talk to me I would not have to speak to other folk. He was very insecure about the relationships that I developed with people in the church.

I then decided to really open up. I could not take it anymore. I said that this man does not pray with his family, or speak to his wife and then has the nerve to stand in a pulpit and command people to live righteous lives. He needs to be examined. One of the officers interrupted because she discerned that I was going to let loose everything. Another officer got up and whispered something in his ear. They asked me to leave the room. I was furious. I had given up the Holy Ghost and was ready to go back to fighting in the flesh.

A lady walked up to me, gave me a hug and said that she had something for me. She reached in her purse and gave me a tape. I thanked her and placed it in my purse without looking at it. An officer came out and enfolded me in her arms and whispered in my ear, "God sees all of this; don't worry and don't give up." I asked her if she could go back in there and ask if it was okay if I left. She did and they released me. I was sad and mad. I called my children and we were on our way home. My daughter asked me "How was your meeting mommy?" I looked at her and looked to the road again as I was about to burst out in tears. She said, "Mom, so who dared to call you a bitch?" I stopped the car and asked her how she knew all this. She told me that Mr. Tonka had asked some folk to keep them away from the room where the officers were going to question me. I asked her whether they were present when he asked them. She answered yes. I cried and my son told me how they made their way downstairs after the people had left and they heard me being questioned about being called a bitch.

We got home. If I had had a gun that night, I would probably have shot Rezin when he walked into the house. He came home ninety minutes later. It was on. I could not contain myself. I said, "You need to go for an Aids test you faggot. God is going to kill you." He stood chest to chest with me, and I did not have one scared bone in my body, but I was waiting for him to make the first move. He left.

God got him that night. He was as sick as a dog all night long and could not go to work the next day. I repented before the Lord that night and begged for his forgiveness. I received his forgiveness and continued my night in the Lord peacefully.

The next day I went to Rezin and asked him to forgive me for last night. He tried to say something, but he could not because he had to run for the bathroom. I called his secretary and asked her to call him and asked him if he needed anything. She told me that his personal officer was on the way to deliver some goodies to him.

I took my children to dinner that night and then we went to Bible Study. Rezin was not present because he was still sick. People testified that night how they missed Ash Wednesday service the previous night, and how we should spend more serious time praying for the church.

The next morning I decided to take the children to school. I was on my way home when I stopped in the parking lot of McDonald's and just had a good cry. I read Psalm 91 and was on my way back home.

We had a seventy thousand dollar certificate of deposit that had matured. I made my way to the bank and closed the account. I took the money to another bank, deposited it into a new checking account made out in my name. I purchased three tickets for the kids and myself to South Africa for their spring break. Rezin had no clue.

I was thankful that February was over. Could it get any worse? I had made it by the grace of God.

Chapter 14

Small pots boil quickly when they are on the fire,
and so do little men with quick tempers.
Larger vessels require more time and heat before they will boil,
but when they do, it is a boil indeed, not soon forgotten or abated.
OSWALD CHAMBERS

"And patience develops strength
of character in us
and helps us trust God more each time we use it
until finally our hope and faith are strong and steady."
ROMANS 5:4 AMP

God Sits High and Sees Low

I was called all kinds of names as a child. Mom taught me a rhyme.

> Sticks and stones will break my bones
> but names will never hurt me.
> If I die you will cry
> remember all the names you called me.

I was taught to use that rhyme rather than getting into a physical fight. My mother also taught us how to laugh at people who made fun of us or who insulted us. My family could make a joke out of anything. Those who were trying to insult us always left feeling worse because we could laugh them into shame.

On a daily basis, Rezin would have an insult or a name to call me. I would sing in a high pitched tone, sticks and stones will break my bones but names will never hurt me... followed with much laughter. Rezin would scramble out slamming the door closed behind him. I was supposed to be upset, but he left upset.

When he came back later, I would welcome him with a big silly grin on my face. Through the name-calling and insults, he tried to create an identity crisis for me but was not successful. Some insults did hurt, but the Word of God was my shield against all the fiery darts of the devil. My *survival* tools were laughter, singing, journaling, praying, praising and the Word of God.

It was March 1st, and my daughter had questioned her dad about taking me before the church board. His explanation to her was that I had said something very mean to him, and that I would not apologize to him. She asked me to please apologize so that I could be put back in the pulpit. I told her that her daddy should be discussing the matter with me and not with her, and that I did already apologize.

Rezin had been sleeping on the couch. It was March 4th. I was getting ready for bed. I saw Rezin heading for my son's bedroom. I prayed quietly that God would convict him. I had turned off the lights and was dozing off, when I heard the footsteps running towards my bedroom. It was my son. He got into my bed and I allowed him to sleep there. The next morning he told me that there was an evil presence in his room last night. I asked him whether there was anyone in his room. He answered no, he just ran down to my room when he felt the presence. I never told him that his daddy was in his bed that night.

On March 5th, I had just returned from Barnes and Noble. I walked into my bedroom, and the door slammed closed behind me. I was shocked seeing Rezin standing there with blood red eyes. He scared me for a minute. I walked into the bathroom and locked the door behind me. He started using foul language and was becoming very loud. I knew the children could hear, so I came out of the bathroom. He asked me what I had done with the seventy thousand dollars that was in the bank. I calmly answered I closed the account and put the money away safely. He was furious because I would not tell him where the money was. He told me that it was not fair, and that I should give him half of it. I just ignored him and started humming.

All through my marriage I allowed him to handle the money. We should have been rich beyond great measure. The years that I worked, I gave him my check without even looking at it. He handled it. I assumed that we had the same ideas and opinions about money. His mother told him once that I was the business minded one in the family, but she would not allow me to nurture it. When I stopped working, he decided to take my name off the checking account. Credit cards were all in his name and later in his and his mother's name. I was watching the finances that were being spent between his mother and him. He was buying plane tickets for himself and Tabeal and also paying for their lodging.

I was in the computer room one evening while he was signing in. He was very secretive about his e-mail. I was watching closely as he was typing in his password. He never opened his e-mail while I was in his presence, so I decided to leave. When he left the house, I went downstairs to see if I got the correct password. I typed in the password and it worked. The password was "amazing." I tried the password "grace" for another e-mail address that he had. It worked. The information that I received was rich and came in very handy the next month.

Grandma moved in with us in July, 1998. Grandma came with eighty thousand dollars. She received twenty one hundred dollars per month for social security and pensions. I suggested that we put all the money together and save. I wanted us to pray over the tithes and offerings so that we could be in agreement with God's financial plan for our lives. He did not want to hear it. He was more concerned with his mother's life and finances. He decided that I should use grandma's monthly income toward the house. I used the money for the purchasing of food, clothes, and whatever necessities were needed. Since 1998, he had not given me a penny towards anything in the household. Grandma, my covering in Christ Jesus, took care of all of us. Whenever I questioned him about savings, he would always say that it was none of my business. Whenever he went out of town he would leave me only a hundred dollars - even if he was gone for more than two weeks at a time.

I watched bank statements coming in. The credit card that he and his mother used ranged from seven thousand to twenty-one thousand dollars a month. It had to be paid off monthly. It was 2004, and the campaign needed money again. I purposely took the CD out so that it could not be used for that purpose. He wanted to know where I had deposited the seventy thousand dollars. It was safe and I was not going to tell him. Money is satan's greatest weapon to bring strife and pressure in marriage. So for the last seven years, grandma had been supporting my children and me financially.

On March 8, Rezin and I had to attend a church meeting in Tacoma, Washington. God's Name to me that day was "Helper." **"The Lord is with me. He is my Helper."** (Psalm 118.7) Rezin was in the shower at 4:50 that morning. My daughter came downstairs at 5:10 and started getting ready. Rezin was getting ready to leave, when I told him that I was riding with him to the airport. Our flight was scheduled for departure at 8:20am. Rezin normally took the children to the bus stop, but refused to do it that morning.

I had stepped out of the shower, washed my hair and still had to dry it. He left to pick up Tabeal to give him a ride to the airport. I prayed silently, and God reminded me that He was my Helper.

I took my daughter to the bus stop and waited till someone came and stood with her. I left and when I stepped in the house, my son had packed my suitcase. He had taken everything off the bed and put in my suitcase. It was 6:40. I dried my hair and got dressed.

I thanked my son and soon we were on our way to the bus stop. His bus normally arrived at 7. That morning it did not show till 7:15. I was supposed to be checked in at the airport at 7:20. I sat in my car and said aloud, "God thank you for having been true to Your Name thus far. Now please open the roads for me and let me travel in your safety so I can make it for this flight. Thank you."

God granted me traveling mercies to the airport. I got there at 7:40. I still had to go and park my car but decided to check in my luggage first. As I took the suitcase out of my car, a sky cap came running towards me. He took my case and asked me where I was going. I told him my destination and he went ahead of me. I had left my purse in the car. I turned back to get my identification. When I turned around the sky cap was standing there with my ticket in his hand. I thanked him and said that he was God's right hand. I had eight dollars to my name and gave him five dollars of it. I asked him if he thought that I would make it back from the parking lot in time for my flight. His exact words were, "The Lord is with you." I got in my car, thanked God and went to the parking lot.

When I entered the parking structure, a lady peered out of her truck and told me to follow her to a parking spot. When I parked and looked in my rearview, the shuttle was waiting on me. I let out a loud scream "Thank you God." I got to the gate at 8:16. A pastor and his wife were standing on the outside praying that I would be able to make it.

I entered the aircraft, and there in First Class was Tabeal and Rezin. I said to Rezin, "God is so Good, He is so Good." He would not look up. I found my way to my seat. Rezin called me on his cell phone in the plane to let me know that I might be going to Tacoma, but I did not have a place to stay. I looked up to heaven and said, "God you are my Helper." The pilot came on and informed the passengers that the aircraft was being moved to another gate as we were experiencing some technical problems. I thanked God.

I called the hotel and placed my name on the reservation with my husband's. We sat at the gate for another thirty minutes and when the plane finally took off, I was asleep. When we landed in Tacoma I went to the baggage claim area. Rezin was taking off Tabeal's and his luggage. When my bag came, another pastor reached for my bag and told Rezin he should be getting my bag and not Tabeal's luggage.

Rezin had rented a car. He was indirectly speaking to me by having a conversation with another pastor who was walking with me. He explained to him that he was going to the rental car place to get a car. He indicated that there was no room left for another passenger because he had big Tabeal and another minister with all their luggage. I kept walking towards the shuttle.

I made it to the hotel before Rezin got there. I told the clerk that my husband was on his way, and that he had the credit card with him to reserve the room. She asked me my name and gave me the key without any question. I was in the room that was reserved by Rezin. If he wanted to move out he could, but I was settled.

I called Bishop Philo to inform him about my shaky accommodation situation. He encouraged me and concluded the call with prayer. I was blessed all day beyond great measure. God's Name was Helper and He was really doing it.

Rezin finally made it to the room. If looks could kill, I would have been dead that day. He enlightened me that I was living in his room and that there would be no spirituality performances in his room. That meant that I could not pray, sing, read my Bible or listen to anything spiritual. I looked at him and did not say a word. There was a knock at the door and it was my girlfriend inviting me to go to lunch with her.

At opening worship that night, Bishop and Rev. Christians called all clergy couples to the altar for anointing. Rezin was sitting with Tabeal. In my heart I was praying that he would be obedient to the leadership. He openly defied them and walked out with Tabeal. I prayed for him. That night he moved out of the room. Where he went I do not know.

The meeting was very uplifting and inspiring. It was just good to be away from the everyday environment. The weather was beautiful, and the people's spirit was so kind. The preached Word was edifying to the soul, and the workshops were very inspiring.

At the meeting, I was asked to accompany a group of missionaries who were traveling to South Africa. Their mission was to go and evaluate the work at an orphanage that Rev. Helga adopted in South Africa. The dates were the exact dates that I had made reservations for the children and me to travel. I was given a stipend of three thousand dollars for travel and accommodation. Several friends placed bills in my hand. I left Missouri with three dollars in my pocket and returned with more than four thousand three hundred dollars. Jehovah Jireh was my wonderful provider.

I had hidden our passes to South Africa and reserved the passes from Atlanta, Georgia. I forgot that we were traveling from Columbus, Missouri. It was six days before travel when I realized that we did not have tickets from Columbus to Atlanta. The prices were expensive, and I could not afford the amount. I decided to drive to Atlanta one day earlier. I made a one-way car rental.

On the night of the 23rd I had everything packed and ready to be loaded in the car the next morning. I went upstairs to look for our passes and could not find them. Rezin saw me coming downstairs and sat looking at me with a silly grin on his face. I knew then that he had something to do with the disappearance of our tickets. He said that I had to tell him where I had deposited the money in order to get the tickets. I waited until 11 that night. I lied to him and said that it was at First Bank and gave him a wrong street name. He immediately called Tabeal and told him where the money was. They called several banks but could not get the information they needed without me giving them more information.

The next morning I sent my daughter to her father to ask for the tickets. I knew he would not want to upset the children. He gave them the tickets. The children and I prayed and left for Atlanta, Georgia. We had a wonderful drive to Atlanta. We had two five minute stops and kept going. We spent the night with Imaan's godparents in Atlanta. The next morning we boarded the South African Aircraft and were on our way.

We arrived safely in Cape Town. A friend brought me his BMW to use while I was in Cape Town. We went to greet my dad and enjoyed a snack. We checked in at the hotel in Cape Town. We were facing the ocean and Table Mountain. The scenery was beautiful. The Southeaster was blowing and it was very windy. We decided to stay awake until eight that evening. I had many visitors to come by and enjoyed catching up on pertinent news in South Africa.

I was sitting in the lobby when I saw my girlfriend entering the hotel. We had not spoken for years. She asked me if we could go to my room. Another girlfriend showed up and she took my children to the waterfront. When we entered my room, my girlfriend informed me that she was single again. She was married to a pastor, and he had left her for another woman. She broke down and cried. I was speechless. While she was in the room, my phone rang. I answered, and it was another pastor's wife informing me that her husband had left ministry and was now living with a Muslim girl. I informed my friend who was with me, and I told her to come to the hotel so that we could all pray for and with each other. I knew then that divorce was inevitable for me.

That Sunday we had dinner at my nephew's home. The whole family was together. My oldest sister was doing my laundry when she decided to hang the clothes on the laundry line. I went outside with her and told her that my marriage was in serious trouble. She informed me that the Spirit had already told her. My sister embraced me and said that God is still God. I told everyone except my dad. I was so entranced by their reaction. No one pointed a finger or said an unkind word, but decreed that it was in the Lord's Hands.

We had a very busy week in South Africa. We met with judges, lawyers, architects, bankers, social workers and political leaders. We worked at the orphanage daily. My girlfriend had a preaching engagement in Piketberg, about ninety minutes outside of Cape Town. I was driving to Piketberg when I fell asleep behind the wheel. God's grace and mercy kept us. I pulled over and slept for ten minutes and then was ready to go again. We made it safely to Piketberg and were welcomed by a beautiful congregation.

On that Thursday we baptized twenty four persons at the orphanage. Fourteen of them were new believers.

We were scheduled to leave Cape Town that Friday evening at 8. It was 2 that afternoon when I decided that I was through working. I was going to spend the next three hours with my dad. I went to his home and sat on his bed. He was talking about everything when I finally interrupted him and said that my marriage was in trouble. My dad went down the wrong avenue. He said that I should humble myself and stop being so stubborn.

I wanted to scream. He had awakened every childhood negative memory about him in me. I wanted to tell him that my mother probably went to the grave without an apology from him. My lips were sealed and I was thankful. The spirit reigned. My niece came in and asked me to join her for a cup of tea. I did.

That evening when I left for the airport, dad told me that I was his most blessed child and that God would take care of me. That was his way of apologizing. I received it in Jesus Name. I hugged and kissed him, and we left for the airport. For the first time my dad did not come to see me off at the airport. He was hurting.

We arrived in Atlanta on April 4th. We spent the night in Atlanta. My niece was so kind to make us plane reservations to get back to Columbus. After arriving in Columbus, the children went to church and I went to sleep. I slept all day.

The children came home that afternoon tired and hungry. My daughter came and awakened me. I turned around and went right back to sleep. She wanted to show me something. I said later.

I went downstairs to the basement and tried to go into the children's playroom. I could not enter. The lock on the door was changed and it was locked. I went back upstairs. When Imaan saw me, she said, "Did you see that?" I asked her what she was talking about. Her father had taken down their playroom and made it into a bedroom for himself. That next Sunday he was preaching about basement Christians and balcony Christians. He said that basement Christians always want to pull you down. He preferred hanging with balcony Christians. The irony of it was that he was in the basement, and I was in the balcony.

Chapter 15

We must be vigilant,
constantly examining our own hearts.
Otherwise we will continue to be the
"Great Pretenders"
Matters of the Heart Devotional for women
JUANITA BYNUM

"But you walked away from your first love - why?
What's going on with you anyway?
Do you have any idea how far you've fallen?
A Lucifer fall!
Turn back!
Recover your dear early love.
No time to waste, for I am
well on my way to removing
your light from the golden circle."
REVELATIONS 2:4-5 MESSAGE

No More Pretense

I had accepted an invitation to preach the Easter 2004 sunrise service at a church in the community. I worked on the sermon while we were traveling, returning from South Africa. The sermon was ready to be preached. The only thing it needed was a sermon topic. It was April 7, 2004 when I was awakened at 2 in the morning. My spirit said, "Happy endings." I was confused, thinking that maybe the troubles with my marriage would be over by morning time. I thought about it and decided to use it as the sermon topic.

I went back to sleep and I was awakened at 5:10. I got up and turned on my praise music. My daughter was getting ready for school when I noticed Rezin entering the bedroom dressed as if he was going somewhere. Imaan was ready to leave. Imaan and I prayed, and Rezin escorted her to the bus stop.

At 7 a.m. my son came into my room and said that he was ready to leave. I asked him where his dad was. He informed me that his father had left for Los Angeles. I took Niamke to the bus stop and saw him off to school.

When I came back to the house, I unlocked the door and Jehovah Shalom himself welcomed me. I felt so relieved and free. I said, "God thank you for the spirit of peace that is here. Please let me experience your peace all day long." I did my morning meditation and got busy around the house.

At 10 a.m. there was a knock on the door. When I opened the door a lady in denim shorts and a white top was standing there. She asked to speak to Mary. I told her that was me. She shoved a stack of white papers into my hand and left. I was served with divorce papers.

I turned back into the house and audibly said that I would contest the divorce. The spirit answered back and said, "There will be no

peace." It was as if someone was standing right next to me. I said,
"Was that You God?"

I sat down and stared at the papers. I started looking back over my
married life. I had been waiting for things to get better.

God's standard for marriage is for one man and one woman to be
totally in love with each other. I loved him, but it seemed that it
was never returned. I believe that my marriage was based on duty
and responsibility only. We had two children and sixteen years of
marriage. We were living as roommates. We slept in the same
king size bed but so far apart of each other. Our relationship, I
realized, was much less than what God intended. I had been his
cook, his housekeeper, his hostess, his laundress and roommate. I
was his slave and that was it.

Marriage is based on romance and commitment. It hardly
happened. His commitment was to himself, his mother, Tabeal
and the church. There was no commitment to me and the children.

Our communication had become blunt, sarcastic and very critical.
He did not want to be my friend and did not care about my needs
and wants. There were hardly times of tenderness, patience and
romance. I was his slave and not his wife.

Sexual love is to be enjoyed. God invented sex for marriage. I
was blind to his faults and weaknesses. We had had five thousand,
eight hundred and thirty five days of marriage with less than two
hundred days of lovemaking. He could not look into my eyes
anymore. He had opened the door to satan a long time ago with
pornography and masturbation. It was hard for him to admit that
we were wrong and had to start over.

Finances were his and never ours. He shared money freely with
his mother and Tabeal, but could not share it with me and his
children.

God had placed grandma in my life twenty years ago. She is 102
years old today and still my covering. I truly believe that God has

kept her here for the children's and my sake. We never would have had what we had if God had not placed grandma in our lives.

Our marriage died a long time ago. He was not willing to renew his mind by the teaching of God's Word about marriage and commitment to the family. He did not want me to make it in the things of God. He reduced me to control me, because he did not want to walk on the same plateau that God had placed us on.

He had no respect for me anymore. He would leave town for days and tell the children and not me. He thought that the buying of expensive gifts was more important than communication, quality time, respect, intimacy and love. He was in a spiritually adulterous relationship with his mother and Tabeal, and stubbornly defending his position. He was not willing to make his children and me his number one priority. I believe cleaving was never accomplished in our marriage because the prerequisite of leaving his mother never happened.

My mother-in-law had five sons, but this one, (Rezin) she had raised for herself. From the beginning of my marriage, she continually clung to her son physically, psychologically, financially and emotionally. She used him as a crutch and unloaded all her emotional, financial and physical stress on Rezin. This strangled the chances of the development of a close bond necessary between my husband and me. She had so much influence over her son that he had no initiative of his own but listened to everything his mother told him. She had excessive interest and influence in his life. He would rather that I was offended in times of conflict than his mother. I tried to accommodate her to the utmost. My husband could not become the key to a good relationship between his mother and me.

My children and I never had a real relationship with my in-laws. My children had never heard of their grandmother's experience of saving faith. She had never looked for an opportunity to nurture her grandchildren's curiosity about God. My children had spent more time with my family in South Africa than with his family right here in the United States. They never were our family. I tried to become theirs, but they refused to become mine.

The relationship between Rezin and Tabeal was unexplainable. Rezin accused me of spreading rumors about the two of them. He did not realize that their actions were speaking much louder than words. Tabeal's so-called wife had told everyone that she was leaving her husband because he had been fighting his homosexual tendencies but could not overcome them. Tabeal was dictating to Rezin how he should live his life, when he could get up and move, how to spend his money and what he was allowed to do and what he could not do. All of Rezin's time was being spent with Tabeal. He started walking in the wisdom of Tabeal and not of God. Rezin twisted the truth because his heart was set on hearing a lie rather than the truth. Rezin had become comfortable in living a double standard life.

Rezin was supposed to be responsible to introduce our children to the Word of God. The only time the children heard him reading the Bible to them was in church on Sunday mornings or Wednesday evenings. It was biologically easy for him to become a father, but it was spiritually challenging to actually father our children. I wonder what kind of images they see about God when they look at their father.

My prayer is that God Himself will come down and love me through someone who will introduce my children to the character and heart of God. Not that I have not done so already, but it should have come from the head of the home - the man. I believe this generational curse stops with me. I believe that women in my lineage (who have husbands) will no longer have to be the spiritual head in the household but that the man that my daughter and men that my grand-daughters will marry, will be distinctly sent from God. For my son I pray, that he will be an example of expressing God's love in relationships with others, especially his God-given wife and children. Also that Niamke will commend God's work and faithfulness to be recalled by his children and grandchildren to infinity. For myself I pray, that the lessons that I learned through my mother-in-law I will never repeat in the lives of my "son and daughter-in- love." I pray that I will be able to say one day that I raised my children for God and not for myself. Roman 8:28 says, **"All thing work together for good to them that love the Lord and are the called according to His purpose."**

So I wasted sixteen and a half years waiting for things to get better. While I was waiting the enemy was wasting my life. I stopped living without even knowing that I stopped doing it. Dysfunction had become an institution in our relationship. I had missed the best days of my life. In my heart I knew that my present circumstance was a blessing from God. I took my vows very seriously, but the wedding never became a marriage. I know that God hates divorce, but He loves the divorcee. I accepted the invitation to divorce.

I laid prostrate before the Lord and asked God to forgive me for breaking the vows I had made unto Him. I asked God to protect the portals of my mind. My dad had two nervous breakdowns in his life and since 1966 had been on anti-depressants. I was alone I thought, in this foreign country. I had no blood relatives to support and encourage me. But God had already raised up family for me. When I accepted the divorce invitation, family came forth who were better than blood or in-laws. It was family tied by the blood of Jesus.

Philippians 4:7 was running rampant in my spirit. **"The peace of God that surpasses all understanding will keep your heart and mind in the knowledge of Christ Jesus."**

The phone rang and it was my spiritual mentor. I informed her of the most recent event. She quoted Jeremiah 29:11, **"I know the thoughts I have for you, plans to prosper you and not for welfare, plans to give you hope and a future."** She never spoke a negative word against my husband but prayed for both of us and the children. She implored me to put up the divorce decree till after resurrection Sunday. I complied.

I was watching the Word Channel when a preacher came on. His sermon topic was "The Door out of Boredom." God himself was speaking to me.

I began to reminisce about life in South Africa. My dad was divorced. I never knew of his divorce until I was about eight years old. I remember two young women visiting us regularly, especially on Friday nights. Their names were Grace and Dawn. I always admired them because they were two beautiful black women. I cannot remember as a child having much interaction with them as they were much older than me. We were invited to Grace's twenty first birthday.

It was at this occasion that I learned that they were my half-sisters. I could not understand the relationship that my mother had with their mother. They had the greatest respect for each other and helped each other raise their children. Conflict exists most of the time between the present wife and the former wife. It was not so between mom and their mother. What an example they were.

A lady at the party just willingly shared this information with us. My father was married to their mother who divorced him. It was a family secret and could not be discussed. We used to recite the Ten Commandments in church every Sunday. There was a clause that said, **"The sins of the father is unto the third and fourth generation..."** I would privately sit and ponder who in our family was going to inherit the sins of the father. Well like Job said, **"Everything I feared has befallen me."**

My father had six children. Three of us were married. I was the one chosen to experience divorce. I did not believe in divorce, but I accepted the invitation. I had had enough.

Rezin returned that Saturday. I did not discuss anything with him about the divorce decree.

The children and I had a wonderful Easter Sunday. God blessed us all day long. God was right there with us. The children wanted to go to the Easter Buffet at the hotel. I did not have reservations. When we arrived, the hostess informed me that the only way that she could seat us would be if they had a cancellation. I told her that we were willing to wait. We patiently waited. Fifteen minutes later we were seated. We ate and stayed for two hours. I had asked for the bill several times. Finally, the waiter came back and told me that it had already been taken care of. Favor. I thanked God for the blessing and left.

God saved me through divorce. Throughout my marriage, I considered the institution of marriage as more important than my happiness and health. I was not going to fight God's will by opposing divorce from a bad marriage. God told me long ago that my husband was not going to change. He gave me many options which I ignored.

A marriage should reflect the character of God. We were supposed to be the vessels through which God could manifest His love for us. My marriage publicly did that, but privately we were the worst witness. The saddest thing about it was that our children were watching. It did not matter how hard I tried to please Rezin, he always found something else to berate me.

God is more concerned for the individual than for the institution. I was naïve. He was selfish and always insisted on his own wants being fulfilled. I knew God could restore the marriage to what it was supposed to be, but he did not want it. If he really loved God first, I would have been second - not his mother and Tabeal.

The road to divorce was a long, tedious and ugly one. On a daily basis, Rezin would call me crazy. My response would be that I am crazy for Jesus. I thank God for protecting the portals of my mind. God gave me peace that I could not understand but do understand.

In my peace and contentment, I became effective against the schemes of the enemy. I decreed daily that I shall live and not die. I started living again. Through faith, I came to know God. Through God, I came to know myself again.

Every time the enemy came angrily against me, the Lord gave me the strength and tenacity to refuse his attacks to have dominion over me. 1 Timothy 3 was alive and active in my being. **"God has not given us a spirit of fear but..."** I still had fears but God was, and still is dealing with them.

I thank God for the knowledge that I have gained from my mistakes. Through them, I can now internalize the significance of God's Word and better understand it. In my ignorance, God still blessed me with greater wisdom. I humbled myself before God in prayer. His great teachings were able to find a place in my soul and understanding. I make it part of my daily living. I asked Him for wisdom, knowledge, counsel and might, but most of all understanding. He answered my prayer - not the way I expected Him to - but He answered. I am FREE!

On November 3, 2004 the divorce was finalized. It was "Happy Endings."

Chapter 16

Our present enjoyment of God's grace tends
to be lessened by the memory of yesterday's
sins and blunders. But God is the God
of our yesterdays, and he allows
the memory of them to turn the past into a
ministry of spiritual growth for our future.
God reminds us of the past to protect
us from a very shallow security in the present.
OSWALD CHAMBERS

"You shall not go out with haste,…for
the Lord will go before you,
and the God of Israel
will be your rear guard."
ISAIAH 52:12 NIV

Connecting

Mother Teresa said, "Be sure to teach families how to pray all together - father, mother and children. For the family that prays together stays together, and if they stay together they will love one another as Jesus loves each one of them...I will be praying that the Lord will bring peace into the world through the Love of fathers for their families."

Through all the pain and trials of my experience with my dad, God's light still shined. Dad kept us together by prayer. Through prayer, dad acknowledged that God was His only Hope. Rezin refused to pray with his family, so we could not stay together.

I had received so many blessings and knew the Word of God, but I really did not know God. My relational bumps in life taught and enabled me to enter into the closest relationship with Jesus Christ. It was when I thought I was lonely that He would show up and give me all understanding and compassion.

The cares of the world and deceitfulness of man will choke the life of God in us. I always looked for God in relationship with others. It started with my dad, my brother, my husband, my mother-in-law, friends and the church.

I forgot and neglected my own personal relationship with Him. That which was represented as Godly was always a contradiction to what I had been taught about God. I had thoughts that had been planted in the subconscious mind as a child that was so much a part of me.

I too, started living a lie that was comfortable and convenient. I made concessions to accommodate the dysfunction. It met my needs. I was more willing to live the lie than be willing to trust God and step out by faith. I was still being sustained by the Word. At church I would shout heaven down and go back home to live in hell.

I became desperate in seeking God while all the time, He was relentlessly seeking after me. I was left to my own devices. I am so glad that rather than finding a tradition, I found my own personal relationship with God. The unhealthy relationships that I had experienced were all part of some higher plan. Nothing on earth happens without God's permission.

God has a plan and will not rest until He fully accomplishes the purposes of His heart. God created my life with purpose and led me to experience that purpose through a relationship with Him. Most of us seek fulfillment in life. God gives us the most fulfilling life. He says, "I have come that ye might have life, and have it more abundantly." I have learned how to be content whether I am abased and abounding.

In California, my favorite scripture was Psalms 125:2, **"As the mountains surround Jerusalem, so God surrounds His children forever."** In Columbus He reminded me, that He was not only a God of the hills and introduced me to 1Kings 20:28, **"This is what the Lord says, because the Arameans think the Lord is a god of the hills and not a god of the valley, I will deliver the vast army in your hands and you will know that I am the Lord."** Columbus is a valley geographically. It is in the valley that Psalms 23:4 becomes alive, **"Yea though I walk through the valley of the shadow of death I will fear no evil, for Thou art with me Thy rod and Thy staff they comfort me."**

All through my life God has never been remote or distant. He was right there with me.

A relationship with God is a lot like being married. I am divorced from man, but I am married to the Son of the Living God. This relationship will last for all eternity. It is growing daily. It has its ups and downs, its highs and lows, its joys and pains. But I get to know Him better everyday.

I decree and declare every day that "as for me and my house we will serve the Lord." I am not interested in the things that are seen as much as I am interested in developing that which is unseen. In Jesus we find the greatest depth of love, the fullest portion of joy and the greatest measure of peace.

Earlier in the book I told you about a poem that I learned while my pastor's wife, Mrs. Jantjies was reciting it. I still remember it to this day and it all makes sense. I do not know who the author is, but the name of the poem is

"TOO LATE."

It's sometimes too late to be sorry
Yet it's never too late to be glad
Though it's often too late to worry
Over things you might have had
So don't let too late be your master
And don't let too late be your fate
For the saddest two words in all the world
Are the little two words
Too Late.

I am so glad that it is not yet too late for me. God had me to memorize it for such a time as this. God patiently taught me the art of living. I was just very slow. I heard God. I believed. I substituted sight for faith. I became still, and I knew that God was God. I received peace. The peace of God equipped me with an indestructible joy through the divorce process. Now I have knowledge. This knowledge makes me strong. God has given me power. When you have power you are Free.

God chose through my painful relational bumps to reshape and refine me. "But the pot He was shaping from the clay was marred in His hands. So the Potter formed it into another pot shaping it as seemed best to Him." (Jeremiah 18:4) It was in His Hands that I learned the most sublime lessons of self-sacrifice, humility, obedience, boldness, surrendering and love.

I discovered for myself that the world is a lie. Pain is no longer my constant companion. You the reader can probably easily point out my foolishness, but I was in the middle of it and it was not so easy to see. I have accepted God's truth and try daily to live accordingly. I've read Deuteronomy 24:1-5 and 1 Corinthians 7:14. I am never going back. I am enjoying God's peace.

So hear what Christ Our Father says, "You shall love the Lord Thy God with all thy heart and with all thy soul and with all thy mind. This is the first and great commandment. You shall love your neighbor as yourself. On these two commandments hang all the law and the prophets." God loves me and you. I love God with all of my heart and all of my soul and all of my mind all of my strength and all of my expectancies. I love myself again, I love my neighbor and my enemies.

Through all the relational bumps, I developed an everlasting relationship with my Heavenly Father. I now walk in the authority of the King and rise as more than a conqueror in every area of my life. My relational bumps connected me to God.

Hail Mary, full of grace the Lord is with thee, blessed art thou amongst women.

This writing of this book was completed
December 31, 2005
@ 10:31a.m.

THANKS BE TO GOD!

This book is the fulfillment of a prophecy that was spoken into my life in 1974. My Tenth grade (standard eight) English language teacher, Mr. Bernard Johnson who taught at Salt River High School, said that I was going to become an author. This is the first of many more to come. Thank you, Mr. Bernard Johnson.

I have since left the denomination that I belonged to (in good and regular standing) and have since joined Shalom Church (City Of Peace), where Dr. F. James Clark is the pastor and founder. The name of the church is so accurate and appropriate. I found Peace and wholeness at Shalom Church.

Dear Dr. F. James Clark,

When I asked you to write the foreword to my book, I did not expect you to say "yes," but you did. You did this despite the 7,000 plus members you have to pastor on a daily basis, despite the fact that you were trying to get your own book published, (*HOSPITALITY*) despite your traveling engagements that you had to fulfill, despite the fact that you were entering into the building phase of a $10,000,000 church edifice, despite the fact that your wife became ill, despite the fact that you still had to prepare yourself for preaching, teaching, and praying for Shalom church and probably many other reasons that I do not know of. Pastor you said yes and your word was your honor.

I thank you for being the man that God has called you to be. You have surpassed them all. Thank you for your kindness and hospitality towards me. I thank God that the world is not a stage to you. Oh that God would continue to bless you and Mrs. Clark indeed.

Maureen S. Eckert

Dear Lois,

How can I thank God for the friendship that we have developed? I am blessed to know you. You encouraged and embraced me as if you had known me forever. When we met a year ago at the Shalom Church picnic, our spirits connected immediately. I know we will be friends forever. Continue to fill the kingdom with love, mercy, compassion, unselfish service and loving devotion to the Most High God. Be blessed forever.

Thank you so much. I love you with the love of the Lord.

Maureen S. Eckert